W9-CED-460

Praise for Solution Selling

"We have trained our sales executives in Solution Selling. Everyday our salespeople match right solutions to their customers' particular business problems—some of our services result in 30% to 40% productivity gains. That's because Solution Selling methods have helped us to develop the correct application to a properly diagnosed problem."

DON LAVOIE— Vice President and General Manager, TRW Business Credit Services

"Solution Selling is the way to sell sophisticated services in the 1990s. By proactively selling solutions and helping our customers solve problems we'll be able to continue our successful growth rate. Our Solution Selling Trainer achieved instant credibility with our sales staff."

RAY BECKER— Executive Vice President, Keane, Inc.

"Solution Selling allows us to add the way we sell to our list of competitive advantages."

PHIL ALTMAN— Senior Vice President, Great Western Bank

"Solution Selling has enabled us to dramatically cut the learning curve for new salespeople."

DOUG GORMAN— President, Information Mapping, Inc.

"Solution Selling has provided the tools for us to manage the sales process and grow at well over 50% a year with a solid profit margin. It gives an organization the structure to sustain that kind of growth over the long term."

JOHN THRON— President, Programart

"The principles of Solution Selling have not only altered the way we think about our relationship to our clients, but it has helped us to become co-authors of our clients' business strategies. It is a wonderful, human approach to selling."

MARY ELLEN TEARNEY— President, Tearney & Tearney

"Solution Selling focused our sales force on the customer's value and vision. This increased average order size for our experienced salespeople as well as business knowledge and confidence among our newer salespeople."

LAWRENCE S. BREWSTER— Vice President, North American Field Operations
Sales Technologies, A company of The Dun & Bradstreet Corporation

"Solution Selling is *the* quality approach from a sales perspective. Many of the usual buyer versus seller problems disappear because Solution Selling is about how buyers buy. It enables our salespeople to do it right the first time and avoid reworking presentations."

MERRYLUE LANGDON— Sales Trainer, TRW, Business Credit Services

"Solution Selling provides a readily understandable approach to mastering the complex 'consultative sale' in a way that benefits both seller and buyer. The art of selling is reduced to a set of practical skills which shorten the cycle and increase the win percentage."

ROBERT A. NERO— Vice President,
Information Technology Division, LEGENT Corporation

"The part of the model that has helped me most is the call debriefing. We use the call debriefing to see if we have missed anything in the sales cycle and to understand why the buyer is buying. We then identify the tactical steps to create our strategy. We have also gained more awareness of being 'column fodder.' We can look at the account more realistically knowing that part of the process of the prospect's organization is to make all of the vendors feel like they are winning."

SHELLY SCHOENBERGER— Director of Sales, AAC Corporation

"Solution Selling has fit nicely into Lawson Software's quality process management philosophy. This 'quality' selling process has enabled Lawson to increase revenues in addition to maintaining our industry leading 97% client satisfaction rating."

DON SLUSARSKI— Vice President of Sales, Lawson Software

"The most effective way to take advantage of the Solution Selling process is by getting commitment from the top. And I mean from the CEO. Everyone in the company is involved in the sales process and it is the most important activity of any company. If the CEO doesn't understand the need to take a hands-on leadership role in this, the results will be diluted. Don't let the CEO tell you he or she doesn't have time to take the course. They don't have time NOT to!!"

RICHARD EARNEST— President, Earnest Enterprises

"Solution Selling provides a sales force with a reproducible process, from the initial phone call, to techniques for face-to-face sales calls, to letters for controlling the process, to getting the contract signed."

JIM COLLIGAN— Vice President, Sales, Data Forms Co., Inc.

"Accurate sales forecasting is fundamental to developing a solid business. Solution Selling provides the basic for accurate forecasting."

PATRICK GEHL— CEO, J B Systems, Inc.

"The Solution Selling program is the most complete and effective program for sales and sales management training I have seen. It treats the sales, process as a system which, of course, it is."

JAMES G. SPENCER— Vice President, Sales & Marketing, Figgie International, Inc.

"Solution Selling is an excellent vehicle to teach new salespeople critical sales skills and allow experienced salespeople to fine tune their skills. Solution Selling is the best methodology I've seen for placing emphasis on business issues rather than product."

DAN GORSKI— Sales Manager, AT&T Global Business Communications System

"My staff now address their buyers' needs, shifting concerns, and phases of buying. Solution Selling has brought immediate results to our sales performance."

RANDY WELLEN— Senior Vice President, Great Western Bank

"There is no magic to Solution Selling. What it provides you with is a sound methodology that concentrates on solving a client's business problems and a structure to measure the sales process and make necessary correction to close or walk."

**GEORGE LANGAN— Vice President, Marketing,
LEGENT Corporation Information Technology Division**

"Solution Selling was all I had hoped for and more! Our team now has a shared sales method for consultative and services marketing, a shared nomenclature for the process, and a belief in our abilities to identify new opportunities and turn them into dollars."

LARRY PASTOR— Business Unit Executive, IBM

"In counseling my clients to find the best answers to satisfy their insurance needs, Solution Selling is invaluable! Holding back the specific product or service until the need is thoroughly diagnosed means a more complete solution and a happier client. An excellent course!"

BLAKE GRAEBER— Senior Vice President, Marsh & McLennan

"Solution Selling has taught me how to keep my product in my pocket and fully understand my clients' situations. This has helped me increase my ability to handle—in a very successful manner—more complex financial situations that my clients have."

CHRIS DAVIS— Vice President, Wheat, First Securities, Inc.

"The principles of Solution Selling have been critical in helping us focus our business development efforts. When we enter a proposal situation, we now ask each other whether we are the Column A provider or whether we are 'column fodder.' We sometimes discover we are . . . and more than once we declined to respond to an RFP. This has saved us time and money and we focus on more fruitful areas.

Solution Selling has also helped us to think much more strategically about the kinds of information we need to get from a potential client. . . . We now ask questions that turn latent need into pain. Once we discovered the pain, a level of trust builds as the prospect continues to reveal more problems or missed opportunities. This trust often becomes the basis of a mutually beneficial business relationship."

WARREN SMITH— Marketing Manager, Coopers & Lybrand

"I especially like the Solution Selling process for Great Western Bank because it naturally complements our commitment to excellence. Now, instead of selling the product of the quarter, we are helping our customers discover and identify what they need."

MICHELLE MARIE MADDOCK—First Vice President, Great Western Bank

"Solution Selling is the most comprehensive sales and sales management process available today. Mike Bosworth has the best understanding of the sales process in corporate America."

JEFFREY M. FISHER—Senior Vice President, Symix Computer Systems

"No bank or financial services company truly gains a competitive advantage through the products and services it offers. We can only hope to gain an advantage through our people and our own sales process. I believe that the Solution Selling process will not only differentiate Great Western Bank from our competitors, it also helps to create a set of values, skills, and phraseology on which we can build a customer-driven sales culture."

MICHAEL S. SHALLANBERGER—Vice President, Great Western Bank

SOLUTION SELLING
Creating Buyers in Difficult Selling Markets

Michael T. Bosworth

McGraw-Hill

New York   San Francisco   Washington, D.C.   Auckland   Bogotá
Caracas   Lisbon   London   Madrid   Mexico City   Milan
Montreal   New Delhi   San Juan   Singapore
Sydney   Tokyo   Toronto

McGraw-Hill

A Division of The McGraw-Hill Companies

Solution Selling® is a trademark and service mark of Michael T. Bosworth, Post Office Box 9305, Rancho Santa Fe, CA 92067, registered with the U.S. Patent and Trademark Office.

© MICHAEL T. BOSWORTH, 1995

All rights reserved. No part of this publication may be reproduced, stored in a retrieval system, or transmitted, in any form or by any means, electronic, mechanical, photocopying, recording, or otherwise, without the prior written permission of the publisher.

This publication is designed to provide accurate and authoritative information in regard to the subject matter covered. It is sold with the understanding that neither the author or the publisher is engaged in rendering legal, accounting, or other professional service. If legal advice or other expert assistance is required, the services of a competent professional person should be sought.

From a Declaration of Principles jointly adopted by a Committee of the American Bar Association and a Committee of Publishers.

Library of Congress Cataloging-in-Publication Data

Bosworth, Michael T.
    Solution selling : creating buyers in difficult selling markets /
Michael T. Bosworth.
        p. cm.
    Includes bibliographical references (p.   ) and index.
    ISBN 0-7863-0315-8
    1. Selling. 2. Sales management. I. Title.
HF5438.25.B67   1995
    658.85—dc20   94–10543

Printed in the United States of America
    12 13 14 15 16 17 18 19 20

Acknowledgments

Sellers—whether whole businesses or individual salespeople—have available today the information and experience needed to sell successfully. However, a vast distance remains between smart buyers and most sellers. By "sellers" I mean CEOs, CFOs, marketing people, sales managers, salespeople, and product and service experts. With this book I hope to add to the body of knowledge about how to create buyers. But my first aim is to present *Solution Selling* and thereby increase the supply of expert sellers, that 20 percent—in the jargon, the Eagles—who account for 80 percent of most sales results.

This book is the result of many people and many experiences over 20 years. It began when I left college and joined Xerox Computer Services to pursue a technical support career in information systems. Surprisingly, that was not to be my career path. I changed it—reluctantly, at first—to selling and sales training. Now I am grateful for the suggestion that I try selling, and I am grateful for the encouragement and wisdom of all the people who inspired me along this worthwhile journey.

I applaud my clients and friends of *Solution Selling* and the thousands of attendees who have taken this material and used it in the marketplace. Their results and feedback are a great encouragement to me and to my associates who conduct *Solution Selling* seminars across America and internationally. Graduates of *Solution Selling* are creating buyers in difficult markets—everyday I hear of *Solution Selling* graduates who have increased their sales and improved their personal earnings. They are proof that honorable selling need not be an oxymoron. Sellers can align with buyers and create a common vision of a useful shared solution to a problem.

For this book and its contents I am grateful especially to several people:

> To my wife (and chief editor) Sally, and to each of our children, Brendan, Brian, and Shiloh, for accommodating my life of extensive travel and activities outside our home. You each help me immensely.
>
> To my mother and my sister, gone but not forgotten.

To my brothers, Steve, Sam, and Dick.

To my valued associates in *Solution Selling*®, especially: First to Keith Eades, Mary Ann Cluggish, and Bob Junke—my pioneer affliates. To Rebecca Fritzson, Phil McCrory, Bob Populorum, John Linton, and Michele Wrzesinski—for creating buyers for our business. Your seminar teaching, consulting, and speaking engagements are an essential part of our progress. Many of you have made valuable contributions to *Solution Selling* course material and seminar formats. I am indebted for your constructive feedback.

To "Mac" McLoughlin who—with unfailing wit and energy—assists me in my part of the business, consults, and teaches at my public and private seminars. He is a coach's captain without equal. His assistance gives my life structure, and that has allowed me to do what I like best to do: teach, consult, and continue to develop *Solution Selling*.

To Merrylue Langdon, who brings an extensive education background to our business, for helping us rise to new levels of coaching competence. I also appreciate Merrylue's insight into the training and educational process.

To Howard Eaton, who is taking *Solution Selling* to banking and the financial services industry and who has assembled our seminar materials, collected client reference stories, and helped write and creatively market this book.

To managers, peers, clients, and friends who over the years have supplied inspiration, motivation, and material for stories—in no particular order: Jim Campbell, Bob Foster, Allen Hoey, Dan Long, Mike Kenney, Tom Wells, Marketta Silvera, Jim Hall, Larry Brewster, Ted Hill, Jeff Fisher, Bob Brown, Dave Crabtree, Bob Whelan, Phil Yarbrough, Jeff Berman, Jane Coutts, Karen Hillegas, Steve Levine, Bill Watkins, Richard Earnest, Rose Lane, Bill Hammon, Richard Levak, Doug Gorman, Gary Walker, John Sturm, Dave Ehlke, Dennis Neary, Eli Szklanka, Lisa Nirell, Lorraine DePolo, Larry DeFazio, Kay Dodd, Dag Forssell, René Jacobs, John Holland, Charlie Palmer, Bob Parsons, Marv Perel, Kathryn Tidyman, and Vito Tanzi.

To Carol Rogala, who—after attending one of my public seminars—decided to publish this book, and for helping me sell it in ways and in markets that suited our business and hers.

Contents

List of Figures

Introduction

In my seminars, I ask, "When you were growing up, how many of your mothers had a vision of you with a career in sales?"
The audience laughs.
Then I ask, "What adjectives would your mother use to describe salespeople?"
The audience laughs louder, and replies with sleazy, pushy, dishonest, etc.

This book, which grew out of a seminar that I originated and teach nationally and internationally—and which my valued associates also teach—is about selling to buyers who now enjoy plurality of choice, who have expertise, who compare, who are trained negotiators, who demand satisfaction, and who litigate their disappointments.

When you go through this book, you will notice that I use the margins occasionally to describe a transaction between a seller and a buyer, or to offer an additional dimension to a concept. We have purposely allowed wide margins throughout the book for you to use for your personal comments and notes. I encourage you to mark it up. Write your comments and notes in the margins. Use them to help you implement the ideas, concepts, and process within.

This book is about making *the way you sell* as big an advantage as your product or service. Since most buyers have a negative impression of salespeople, one of the best things salespeople can do is to sell in less stereotypical ways.

Most people love to *buy* but hate to feel "sold." Feeling "sold" means feeling like you have lost control—been taken advantage of, coerced, or manipulated. Most people have had an experience in their life where they have come away from an encounter with a salesperson feeling that the salesperson controlled them. That is why salespeople have to live by Napoleonic Law: You are guilty until proven innocent. Salespeople are guilty by association of all the sins that other salespeople have committed on their buyer.

Many jokes are told at the expense of salespeople—I think that salesperson jokes rival lawyer jokes in both disrespect and number. Today, from the beginning of a call introduction to getting buyer commitment, we face buyers who have been abused by almost every smooth-tongued scheme, intrigue, conspiracy, price manipulation, connivance, contrivance, deceit, deception, dishonesty, fraud, lie, double-handed machination, maneuver, ruse, ploy, finagle, sleight-of-hand, trick, and trap known and practiced in the marketplace. No wonder buyers are suspicious. And they are right. "Joe Isuzu" and clones of "Joe Izusu" and clones of clones of "Joe Isuzu" abound. Therefore, this bears repeating: *Buyers are suspicious.* Face it, your buyers carry psychological baggage left over from previous encounters with sellers. Plan on that. Few businesses, executives, salespeople, and marketers consider this problem.

Most businesses and salespeople *lead* with their product or service features. And consumers have been, still are being, and will continue to be "featured" to boredom and confusion—into a state of inertia. We can deal with this to our advantage. If you genuinely want to differentiate yourself, your product or service, your business, then you must learn to become different by the *way* you sell. *Solution Selling* is about making yourself different.

It is the responsibility of the whole business to sell, to be in "sales." Marketing is about selling. Your CEO, top management, middle management, CFO, and entire staff are together in your business's entrepreneurial responsibility to create a buyer and make a profitable sale. We must plan our products and services from their design beginnings to their point of sale and on through to aftermarket service and repair with *Solution Selling* in mind.

This book is for *any* business or organization that sells: small, big, wholesale, retail, new, old, utilities, banks, information industry businesses, automotive, financial services, consulting, professional services businesses, and others. From sole proprietorships to huge corporations, if your business or organization sells something, this book is for you.

Solution Selling is an action program for action owners, executives, salespeople, and employees who grasp the fact that the two entrepreneurial functions of a business are *marketing* and *innovation*. This book contains many of the sales and sales management principles, concepts, and strategies taught in *Solution Selling* seminars and workshops.

Solution Selling provides entrepreneurial concepts for tactical selling and tactical marketing. *Solution Selling* provides essential strategic tools that can help you make your business even more entrepreneurial. Although strategic marketing—which deals with potentials—is important, in matters of the bottom line, success boils down to tactical marketing, which is about actuals: Creating demand for today's products and services today.

FIGURE 1
Situational Fluency: Integration of Knowledge and Skills

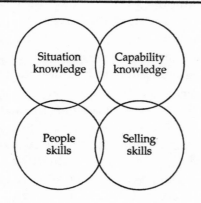

Solution Selling is for change agents, bold people, visionary people, executives, and salespeople who understand it is in their interest and in the interest of their businesses to align with buyers—*to create buyers*. It's for people who want to learn *Solution Selling* and who want to go out onto the great stages of the marketplace and honorably empower buyers.

Solution Selling can enable you and your business to be different from your competition—to become aligned *with* your buyer. Many of us sell products and services that are difficult to differentiate from our competition's. I have learned that *the way you sell* can be a key strategic differentiation point between you and your competitor. Some of these strategic tools include key concepts that you will find discussed throughout this book.

Situational Fluency. In Figure 1 you see four circles that intersect. I use this diagram to help people understand the transaction that occurs between a buyer and a seller. In order for a successful sale to occur, the seller needs *situational fluency:* Knowledge of how the buyer operates with and without his product or service and knowledge of what specific product or service capabilities in his offering match *situationally* with the buyer. With the complexity of some of today's products and services, it is very difficult for a single human being—buyer or seller—to understand and comprehend all of the options, configurations, and applications available. Superior sellers are able to organize their knowledge situationally. A "situation" is when a specific person in a specific function needs a specific capability at a specific point in time. Superior sellers are able to *integrate* their capability knowledge with their knowledge of their buyer's situation(s).

The bottom two circles bring the buyer again into the equation. Superior sellers are able to align their selling methodology with the buyer's level of need and progress through her buy cycle. Many companies spend enormous amounts of money training their people in people skills, selling skills, product knowledge, and situation knowledge. What they have been unable to do for their people is help them achieve situational fluency. Even superior talent can take an inordinate amount of time to achieve sales success with today's complex, conceptual products and services. *Solution Selling* will give you and your business a "map" that will allow you to achieve situational fluency—to integrate knowledge and skill you already have with communication skills that keep you aligned with your buyers.

People buy from people. Superior sellers (I call them *Eagles*) have intuitive relationship building skills; they emphatically listen, they establish sincerity early in the sales call, and they establish a high level of confidence with their buyer. Sincerity and competence blend together to establish trust. Many people also believe that if the buyer likes the seller, the odds of success go up.

In this competitive world, I believe we have to give our competitor the benefit of the doubt that she will be likable, sincere, competent, and trustworthy. The additional factor we will bring to bear in this book is that people buy from people who *empower* them—salespeople who help buyers feel in control of their buying, salespeople who help their buyers see themselves gaining control of their problem, salespeople who help buyers see themselves enjoying the benefits of their product or service. People buy from people who can create *visions* for them.

The most difficult challenge we face in our *Solution Selling* workshops is teaching sellers to create what we call *action visions* for their buyers: that is, painting a mental picture for the buyer where she can see herself actually using the product or service in a specific situation.

A "Solution" Is Equivalent to the Buyer's Vision. Sellers can learn to facilitate the buyer's buying process so that the "close" becomes a "nonevent"—the next natural step in the buying process. Completing a sale is about moving the buyer to *visualize* future satisfaction with the bias of our product or service in mind. The buyer acquires an *action vision* of being able to solve her problem or to satisfy an unfulfilled desire. When a buyer has an action vision, she has a picture in her mind of *who* (the buyer or someone in the buyer's organization) will be taking *what* action (specific), *when* in time (some triggering event) *via* the seller's capability.

For example, if a seller was trying to sell an order processing system to a vice president of sales of a manufacturing company, an action vision question might be: *"What if your order processing people* [who] *could have a "window"* [seller's product capability] *into the production line so they could promise* [what action] *your customers an accurate delivery date while they are on the phone* [when in time] *with the customer?"* When sellers create such action visions, they demonstrate situational fluency to their buyers.

When the buyer has an action vision, the next logical step is to *take action.* Completing the sale and price negotiating become natural and agreeable sequences in the buy cycle.

There are three levels of buyer need with respect to the seller's products and services. The three levels are **latent pain, pain,** and **vision.** The buyer can be at any of those levels.

A buyer can be at latent pain—unadmitted pain and no vision of solution even though the *seller* has a clear picture of the need and how her product or service could help that buyer. Most sellers I work with tell me that they can see the buyer's need for their product or service in minutes, sometimes seconds, of a first encounter with a buyer. The reason? The seller has *expertise*—personal experience seeing others successfully using her product or service. The buyer, on the other hand, has no idea how this product or service could benefit him or his business. The two primary reasons for latent needs are ignorance—unaware a better way exists—or rationalization: He tried to solve that problem before and was unsuccessful.

If the buyer has what we call *pain*—discomfort or dissatisfaction with the current situation—he will be motivated to seek a solution *if* he thinks a solution is possible. In *Solution Selling* workshops we compare the human brain to a computer—both with "foregrounds" and "backgrounds." According to some very knowledgeable people I have worked with, most people have between five and nine "slots" in their foreground. The challenge sellers and marketers face is gaining *mindshare* of the buyer—occupying one of those foreground "slots" with an issue that their product or service can help the buyer address.

The third level of buyer need is vision—vision of a solution. A buyer is most likely to *volunteer to buy* when he has a vision. A vision of *who* will be taking *what* action, *when* in time via a specific capability. The seller's challenge is to make that vision include her product or service. When a buyer has latent pain or pain, the seller can *create* a vision for the buyer. When a buyer has an existing vision, the seller can reengineer that vision, adding the seller's aura and product or service bias to the vision.

The number one selling problem I encounter is an alignment problem—alignment between seller and buyer with respect to these three levels of need. The seller's expertise and experience allow her to see a "solution" more quickly than a buyer. This same expertise and experience can become her enemy if she does not control her enthusiasm. Remember, the buyer may not even believe the problem is solvable. When the buyer is at the latent pain or pain level and the seller has a vision, the seller will be very tempted to *project* her vision onto the buyer. Sellers need to be careful not to use "You need . . . " statements. "You need" statements cause the buyer to feel overcontrolled. In this book you will learn how to control your expertise and enthusiasm and make it your ally.

Diagnose before you prescribe.   Any time you say to your buyer, "You need . . . ," you are prescribing. Anytime you are talking about *your* company, *your* products, or *your* services you are prescribing what is good for them. In medicine, doctors who prescribe before they diagnose frequently get slapped with malpractice lawsuits, because they make mistakes. Furthermore, patients expect and *want* their doctors to diagnose their aches and pains. Health is personal and it demands a personal relationship. Buying is personal, too. However, many businesses today say to their customers, "You need . . . " Few salespeople are able to truly diagnose their buyers. Instead, sellers lead with their company, product, and service presentations assuming the buyer will be smart enough to see the value of their offering.

People are impatient. Once a seller knows something, it's hard for her to have empathy for those buyers who do not know what she knows. As sellers, our selling language is filled with impatience: "*So you have too many credit losses. I have just the thing for you! Our credit model scoring system will help you reduce your losses and keep your risk exposure low at the same time.*" All the buyer said in this example was "*I have too many credit losses.*" Seller impatience—I call it "premature elaboration"—kills many sales. It is counterproductive to building a relationship with the buyer. "Eagle" salespeople intuitively know they need to be patient. They ask questions of the buyer, methodically diagnose the buyer's problem, and step-by-step participate with the buyer in building a vision of a solution—biased, of course, with their product or service. You will learn how to emulate that patience in this book.

Power buys from power. The light bulb in my head turned on about thirteen years ago when I was working for Xerox Computer Services. I was reading a survey of American purchasing managers that showed these professional buyers prefer to buy from salespeople who have the most "command over their company resources." This makes perfect sense if you think about it. If a buyer's name is to be on a purchase order committing her organization to a large expenditure, what is the probability she would ask herself before she signed that purchase order, "What can go wrong here?" Part of her mental risk management process might include listing the things that could go wrong and then asking, "If one of these bad things happens (not delivered on time, broken, poor training . . .), what will I do (to regain control)?" Most people I talk to tell me that the first action thought that pops into their mind is to *call the salesperson:* the salesperson with *command of company resources,* the salesperson with *power.* If a buyer perceives that a seller does not have the power to complete the sale with satisfactory delivery, that seller will likely encounter difficulty getting the buyer's commitment.

Power is a two-way street: you and your buyer each have power and it is important that neither of you lose power or take power away from the other. On two-legged and four-legged sales calls—or however many legs you take on a call—I see many sellers lose power or credibility because of "guru" or sales manager "take-aways." A common take-away is when the sales manager leans into the sales transaction and says to the buyer, "What she means by that is. . . . " From that utterance, the seller loses credibility. Now the smart buyer will want to work with the sales manager, since she seems to know more and because she has *title* power. Since the sales manager *took away* the power, the manager will now have to close the business.

Words can reduce a seller's power. I come down hard on "wimpy" words and phrases in my workshops: "Maybe," "possibly," "perhaps," "we *might* be able to." Qualifiers like these diminish a seller's personal power. In *Solution Selling* workshops we work hard to help sellers maintain their power. This book will help you avoid power reducing words.

There are three phases of buying.   Sellers must also learn to align horizontally with their buyers. Buyers frequently shift between three major buying phases and you can learn to identify them and then to adapt to your buyer's concern.

The three phases of the buying cycle are:

Phase I. Define needs.   The buyer asks, "Do I have a need?" "What must I do to take care of it?" "How much will it cost?" If the seller meets the buyer in this phase, she can establish trust with the buyer, get the buyer to admit to having a problem, and lead the buyer to a vision of a solution that includes her offering.

Phase II. Evaluate alternatives.   The buyer who now can envision capabilities needed to solve her problem must analyze and compare available products or services to her vision. She must justify the cost. Buyers will ask, Is there really a match for my vision? Which one is best? Can I afford it?

Phase III: Risk evaluation and action.   Once a buyer concludes that there is a potential solution and that she can afford it, she enters Phase III—the consequences. Now the buyer is suddenly concerned with the risks of buying versus not buying, and she must justify price. Now the buyer asks, Should I buy? Does the seller have command over her resources? Am I getting the best price? What if I delay? Will they be responsive after I sign the contract? What if I do nothing?

Within these three phases of the buy cycle, buyers consider a whole mix of needs, potential solutions, costs, and risks. It is critical for sellers to stay in alignment with their buyers through each phase. *Many potential sales are ruined because the seller did not stay in alignment with the buyer's behavior.* This book will help you consciously stay aligned with your buyers.

Make yourself equal before you make yourself different. Businesses and salespeople usually compete fiercely. Most buyers look at more than one alternative. If you are not the first seller the buyer deals with, it is important for you to make yourself equal with the "leader" *before* you attempt to become different. Our competitive nature often causes us to attack our competitor's offering before we make ourselves equal to the original vision. If we succumb to that behavior, we disregard something very valuable to the buyer—her *vision*. Later in this book you will learn vision reengineering (while avoiding the competitive battle as long as necessary) to deal with this critical selling issue.

Don't close before it is closeable. Too many sellers destroy a valuable relationship by attempting to close their sale before it is closeable. At the beginning of my workshops, I sometimes ask attendees if they have ever gone on a call, expecting to get a signature, when they did not get it *that day*. Most hands go up. I then ask them to quote the buyer's reason for not signing that day. What attendees realize is that most of the time they were closing before it was closeable.

Such selling *mis*behavior is not caused just by inexpert selling; it is also caused by poor management. Does senior management ever force its salespeople to close prematurely? Because some executive or CFO or sales manager is trying to increase sales or increase profits or make a quarterly goal, many salespeople are forced to destroy valuable relationships by being *ordered* to close—before a sale is closeable. I find that most senior managers applying the pressure are doing so because they have a gut level belief that the front-line salesperson doesn't really have control over when the buyer will buy. In this book you will learn how to create the "perfect time to close" and to predict future business more accurately by being able to target when the buyer will be ready to buy.

I am trying to change the definition of selling to "helping people buy"—facilitating the buying process. Ideally, if you are the one helping them buy, they will want to buy from you. Many times in this book we will discuss the concept of *honorable selling*. Honorable selling does not have to be an oxymoron. For now, let us say that in order for selling to be honorable:

- The seller must believe that she can truly bring value to the potential buyer.
- The seller must be willing to tell the truth about her product or service.
- The buyer must feel good about the process.
- The buyer's expectations are met.

The point, the buyer must feel good about *the process,* is important. As I work with an increasing number of clients who tell me that they sell a "commodity," I realize how critical the process is. I tell my clients that the best seller executing the best process will win. I tell them they should be able to win with a *reasonable* product or service. If the seller is selling a conceptual, intangible product or service to a nonexpert buyer, she can win with a process. You can win with a process. This book is about a process.

Michael T. Bosworth

10 FACES OF PAIN

Solution Selling is not just a methodology for bag-carrying, on-quota salespeople. Thousands of consultants, engineers, Ph.D.s, CEOs, professional practice partners, sole proprietors, and entrepreneurs have participated in *Solution Selling* workshops. It never ceases to amaze me how these "nonsalespeople" react to the sales process. The comments I hear most frequently are, "I had no idea how tough the job of a salesperson really is," and "I'll never degrade salespeople again." In this section, 10 Faces of Pain, I want to take you out into the real world of high-difficulty selling and give you a sense of some of the extremely difficult situations sellers face on a daily basis. With the 10 Faces of Pain I am setting the stage for Part II—Strategies to Facilitate, Influence, and Control the Buying Process. Each selling situation highlighted in this section will be addressed specifically in Part II.

10 Faces of Buyer Pain

Pain, "*. . . the distress or suffering, mental or physical, caused by anxiety, anguish, grief, disappointment, etc. . . .*"

Webster's New World Dictionary,
Second College Edition

I am frequently asked how top salespeople (that 20 percent who produce 80 percent of the results—I call them *Eagles*) achieve their outstanding results. I usually reply that if they could replicate it, the business world would beat a path to their doorsteps. Of course, then there would be no *Journeyman* salespeople—that 80 percent who produce 20 percent of the results. Most Eagles are surprisingly unaware of how they do what they do so well; consequently, they are unable to transfer these precious selling talents to others. In fact, few people can teach anyone else how to sell like an Eagle, and this is a problem for most businesses. I believe that a good Journeyman can be trained to consistently outsell an Eagle salesman who is "winging it."

The question is, "If most Eagles cannot teach selling, who can? And what is to be taught?"

It is clear that we need a model—a model of how the eagle sells that can be taught to journeymen. In order for you to appreciate the *Solution Selling* model, I ask you first to examine the *10 faces of buyer pain.* Each of the 10 faces of buying pain illustrates those points of stress between sellers and buyers. Trying to facilitate the buying process is often an uphill road. Each *face* is connected to the buying process: the three levels of buyer need, shifting buyer concerns, and how buyers buy. Each *face* has problems. When you read the stories, see if you can find the selling problems. Each face portrays common selling faults associated with salespeople.

I like to think of the sales process as similar to a fine play in which all the actors or artists are engaged in a working dialogue. Competent actors practice their lines before going in front of an audience. Sellers can also think of themselves as artists, trained artists who know how and when to use the right words.

You will find that I use scripts freely throughout this book. I find that scripts illustrate well the language and skill of the seller's real-world marketplace. Scripts work into role plays that are critical to the seller's trade. Scripts provide a tool to practice key concepts. Products and services are a seller's props—some better than others but getting a sale is usually reduced to sincere, competent, trained salespeople and *great* scripting. A smart director helps too—one who knows how essential it is to rehearse. So not only are the sellers key players, but their managers are too.

When you read the following sections, think carefully about the selling challenges represented by each *face*.

FACE #1—LATENT PAIN TO PAIN

A seller's "conceptual" sales territory is filled with buyers who have latent needs or "pains" for his products or services. Later we will learn about conceptual sales territories. A buyer has a latent need either because of ignorance or because he has rationalized an active pain as unsolvable and therefore pushes the need to the back of his mind. In other words, many buyers recognize a need (pain), attempt to act on it, and, finding no satisfactory solution, relegate it (deprioritize it) back to a latent need. Buyer #1 is such a buyer.

Situation. John is a 42-year-old healthy male, married with three children. He is a decisive entrepreneur.

Critical issue. John is balding.

Reasons. The following interview uncovers the reasons why baldness is a critical issue. The interview reveals the buyer's level of buying need, his previous phases of buying, and his current concept of a solution.

You have a problem? Tell me about it.
Balding is the problem. I want hair—here on the top of my head. I lose more hair every day.

When did balding first become a problem?

In my early thirties. Actually, I was about 31 when I began to lose my hair. It was a depressing discovery, because I thought I was too young for balding to begin. I searched everywhere for solutions that would either prevent further hair loss or replace lost hair with new hair.

You said it was depressing. Why depressing?

I wanted to have hair. I wanted to be "normal." I want people, especially women, to see me with hair. I want hair—you know, the normal reaction of a balding man.

Solution.

Then what?

I refused to accept it passively. I looked for remedies, for solutions.

What did you find?

Witch doctors, everywhere. I looked into the pharmaceutical or near-pharmaceutical formulas—any kind of snake oil that promised hair restoration. I literally tried everything. Anything and everything. Bottles of concoctions. My hair was continually drenched in someone's commercial promises.

And?

Nothing worked.

What did you want?

Full and healthy growing hair with no damage to my head, although I certainly worried about some of the stuff I poured over my head. I'm probably lucky to still have any hair. God only knows what I poured on top of my head.

Did you try other approaches?

Yes, I looked into surgical procedures. For instance, one procedure remains a vivid memory. It involved cutting and removing the bald skin on the top of my scalp, then joining the edges of the skin left by stretching them up to the center of my head, and sewing the ends together. Of course, then I would have hair on the top of my head—real, living, growing hair. Hair that used to grow over my ears would be growing on the top of my head. I rejected the procedure. Too drastic, too bloody.

Then I examined hair "plugs," which involved taking plugs of scalp with hair from the abundant hair areas of my head, then plugging them or inserting them into the bald area. This is also a long and bloody procedure, requiring frequent visits with intervals of pain mixed with sheer ugliness.

In the final analysis, I decided against all surgical remedies. They were too drastic and I lacked the stomach for them.

Did that end your search?

No, next I examined a whole field of toupees. After several attempts and fit-tings—some even involved sewing the toupees to your scalp—I decided that this alternative was unsatisfactory, too. I have seen my share of poorly matched hair pieces. How many times have you snickered at some desperate guy's lifeless, shabby, tacky, mismatched toupee? I couldn't bear that.

So, what now?

Now? Nothing. After a full investigation into remedies for baldness, I opted to do nothing, because no remedy offered a satisfactory solution. I put the whole problem in the back of my mind. Hey, life goes on. That was a long time ago. I've put all that behind me.

[Now the interviewer hands John a fictitious *Wall Street Journal* ar-ticle entitled, "Miracle Biogenetic Cure for Baldness" which reports an early-stage, esoteric research project about a biogenetic cure for baldness. If successful, baldness will become a thing of the past. The buyer is instantly curious, reads the article, realizes the product is not yet commercial, then looks up.]

What do you think of the article?

Incredible. Even though it's still only at the research stage, this is the kind of thing I'm looking for, no doubt. May I keep this article? I want to find out more about the project.

What has to happen for you to be a buyer—if and when they bring it to market?

Safety. It has to be absolutely safe and healthy to use. I don't want to use it and find out later—down the road—that I have developed cancer from it. Personal risk, I guess. I don't want to feel that other health problems would occur. I would not want to take the shots, or however one would receive the treatment, and gain fifty pounds. So safety, and it also has to be reason-ably priced.

So, safety and price?

Yes.

Did that fictitious *Wall Street Journal* article on the biogenetic cure for baldness bring the buyer's latent need back to an active, recog-nized pain? Yes. Having decided earlier there was no satisfactory solution, John had taken his personal problem—for him *pain*—and downgraded its urgency and rank, putting it "on hold" in his un-conscious memory. Why? Because he realized he couldn't *control* the problem. Now it is a latent need. Right? While the answer is yes, do not be deceived. With *hope* for an untested *cure*, John's *pain* instantly reappeared; he became a buyer actively seeking an acceptable solution.

I raise this point early to illustrate that a legion of buyers, like the balding man, live with *latent* needs, needs that, on the basis of your product's or service's merits and quality (physical and psychological), can be developed into sales. This buyer lives in your conceptual sales territory. It's up to your business and you to uncover such buyers—to create *hope* for them. Then—and only then—can you lead them to a vision that your product or service could be an acceptable solution for them.

Your conceptual sales territory is much greater than you think. You will learn how to prospect in this sales territory.

FACE #2—PRICE NEGOTIATION

Smart buyers are aware of a seller's deadlines and often exploit that knowledge and use shrewd buying strategies. Face #2 portrays the scenario of a smart buyer and an unprepared salesperson who is caught with a last minute demand from the head office to increase sales because it is "September 40th" at the end of the third quarter.

Situation.   Harry Gillespie is the vice president, administration of MASH 1955, a health maintenance organization (an HMO).

Critical Issue.   MASH customers and merchants (retail pharmacies) are unhappy.

Reasons.   MASH customer records are administered manually. MASH's administration staff go home after 5 PM. However, because MASH is a 24-hour care facility, 30 percent of MASH's customers use the facilities after regular hours, usually between 6 PM and 9 PM.

After 5 PM, pharmacies cannot obtain information from MASH about its customers' coverage. Many pharmacies have experienced losses by extending credit to unqualified MASH customers, and consequently refuse to offer after-hour services to MASH customers.

An HMO started up across the street. It is successful, mostly because of MASH 1955's problems. Pharmacies can verify coverage 24 hours a day. Now MASH has to solve its critical issue.

Solution.   The MASH board formed a buying committee consisting of the entire board of directors. The buying committee has asked Buyer #2, Harry Gillespie, to find solutions and to come back to them for a decision.

Harry has selected Mary White's interactive voice response system. Her product has been cost justified, and now only price negotiations remain. MASH has decided to buy.

The buying committee knows that the seller's company's fiscal year end is the three days, so with that in mind, they invited her down to their headquarters for the price negotiation meetings. MASH 1955 is in Charlotte, North Carolina, and the seller's company is in Princeton, New Jersey.

The meeting was set for 3 PM, Friday, and the last airplane flight to New Jersey out of Charlotte is at 5:45 PM, barely allowing Mary time to get from the meeting to the airport. (Do you think the buyer is aware of the flight time?)

Mary White is a single parent with two children. It is imperative that she return that evening to Princeton. She agreed to the appointment time because her company is under pressure to increase sales revenues. Her instructions were, "come back with the deal."

The price negotiation meeting.

[It is 4:25 PM. Harry Gillespie, the vice president, administration, chairs the MASH buying committee. All members are present. The meeting started an hour late because one member could not show up until 4 PM. Mary is worried about her airplane connection.]

Mary: So, as you can see, we have done everything you asked. The contract is approved by legal, and you, Harry, have it there in front of you. My company feels its price is competitive.

Harry: Mary, we like your product. Your demonstration—was it three months ago?—settled that issue. However, we want your price discounted.

Mary: That's difficult. We have already included a 10 percent discount.

[Mary looks at her watch. It is 4:40. Her company has told her to get the contract, no matter what. It is their year end and the CFO wants sales revenues to look good.]

Mary: How long does it take to get to the airport?

Harry: Only 20 minutes. You've got lots of time. We'll drive you there. We need another 10 percent off your price.

Mary: Ten percent? I can't do that.

Harry: What can you do?

Mary: Even at 5 percent my boss will be upset . . . but, I tell you what, I'll phone my office and see.

[Mary leaves to telephone her office, swearing to herself. She has to get home to her kids. However, her boss has already left for the weekend and she cannot discuss MASH's price demand with him. She remembers his parting instructions. It is 4:50. The plane leaves at 5:45 and it takes twenty minutes to get to the airport. Mary decides she must leave the meeting by 5:15. Mary returns to the meeting.]

Mary: He's upset with me, but I can do the extra 5 percent.

Harry: So, including the 10 percent—and with that 5 percent, that's 15 percent. Right?

Mary: Right.

Harry: I think we're almost there. Mary, we'd like to meet privately. I have to poll the members. It's only a formality, so would you step outside the room for a minute?

Mary: Of course.

[Mary steps out, looking at her watch, which shows 5:03. She is exasperated and resents the pressure. She wonders, Why does my company always do this to me? Year end pressure for sales. Mary has no wish to spend the weekend in Charlotte away from her kids.
    The committee calls her back. It is 5:12 PM.]

Harry: We like your price.

Mary: Great.

Harry: However, Mary, there is just one more thing. Just one more thing and then we'll be through.

Mary: What's that?

Harry: We want you to throw in your latest voice conferencing software module free as part of the deal.

[The software package sells regularly for $12,000. What the hell, Mary thought; she has to come back with the sale and, if she stays any longer, she will miss her flight. Mary will not earn a commission, because the price is below cost.]

Mary: Done.

[Harry shook her hand jubilantly. Mary made the changes in the contract and Harry signed. The driver was waiting and Mary rushed to the airport. The time was 5:18 and Mary was a nervous wreck—happy to be on her way to the airport, unhappy with her sale.]

How many times will profits be killed by company year ends, executive pressure, and lack of negotiating skills? What's to be done? For one thing, not only sellers but the whole organization need to reappraise their selling habits.

This was not a good price negotiation. The seller made serious errors—at least two *faux pas*. First, the seller did little precall preparation and did not anticipate or manage her time pressure. She had options. And, second, the seller gave concessions without *first* asking for concessions in return.

FACE #3—COLD CALL "WINDOW OF OPPORTUNITY"

Sellers hate to telephone prospect. Most would rather go to the dentist for a root canal. They do their best to leave telephone prospecting to the last moment or avoid it altogether. Face #3 portrays a telephone cold call prospecting effort.

Situation. Michele is the vice president, sales, of AAA Copiers Inc. (fictitious), a Fortune 500 public company that distributes and sells third-party office equipment under its own corporate name, primarily office copiers and fax machines.

Critical issue. The company has not been meeting sales goals.

Reasons. AAA has been losing market position in an important product line. They are experiencing heavy competition with regard to that product line. Revenues and profits are under pressure, and selling costs are high. Customers have become confused and disenchanted with AAA's problems and confusion, and the industry is known for its fickle customers.

Michele, the VP, sales, manages 1,500 salespeople who are geographically dispersed, and the sales force has a wide range of selling experience.

Product education is not uniform. Because of product complexity and frequent product and price changes, the sales force finds itself selling outdated products at prices that differ from region to region. Company technical experts are frequently unavailable for customer demonstrations and trainings.

Technical training costs are excessive. AAA uses a small group of technical experts for a number of sales purposes: product sales education, sales demonstrations, buyer training, and office equipment exhibitions and shows. They travel a lot and their expenses are high.

Problems extend throughout the organization. The VP, finance, is impacted by missed revenue targets, high and rising travel expenses, and falling profits. The VP, marketing, is reeling because product marketing managers are living on airplanes, product roll-outs are costly, and market share is eroding. The CEO has to answer to a critical investment banking community, the stock price is falling, and capital markets are unimpressed, affecting the company's ability to finance new innovation and growth.

Michele's inability to meet or exceed sales goals affects the entire company. She is searching anxiously for solutions.

Solution. The seller, Mike, a sales rep with NNC Business Television Inc., sells satellite business television. Mike assumed Michele had problems that he believed his products and services could address and help solve. Wanting AAA Inc.'s account, he decided to prospect her business. The buyer has not considered satellite business television technology.

Mike "cold calls" Michele on the telephone.

Mike: Michele, this is Mike Adams, with NNC Business Television. We have been working with office equipment companies for the last 10 years. One of the chief concerns we are hearing from other sales executives is their frustration at not meeting sales goals because of poor communications with their sales staff regarding frequent product and price changes. We have been able to help our customers deal with this issue, and I would like an opportunity to share with you how.

Michele: Tell me more.

Mike: Do you have time to talk now, or would there be a better time for me to call you back?

Michele: I have a few minutes right now.

Mike: What I would like to do in those few minutes is introduce you to NNC and tell you about another office equipment company with which we have worked. I would then like to learn about you and your situation. At that point the two of us will be able to decide whether or not we should proceed any further.

Michele: That's fair.

Mike: Good. Michele, NNC Business Television is in the business of helping companies with national distribution operate more productively and profitability through products and services we provide.

NNC was founded in 1982. Since that time we have had steady growth to where our revenues exceeded $300 million last year. We have many Fortune 1000 customers, and our customers are important to us. We get feedback from them via regular customer service reports and by independent audits. Some of our customers include EDS, Minolta, Exxon—

Michele: Big names.

Mike: Yes. A particular situation you might be interested in, Michele, is another office equipment company. Their vice president of sales was missing his sales quota. The reasons included difficulty training salespeople on the latest technological improvements and with uniform product pricing between regions. What he said he needed was some way to train his salespeople more quickly on their company's latest product technologies at a reasonable cost. He also wanted a way to communicate with everyone at the same time to eliminate the information float problem. NNC provided them with those capabilities, and the result was an 8 percent jump in sales and an increase in aftertax profits by over $600,000.

Michele: That's impressive, Mike.

Mike: I agree, but enough about NNC Business Television, Michele. Tell me about your business situation.

Michele. Mike, this sounds very interesting to me. I want to talk with you, but I really have to go now. What if I clear 40 minutes tomorrow morning, say, between 11 AM and noon? Then we can figure out whether we have common interests. Okay?

You bet it's okay! And that's because it was a good prospecting telephone call. Mike was granted the meeting because he proved to be competent and sincere. The buyer concluded the seller had expertise and was trustworthy.

In today's world of costly travel expenses, telephone prospecting saves unnecessary expenses, adding to profits—if it's done right.

Mike still has a long way to go. Since Mike's capability is to provide satellite business television services, how will he develop a vision of a solution for Michele and get it biased with his product? Now that he has established rapport and has completed his call introduction, what's next? How will he get Michele to admit all of her pain, its complications, and its interdependencies? Can he stay in alignment with her? How will he compete against the competition? He knows, and you know, Michele cannot buy without price comparisons and senior management approval. How will he gain access to power? How will he control the selling process all the way to a signed agreement?

FACE #4—ORGANIZATIONAL INTERDEPENDENCE AND ACCESS TO POWER

tough

Some buyers are only "sponsors." They do not have the *power* to spend money. Smart sellers see that and work to find the "power sponsor." Power sponsors have the political power (regardless of title) to obtain the seller's product if they believe it is right for their organization. The power sponsor may not even be inside the buyer's organization.

Situation.   Clarke Johnson is the superintendent, administration, of School District 24, a metropolitan secondary education school district.

Critical issue.   The state has threatened to reduce the district's funding.

Reasons.   School District 24, as do other school districts, receives funding based partly on the results from student standard testing and expeditious reporting. The higher the test scores, the greater the funding; the lower the test scores, the lower the funding. Because of a combination of low test scores and late reporting, funding cuts threaten the district. Jobs are at stake.

There are two reasons for delayed testing and test reports. It's a complex process. First, tests are now manually rendered, scored, and collated. Second, test results are reported manually and sent by surface mail to the state. Late reports are counted as "no report" and the district receives less funding.

The district is highly interdependent. Problems in one area can produce problems in another. District 24 has received written criticism by state administrators. This creates pressure on the board of education to solve the problem—pressure from teachers as well as parents. The district superintendent is charged with solving the problem. Buyer #4 must either solve the problem or be replaced.

Solution.   Clarke Johnson, the superintendent, hired a consultant, Joan Smith, to assist in problem definition, solution alternatives, and the writing of system specifications. Clarke was pushed by the board of management to buy a computerized testing and test score report system recommended by Joan.

Before a final request for proposal (RFP) is to be mailed, they want an independent vendor to help write the buying specifications. Joan chose Kemp Kramer of National XX Systems, because she appreciated the ability and reputation of Kemp and his firm.

Clarke is aware of the seller's company and, at the urging of Joan, arranged a meeting with Kemp. Clarke dislikes salespeople; they make him nervous. He is suspicious and distrusting of salespeople—he doesn't want to do business with a "Joe Isuzu," the television car salesman.

Kemp is eager to "set" the specifications, thereby establishing himself as the #1 vendor. To do this, he must get the buyer's participation, that is, to admit to the problem and to develop a vision of a solution that Kemp wishes to bias with his product.

A call introduction.   [The meeting includes Clarke, his CFO (who reports to him), Joan, and Kemp. Kemp was told he could include a "demo," which meant he was free to bring a technical expert. Kemp came to the meeting alone.]

Kemp: Good afternoon, Kemp Kramer, with National XX Systems.

Clarke: Clarke Johnson. Kemp, meet my colleagues . . .

[The CFO and the consultant are introduced, and everybody sits at a conference table.]

Clarke: Kemp, we know exactly what we want.

Kemp: Good. I would like to hear what you want, Clarke.

Clarke: I don't want a big sales pitch. We've done a lot of work here already, and we know pretty much what we want. See? Joan, why don't you take this part of the meeting?

Kemp: Joan, may I ask something first?

Joan: Sure.

Kemp: First, why not tell me what the problem is, and then what you see as the solution? That way I'll understand better what you want.

[Kemp takes out a notepad and makes notes as Joan talks.]

Joan: The problem is the school district may have its funding cut by the state.

Kemp: Is that your primary critical issue?

Joan: Yes. We want a software product that can operate on our existing computer hardware system. We don't want to reinvent the wheel or pay a lot for unnecessary new computer equipment. We need software capability that delivers computerized test scoring, calculates test scores, collates each school's results, and compiles them into standard testing reports and curricula analysis. All of this has to be in accordance with state educational standard operating procedures. Oh, and the system has to be easy to operate.

[Kemp is handed a copy of District 24's RFP. He scans the table of contents, turns to the Specifications & Requirements section, and reads the specifications requirements.]

Kemp: I see.

Joan: We want you to take this away and study it, analyze it, and get back to us with your comments and recommendations.

Kemp: Okay.

Joan: We would like to meet again in three days. Is that enough time for you?

Kemp: Yes. Joan, I'm confident we can work something out that will match exactly what you want—

Clarke: Kemp, we know what we want.

Kemp: Clarke, you've explained you can't get timely statistical reports. Would you explain for me how your present testing and test report systems—

Clarke: It's all in there, in the RFP, Kemp. I think it's best we wait until you've had time to read the RFP, then in our next meeting we can answer any questions you may still have. Right, Joan?

Joan: Right. Kemp, after you've read the RFP, if you want, maybe you can call me.

Kemp: Thank you . . .

The seller is struggling, because the buyer is setting up road-blocks that thwart attempts to establish alignment. Joan appears to be the "power sponsor." What should Kemp do?

A vendor is not selected yet, and the seller has a chance to bias the buying requirements with his product's capabilities. How can Kemp overcome Clarke Wilson's "Joe Isuzu" bias of salespeople? How can he get Clarke and Joan to share a vision of a solution that will incorporate his product's capabilities? How can he differentiate himself and his company from the competition that will be used when it comes time to negotiate price?

FACE #5—PRODUCT OR SERVICE VIEWED AS A "COMMODITY"

Sellers must align with their buyers. Frequently, the seller must earn that alignment. Our seller in Face #5 has an opportunity to become different in the eyes of his buyer.

Situation. George Dudley is 34 and married.

Critical issue. George is unhappy with the poor personal service of his present bank—Bank XXX.

Reasons. George and his wife are co-signers on a home mortgage, two car loans, and a VISA credit card. They keep a savings account and two checking accounts.

His present bank was acquired by a larger bank, Bank XXX. Many of the branch staff who knew him are gone or are leaving. Bank XXX service has deteriorated: the merged banks combined three branches into one big branch. Now customer lines at teller windows are long, and teller staff are inexperienced temps.

George believes all banks are essentially the same. He believes that they are elephants that lumber along with bureaucratic systems. In the past, services have been hard to understand, and he has been subjected to delays and to a humiliating turndown. George and his wife feel bank services are offered without personal service.

Vision. George sincerely wants personal service. He wants a bank relationship.

George has decided to change banks, so during a lunch break, he has gone over to Bank ABC, determined to explore its services and banking policies. Bank ABC is a retail branch federal savings bank.

An ABC Bank branch.   [George walks into the bank lobby and is met by Renae Adame, a financial services rep (FSR). Sensing he is a new buyer, she introduces herself.]

Seller: Hi! My name is Renae Adame. I work here.

Buyer: Hello, Renae, I'm George . . . George Dudley.

Seller: Good afternoon, George, can I help you? I don't think I've seen you in our bank before.

Buyer: You haven't. First time here.

Seller: Perhaps you would like to sit down—over there at my desk?

[Renae motions to a desk in the new accounts area, and they sit facing each other.]

Seller: We can talk more comfortably and confidentially here. How can I help you? Did you want to open a checking account today?

Buyer: I'm not sure. Right now I bank with Bank XXX. My old bank was acquired by them, and the service has gone from just fair to poor. So, I'm looking for a new bank. I want to do business with a bank that cares about my account.

Seller: We can solve that problem. We would like to have your business—

Buyer: Please, call me George.

Seller: Okay, George. Right now we have a special promotion. I can show you a checking account where you get no-service-charge banking for three months.

Buyer: If I go over to the_____ Bank and do the same thing, I can get no-service-charge checking for one year.

Seller: Yes, that's true. But, if you open a mutual funds investment account with our bank's subsidiary, you can get a checking account with no service charges forever—as long as you maintain the investment account.

Buyer: Mmm. Why don't you tell me how you're different from other banks and . . . I see a number of brochures here on your desk.

[She takes three brochures and hands them to him. Bank efficiency experts have done time studies—the experts concluded that an FSR should not spend more than seven minutes with a prospect, so she looks at her watch mindful that she is under the seven-minute limitation with her buyer.]

Buyer: Are you a regular bank? Aren't you an S&L?

Seller: Obviously we're a bank like any other bank. We're just like
Bank XXX. We're $21 billion in size and we have been operating for a
long time, and . . .

"Perhaps . . . " Blah. "We can solve that problem." Blah, blah.
"We're just like Bank XXX." Blah, blah, blah. Renae is a "feature
creature"—"spray and pray." Did Renae maintain power? Did she
make herself equal to Bank XXX before she attempted to make herself different? This sale went wrong early and fast. Renae and Bank
ABC are in a steep death spiral.

The seller is not in alignment with the buyer. The seller is "featuring" the buyer to death. And what's this seven minutes stuff?
Seven minutes for a buyer who is being asked to give the bank an
adult lifetime of business? I doubt the efficiency experts ever had
to sell anything except themselves for promotion up the corporate
ladder.

The buyer is not even close to buying! What is the seller to do?
The buyer is early in his buy cycle and, given the buyer's attitudes,
the seller has not established rapport. First, Renae offers three
months of free checking, then under pressure she offers permanent
no-service-charge checking. Does George think she is sincere and
trustworthy? Why is the seller selling her product's features (we all
know they are the same as most other banks)? Will the seller discover George's "buying committee" (i.e., his spouse)?

FACE #6—REQUESTS FOR PROPOSALS

Here is a tough situation. The seller faces a bureaucratic, large corporate buyer who has issued a request for proposal (RFP).

Situation.   Joe is the vice president, strategic planning, of a
large telecommunications company.

Critical issue.   The company needs an outside expert to develop its annual strategic business plan. An RFP has to be evaluated,
prepared, and completed, also by an outside expert.

The buyer's regular outside audit firm—one of the Big Six—has
a subsidiary consulting arm that has already written the buyer's request for proposal. These same "insider" consultants want to win

the RFP contract, so they have arranged a vendor list against which they believe they can win.

Politics and unfair competition intrude. Although unfair, it is legal and one of the hazards of the consulting business. Everyone knows this is the way the game is played.

Four vendors have been asked to submit RFP proposals. One of the vendors, Andy _____ , a partner in the consulting firm Paradigm Consulting, has received the RFP. He knows the playing field is not level. Andy, after conferring with his partners, decided to attempt to get a face-to-face meeting with Buyer #6, Joe _____, the VP, strategic planning. It is Andy's objective to establish personal rapport with Joe and, hopefully, get an opportunity to slant the RFP assignment in his favor.

The telephone call. Andy (our seller) telephones Joe (our buyer).

[As an aside, the seller's consulting business is in trouble. The firm wins only 1 of every 40 RFPs received. If the business does not improve, the consulting partnership will dissolve.]

Buyer: Hello, Joe_____ speaking.

Seller: Joe, good morning, my name is Andy _____ with Paradigm Consulting, and I am responding to the RFP you sent. It came to me under your letterhead, so I assume you are the person with whom I speak?

Buyer: Absolutely. Hi, Andy. What about our RFP? Is anything wrong?

Seller: No, no, but Joe, after reading it, I realized that it's going to take 40 to 50 hours of work for me to do the kind of job I know you want me to do. It will be difficult for me to get it back to you in the time period you've requested. And I'm sure I'm not the only person who is getting your RFP.

Buyer: Of course. It's a competitive thing. We've mailed several RFPs on this project. Your firm was highly recommended. Although we haven't worked together before, I've been told how good you and your firm are.

Seller: I'm glad to hear that. Joe, are you free to tell me who said those nice things?

Buyer: Why not! Yes, our auditors. They said you were good at what you do.

Seller: Thanks. Joe, before we spend all this time and money, I need to come over and meet with you and—

Buyer: I am prohibited from that, Andy. You know that. It would be a conflict of interest for me to meet one-on-one with you, and our bylaws prohibit that kind of action.

Seller: Joe, before I spend all this money and time—

Buyer: Andy, I absolutely cannot meet alone with you.

This is a tough, tough barrier to cross. How can a seller get by an "insider" consulting firm and get a fair chance? The real commercial world has many similar personal monopolies.

The "rules" prohibit individual meetings. Can the seller devise actions that can shatter such barriers? Unless the seller can establish rapport, interview the appropriate decision makers, and create a vision of a solution (in this case, a finished annual strategic business plan biased by Paradigm Consulting's expertise)—and change the RFP's specifications—then it is highly unlikely the seller will win this contract. What would you do if you were 150 percent of goal? What would you do if you were 30 percent of goal?

FACE #7—FREE EDUCATION

Have you ever dealt with a low-level beneficiary, one who is neither a sponsor nor a power sponsor? A lot of valuable selling resources are wasted by "buyers" who are only keeping current with latest trends, techniques, and technology. Here a seller encounters this problem.

Situation. Auto Fast √ Auto Repair (fictitious) is a regional automotive aftermarket engine tune-up company. Auto Fast √ Auto Repair operates regionally in the huge automotive aftermarket industry: engine tune-up and smog certification services. It is a low-margin, high-volume, high-fixed-overhead, mass-market retail business. Sid Turner, Buyer #7, is the director of training. He has a staff of 10 trainers and, although his services are valuable, the company does not endorse training, particularly from an expense point of view.

Critical issue. Unresolved customer litigation is negatively impacting profits.

Reasons.   Several reasons account for the contingent litigation liabilities: work order service people misdiagnose what customers perceive as the "problem," repair technicians perform
erratically, repair technicians are undertrained, and top management is not paying attention to customers. Neither management
nor the repair station staff are trained in a customer's point of
view. Profit margins are thin. The inside word on the street is that
the owners and their top management are milking the company
for short-term gains. The company's greatest pains are probably
yet to be experienced.

Training—on its own—has decided to interview outside experts
to review automotive technology course curricula. The object is to
upgrade worker technology and work skills. These actions are not
known to top management.

The CFO is told to lower expenses and maximize sales. Any decisions to purchase outside training would be made by the CEO
and the CFO. Although he reports directly to the CEO, Sid Turner,
the director of training, is not part of the "senior management"
committee.

After discussions with the Bureau of Automotive Repair, Sid has
invited three training vendors to meetings at Auto Fast √ Auto Repair with Sid and two of his trainers. One of the recommended outside training consultants is a firm called 2001 Tech Training, and
their sales rep is Les Knight.

A call introduction meeting.   Les has arrived for a meeting
with Sid. They meet in the Auto Fast √ Auto Repair lobby.

Buyer: Les Knight?

Seller: I'm Les Knight, and you're Sid Turner, right?

Buyer: Yes, Sid Turner, Call me Sid.

Seller: Thanks for taking the time to meet with me.

Buyer: Come on upstairs. Let's go to my office where we can talk.
     What a great day. How was the drive up? How about a coffee, Les?

[Sid is entirely welcoming and hospitable, showing Les his company's
car racing trophies, which are enshrined in glass shelving along the
route to his office. After Sid gets a coffee for Les, the meeting starts.]

Buyer: I've heard from the Bureau of Automotive Repair about your
     company, and the head guy up there mentioned your name.

Seller: Right. Yes, we're friends. He told me you had a problem that you wanted to talk about.

Buyer: Yes, it was Steve. I talked to him a bit about a small problem.

Seller: Steve thinks our educational curricula is the best in the state, and he's attended some of my smog certification seminars.

Buyer: Yes, I've read some of your literature, especially the smog certification curricula and training courses.

Seller: Yes, we have great stuff.

Buyer: Hmm. You know, Les, we have a small problem here in our company and it strikes me that you might be able to help—

Seller: Great. Let me show you our training and curricula brochures.

I think the seller has handled himself ineffectually. He positioned himself as power inferior at the beginning of the meeting. Why would a buyer be so friendly to a seller at a first meeting? Most buyers are initially standoffish with sellers, especially at first meetings. Is that normal human behavior? Are *you* that nice to sellers who approach you or call you at home?

How should Les Knight have handled Sid Turner? How does a seller establish rapport and true competence with the buyer? How can Les discover Sid's pain, its complications, and interdependencies? How can Les qualify his buyer and gain access to the real buying power?

FACE #8—BUYER GETS COLD FEET

The buyer has panicked. This is a scary situation common to many sellers.

Situation. Katherine is a 38-year-old married woman earning a middle-income salary.

Critical issue. Additional pension savings are required to supplement an inadequate pension plan.

Reasons. Although the buyer's spouse works, he has no pension plan. He is an hourly worker. Katherine is concerned their joint pension needs will not be covered adequately unless she purchases a supplementary annuity.

The buyer heard of the seller, Tom _____, through a friend. Tom works for an insurance company that specializes in annuity products—products that guarantee a fixed or variable payment to the annuitant in the future.

For over three months the seller and buyer have worked together on a plan for Katherine. She passed health examinations, employment verifications, and other analyses. She has evaluated other insurance alternatives, affordability, and estimated yields.

Last week, she decided to purchase a $400,000 annuity. Then something happened. Communications stopped. Tom made several calls with no response. The buyer has panicked.

A telephone call.   [Tom called Katherine at her work.]

Buyer: Hello, Katherine speaking.

Seller: Katherine, it's Tom _____. What's happened? I haven't been able to reach you. Are you okay? No sickness in the family?

Buyer: Oh, Tom, I'm sorry. I feel so guilty about not returning your calls. No, no one is sick.

Seller: I haven't heard from you.

Buyer: I apologize. It's just that I'm having trouble with this whole annuity thing. Not because of you, but I'm not sure—

Seller: The $400,000 insurance annuity we talked about?

Buyer: Yes. I'm concerned about the monthly paym—

Seller: The payments?

Buyer: Yes.

Seller: But, Katherine, we've gone over that.

Buyer: I know.

Seller: We spent a lot of time covering that part of it. I thought you agreed the monthly payments were affordable.

Buyer: I know—

Seller: And I thought you were satisfied that, along with your expected future raises, you could handle the schedule. What with your spouse's income—

[Katherine is annoyed.]

Buyer: This is independent of my husband.

Seller: Still, he's a backup. Right?

Buyer: This is independent of him, and I also am worried whether I might be buying too much—

Seller: Katherine, we've been over that.

Buyer: That's true, but I'm starting to wake up at nights and worry about the payments and—well, I think I might be taking on too much of a load. What do you think?

[The seller has become concerned the buyer will say no. The seller already has plans for the commission from this transaction.]

Seller: But we walked together through all that stuff. At least a month ago, after you interviewed one of my clients—the one who shares the same situation you have—you felt comfortable with $400,000.

Buyer: Well, I'm having second thoughts. You know what I mean, Tom?

No, Tom does not understand. Has Buyer #8 lost it? The seller has. Tom is out of alignment with Katherine. Tom thought Katherine was going to sign. What's gone wrong? Has a competitor replaced him? Why the panic? How should the seller handle this dilemma? Should the seller drop the annuity amount, thereby lowering the buyer's monthly payments? What options does Tom have to close a win-win transaction?

FACE #9—BOOKING APPOINTMENTS OVER THE PHONE

In telephone prospecting you have 20 seconds to create curiosity—that's the "window of opportunity" on a telephone cold call. Do you use a telephone script that gets you safely through this brief moment? Or are you going to become another failed moment in the brief history of time? Face #9 portrays this problem.

Situation.   Harrison is the president of ABC Bank, an independent retail bank.

Critical issue.   ABC Bank is losing market share to national banks. The bank has $100 million in deposits, is sound, and is marginally profitable. Despite a reputation for personal service, customers are reluctantly leaving. Over the last three years, bank profits have declined. This will eventually threaten the bank's capital base and its ability to meet federal regulations. The bank president is worried.

Reasons. ABC Bank operations are mostly manual. Unlike the big national banks, ABC Bank cannot offer a complete range of financial services. It is losing market share to bigger banks with automated products and services.

In an attempt to compete with larger banks, the bank has decided to lease/buy merchant data processing bank systems, including PC-based platform and teller systems with ATM and merchant credit card processing capabilities.

The seller, Sherri Wall, is a sales rep for an information technology company that sells automated banking systems to small retail banks that cannot afford expensive, in-house data processing and computer systems. The seller's products and services can be customized to each buyer's requirements.

Because it is expensive to travel in relation to the average sale—$30,000—the seller's company does most of its prospecting and buyer qualification on the telephone. The marketing department has given Sherri a list of small banks in the midwest, including one named the ABC Bank.

The cold call.

[Sherri has decided to prospect the account of ABC Bank. She makes a telephone cold call to Harrison Dodge, the bank's president and CEO. The bank is small enough that Harrison answers his own telephone. It is the end of the day and the staff are in the middle of balancing the bank's daily accounts.]

Buyer: Hello, Harrison Dodge, here. How can I help you?

Seller: Hello, Mr. Dodge, have I caught you at a good time?

Buyer: Actually, not really, but what is this about?

Seller: Oh, shall I call back later?

Buyer: It's okay. Go ahead.

Seller: Mr. Dodge, my name is Sherri Wall, and my company was established in 1974—we sell bank systems, and I was wondering . . .

Lets stop right there. This is not a good start. Sherri is in a lot of trouble. For example, she immediately gave away her power: she is selling *reactively*, and the buyer is highly unlikely to develop a curiosity. Sherri could have achieved a completely different, friendly, proactive start.

What constitutes a good phone script? In a few short seconds can a seller establish sincerity and competence? Can the seller arouse the buyer's curiosity—in 20 seconds or less? Is is really possible to *sell* on the telephone? (After all, this is a *prospecting* call.) How long does the buyer have to position his company and its services? Will buyers admit their problems over the telephone? How far can a seller go with a buyer before a face-to-face meeting will be necessary?

FACE #10—BUYER HAS BEEN TO NEGOTIATING SCHOOL

When you negotiate price, does your sale usually become a cliff-hanger? In this situation the buyer has decided to buy, but he has a surprise.

Situation. Frank Johnson is vice president, finance, of Acme Aerospace Corporation (fictitious), a Fortune 1000 company. Frank is concerned with his inability to comply with DoD reporting standards for inventory and project costs required to complete a Star Wars aerospace project. Acme Aerospace's in-house system does not have custom report management capabilities required for this phase of the Star Wars project.

Acme Aerospace is on a short time schedule; thus, money is less the issue than the completion time and a compliant reporting system. They have decided to purchase software specifically written to the DoD requirements. A senior level committee of buyers—the VP, manufacturing; the VP, purchasing; the VP, engineering; the VP, finance; and the director of MIS—has selected a small, dynamic, information technology firm represented by Dave and Mike. The salesperson is Dave and he will call jointly with his district manager, Mike. Dave asked Mike to negotiate the contract signing.

Mike and Dave's company is a venture capital–financed startup operation selling manufacturing control systems that comply with DoD reporting requirements. They are in the seventh month of what they thought was going to be a four-month sale. Dave is personally deep in debt and under pressure to get the contract signed. Their company is in need of working capital. Their venture capital investors are pressuring for positive cash flow.

Frank, the VP, finance, chairs the buying committee. Until this phase of the buying cycle, Frank was the silent member of the buying committee; however, at no time has he opposed the committee's direction.

Three months earlier, the buying committee had asked for the seller's price. Frank asked for a value justification. A total price of $600,000 (Phase I at $450,000 and Phase II at $150,000) had been generally agreeable. Frank participated in the value justification and agreed that his company could recoup their entire cost over nine months. In fact, he confided that he could recoup costs in less than nine months.

The buying committee decided Phase I was to be done first; then, if everyone was still satisfied, Phase II would follow.

Dave has already received verbal approval. They have been selected. They are now at the final step—price negotiations and contract signing.

Price negotiations.

[Finally, Frank called the sellers and invited them to come out for the signing.]

There is a red flag. When they arrive, Frank is alone. This is the first time in the buy cycle that all members of the buying committee have not been present. Frank takes charge and is expansively friendly.

[In this scenario, Mike, Dave's district manager, will be the "seller."]

Buyer:　Sit down, guys, let me get you a cup of coffee.

[The sellers sit down. Frank gets coffee and returns.]

Buyer:　Mike, first let me apologize for the delays. You guys have hit all your deadlines. All of the delays are our fault. I apologize; however, I'm really glad we found you. We think you're a much better alternative than our original choice.

Seller:　Great! We're glad to know that.

Buyer:　I have only one problem left, then I'm ready to do business.

Seller:　What's that, Frank?

Buyer: Your price is totally unacceptable.

[Mike chuckles.]

Seller: You're kidding, right?

Buyer: If you think this is funny, there's the door.

[Frank is not laughing. Frank motions to the door.]

Seller: I'm sorry, it is not funny.

[Mike is no longer smiling. Mike and Dave, the sellers, are confused, because they had participated in the value justification three months earlier, and Frank had personally approved a nine-month payback.]

Seller: Frank, I don't understand. I was there the day we did the value justification. You yourself said the payback was even better than the nine months shown in our pre-proposal. You have known the price for three months. I don't understand what's going on here.

Buyer: Mike, I have a friend at Nu-Tec Computer. I found out how much you are paying for that hardware. I see what you are charging me, and I think you guys are being greedy on that. Regarding the software, I know how much it costs to duplicate a tape. Now I know you have some development costs, but I look at what you guys are making on this and it exceeds my "reasonable person test." I think you guys are making too much money on this. It's obscene, and I'm not going to pay it.

[Mike looks over at his salesperson, Dave. The sight is not pretty. Dave's armpits have sweat all the way down to his belt. His face is green. Dave has elapsed into visions of personal bankruptcy. Mike flashes Dave an urgent "Don't say anything" signal.]

Seller: Frank, the price of my system is a small—

Buyer: Mike, you are not listening. Your price is unacceptable, and I am not going to pay it.

[Frank moves the unsigned contract to the center of the table and pats it softly, almost affectionately.]

Buyer: Mike, drop your price $50,000 and I'll sign it right here and now.

[Frank takes out a pen, resting it on top of the contract.]

This is a tough buyer. What are the seller's options? Frank has apparently gone to negotiating school and appears adamant about price. The buying committee is not present. Mike and Dave are alone with Frank. This *is* the real price negotiating session, and, like two wet washcloths, Mike and Dave are being wrung dry. The contract is on the table in front of them; it is ready for signing. They cannot negotiate an end run around him. This was unexpected. Have the sellers come this far only to find out that they are so far out of buying alignment?

What would you do?

The 10 faces of buying portray the need for planning, preparation, and an effective selling methodology. Early mistakes can lead to early, difficult, or impossible endings.

In over 20 years of selling, managing salespeople, sales training, sales management training, consulting to CEOs and their executive managers, and teaching businesses how to create buyers, I now realize—ever more clearly—that in a majority of selling opportunities, difficulties arise needlessly because of one main problem: *salespeople fail to align themselves with their buyers.* That also applies to the business enterprise itself. Buying decisions are seldom accidental and, in an era of overchoice, businesses and their sellers can learn to differentiate themselves from their competition by the way they sell.

Expert selling is really in the eyes of the buyer.

I challenge you to learn to recognize your buyer's level of need, to learn to create visions for your buyers. Learn to create buyers who not only will *volunteer* to buy from you, but who will return to do business again and again. I challenge you to try *Solution Selling*.

I hope the following *Solution Selling* tools will empower you.

II

STRATEGIES TO FACILITATE, INFLUENCE, AND CONTROL THE BUYING PROCESS

The majority of my personal experience working with salespeople is in the corporate, business-to-business environment. Many of the people with whom I work have experienced a variety of selling programs. I like to ask people how they compare *Solution Selling* to these other programs. The most frequent comments I get on other methodologies and programs is "they taught me to understand, what I needed to do to be effective, they taught me to document what I should do to be effective, but they didn't show me *how* to do it." In Part II—Strategies to Facilitate, Influence, and Control the Buying Process, I will give you the *how*. I will give you the "mechanics of selling" and show you how to get your buyers to take action, to volunteer to buy.

Part II is divided into 10 strategies. I will give you examples of buyer–seller dialogue. I will give you sideline comments and graphic metaphors that will help you understand the process that occurs between a buyer and an effective seller. In Part II you will learn new approaches for generating prospects and new business. You will learn to develop buyer needs and visions that are aligned with your products and services. You will learn how to establish sincerity and competence in the mind of your buyer. You will learn how to anticipate a buyer's change of behavior as she progresses through her buy cycle. You will learn how to gain access to power and how to create tools that will give you situational fluency with power buyers. You will learn how to control the long sell cycle and how to control and facilitate buying committees. You will learn how to come away from negotiations with dignity and money in your pocket. You will learn how to balance the short term with the long term to gain more control and predict future business more accurately.

Recognize the Three Levels of Buyer Need

Buyers will seek to satisfy recognized, active needs—either directly, or, if direct means are denied, sometimes through hallucination and fantasy.

INTRODUCTION

Buyers seek to satisfy any need, either by direct means or through hallucination and fantasy. Borrowing from modern psychology's *reality principle*, in my opinion, we may say that healthy people seek pleasure and avoid pain. Healthy buyers are subject to the same general principles.

Selling is about taking your product or service and developing or altering a buyer's need for it. When a seller personally participates in the formation or alteration of a buyer's vision of a solution, the buyer will most likely want to buy from that seller. Sound easy? Wrong. It is the most difficult challenge we face personally as sellers and organizationally as marketers—how to create a buyer for what we sell.

A study of people's needs presents an amazing array of information and knowledge. For example, A. Maslow developed a system of needs consisting of a hierarchy of seven main divisions to all human motives. I refer to them in my workshops, and I repeat them here.

1. **Physiological needs:** food, water, and so on.
2. **Safety needs:** freedom from threat, security.
3. **Belongingness and love needs:** affiliation, acceptance.
4. **Esteem needs:** achievement, prestige, status.
5. **Cognitive needs:** knowledge, understanding, curiosity.

6. **Aesthetic needs:** order, beauty, structure, art.
7. **Need for self-actualization:** self-fulfillment, self-realization.

Although not everyone agrees, Maslow assumed his hierarchy to be invariant. He argued that the lower (i.e., a number 1 need as opposed to a number 7 need) the need, if unfulfilled, the more *priority* it will possess. For example, a person threatened by a vicious, gun-pointing carjacker is unlikely to be even the slightest concerned about an aesthetic need such as art. Without such an assumption, Maslow's concept of his hierarchal needs would only be a list. His hierarchical need system deserves some attention.

For our purposes, we will deal with different levels of needs. We will study four levels of *buying* need: no need, latent pain, pain, and a vision of a solution. Level zero is where you—the seller—see no potential need for what you sell. For example, an Eskimo does not need ice cubes. An infirm, 90-year-old person does not need a new Mercedes Benz. If from your point of view as a seller there is no buying need, call this level zero, and we will not deal further with it.

THREE LEVELS OF NEED

In *Solution Selling*, there are three levels of buyer need: latent need, pain, and vision of a solution. This is one of the foundations of *Solution Selling*, and it is important to realize that we are working from the buyer's point of view.

Examine Figure 2. I use these three levels in my seminars and we learn to understand them. It is important for the seller to recognize the level of buyer need in order to be able to participate in the buyer's vision of a solution. When sellers learn to distinguish between the three levels of buyer need, the buyer's buying cycle and his shifting concerns will become more apparent and the seller can get alignment easily and quickly.

Level 1: Latent Needs or Latent Pain

The seller recognizes latent needs for his products and services. Latent needs are potential needs for products or services *in the mind of the seller, not the buyer*. The seller sees the need; the buyer does not see the need. Thus, sellers usually operate by projecting their own vision of a buyer's need for their product or service.

FIGURE 2
Three Levels of Need

Level One: **Latent**

Level Two: **Pain**

Level Three: **Vision of a solution**

For our purposes, latent needs are based either in buyer igno-rance or rationalization. In my experience, most latent needs fall into these two categories: Either the buyer is ignorant—they are not aware that what you have to sell even exists—or the buyer has ra-tionalized a solution does not exist. For example, the last time he tried to solve that problem, he concluded that whatever was avail-able was too expensive, too complicated, or too cumbersome, so he decided, "No solution. It won't work for me." His problem exited his attention and he went on to something else.

Many sellers experience difficulty dealing with latent needs and have an unfortunate tendency to commit what I call "premature elaboration." Because businesses and their sellers often have supe-rior product and capability knowledge, they see the buyer's situa-tion, get excited, and say, "You need a way to—, don't you?" Or something to that effect. For example, assume you sell used cars. A buyer walks through your lot, but the buyer already has a car and has no recognized need for another car. The seller knows the buyer's present car has poor reliability, "sees" a potential buyer, and says, "Have I got a deal for you. Look at this real honey here. Only $5,999, and I can get you guaranteed financing." The seller sees a possible buyer need—after all, the guy is on his car lot, right? The buyer, who is killing time, looks at the used car salesperson as though he were an alien. The buyer recognizes no need, no pain. Thus, the buyer's need is latent—even though the seller sees it and the buyer does not. And the seller has grossly "prematurely elaborated."

Level 2: Pain or "Active Need"

In a level 2 need, the buyer recognizes a need or pain but does not know how to solve it. The buyer is unhappy with the existing situ-ation, is uncomfortable with how things are. The buyer is actively trying to find a solution, *if* he thinks a solution is possible. If he believes there is no solution, the pain will be suppressed and become latent. The motivation for trying to find a solution may arise from either physical or psychological needs. Certainly, the need or pain is recognized and unsatisfied, with the potential of a business transaction between the buyer and the right seller.

Level 2 needs are undeveloped needs. That is to say, they have not been processed or developed by any seller. This is an enormously important point, because, unless a buyer has a vision of a solution, he will be forced to trust the seller to solve his problem if asked to buy the seller's product. It is very common for sellers (who easily achieve vision) to ask buyers to take action before the buyer shares that vision. Therefore, the seller must get the buyer to admit pain to him *personally*. This is the seller's proof that the buyer deems him trustworthy—both sincere and competent. In my workshops, we teach attendees to have the patience to "wallow" in their buyer's pain. In fact, at the conclusion of a workshop, we award a "king of pain" and a "queen of pain" prize to the students best at evoking a buyer's pain.

In certain ways, the human brain is similar to a computer. In the computer world we talk about "backgrounds" and "foregrounds." In a manner of speaking, our brain too has a background and a foreground. Most people's foreground—allow yourself to *imagine* it to be your frontal lobes, just behind your forehead—can hold about seven (plus or minus two) subjects or ideas at one time. This appears to be the maximum number of issues, concerns, "balls in the air," or needs most individual human beings can simultaneously manage. This is an important concept for sellers to remember.

For sellers, the paramount issue here is: *Is a problem your product or service could help him address occupying one of the buyer's seven foreground "slots"?* If not, the seller does not have a potential buyer at this point in time.

Using this method of ideation proves useful, especially for sellers who have to work to get their product into one of the buyer's seven "slots." Assume your company sells anti-carjacking devices. If a buyer is considering purchasing a new putter for golf, but hears that someone in his office was killed in a carjacking, then it is likely that his desire to buy a putter will be replaced by a need to purchase some kind of protection that might save his life in the event of a carjacking attempt.

Countless advertising dollars are wasted by businesses trying to sell their products and services. It seems that about 80 percent of all ads I see offer a vision. This approach fails to accomplish a key selling requirement: to take a buyer's latent need and "zip it around" to one of the buyer's seven foreground "slots," giving a buyer a reason to consider buying and therefore relieving his pain. Once the buyer has a pain in his foreground, a vision ad is much more meaningful.

So much expensive time and energy are wasted by countless businesses of every kind and size by "featuring" buyers to death, to a point of mind-numbing boredom and inattention. In other words, sellers fail to give the buyer a reason to pay attention. If the issue our product or service addresses does not occupy one of the buyer's foreground seven slots, the seller is going to have a very difficult time getting that buyer to buy anything.

If the buyer cannot find an acceptable vision of a solution, the pain goes back to level 1 and becomes a latent need. Here is a personal example. Do you remember Buyer #1, in the "10 Faces of Buyer Pain," the bald buyer? I can relate to that person. I have some latent pain. I have a shiny spot up there on top of my head, and the reason I label it "latent"—even though I am slowly losing my hair—is that I have concluded their is no solution. Nothing I could stomach anyway. What would happen in my mind, though, if tomorrow morning's *Wall Street Journal* had an article reporting, "Genetech has isolated the baldness gene in the male, and within the next five years baldness will not be a problem for American men"? Now where is my issue? It would immediately bump up to one of those seven foreground slots. I have not decided to buy yet. I have not determined I can afford it yet. I have not determined whether it's safe enough to do yet, but now I am seriously thinking about it and I am motivated to change if I can find a solution because now I have *hope.*

When we talk about prospecting later, we will learn how to take specific latent needs and move them over to the pain area by creating hope. *The difference between a latent need and pain is hope.*

How do we occupy the foreground brain of our buyer with an issue that our product or service addresses? One of the major challenges to both successful marketing and selling is that single issue. How do we develop buyer need or pain? How do we align buyer need or pain with a capability our product or service can provide?

As Shakespeare wrote, "Ay, there's the rub." Developing hope in the marketplace is marketing's job.

Level 3: Vision of a Solution

At level 3, the buyer has a vision of a solution. The buyer has advanced from latent need to a recognized need or pain, and the buyer has a vision of a solution. An action vision has four components: *who* will be taking *what* action, *when* in time, *via* a capability of a seller's product or service. The buyer is looking to buy. The buyer recognizes a need or pain, can describe need requirements, accepts responsibility for solving the problem, and can "see" the problem being acted upon.

In many cases, sellers meet buyers who have a vision the moment they meet them. The buyer says, "Oh, Ralph, here's what we are looking for: we've got to have a homeowners' policy and we've got to have earthquake insurance, and I've got to have this, this, and that." Or somebody moves from out of state and they have an "I need" list a yard long. By the end of this book I hope you will realize that the worst thing a seller can say is, "I've got it. I've got it. I've got it." It is very tempting to close a buyer with a pre-existing vision. If a buyer walks in and says, "I need, I need, I need," you are tempted to say to yourself: I've got all three of those things; this is going to be a quick one. The worst thing a seller can do is to take the product out and say, "Here it is. I've got it," because what the seller just did is prescribe without diagnosing or reengineering the vision. Even if the seller happens to make that sale, the buyer has no loyalty to him. Vision processing is about taking your buyer from his vision back through the need development cycle, back to the point of original pain or discomfort, and then reconfirming the vision *before* your product or service comes out. Take the time to diagnose, even though you think you already know what the buyer needs.

Diagnosis is key in gaining buyer loyalty when creating, participating, or reengineering the buyer's vision of a solution. You will learn how to do all three. And if you do your job well, the buyer's vision will become aligned with your product or service. Even if the vision is unaltered, by taking the buyer through the diagnosis process, you now "own" that buyer, whereas before you did not. Therefore, the diagnosis process is key for the buyer to buy into you personally—your sincerity, your expertise, and your experience. People want to buy from people who validate them, who understand their business, who see the world through their eyes, who

FIGURE 3
How Organizations Buy

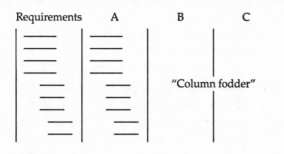

share their vision, and who empower them to see themselves in control of their problem. Sellers must go through diagnosis and vision processing with their buyers.

For our purposes, the seller and the buyer must participate together in the vision of a solution for the buyer to be considered *qualified*. Therefore, to work with a mutual vision of a solution, we must get a buyer to make and to confirm buying capability statements: statements indicating that the buyer accepts responsibility for solving the problem and can "see" the precise capabilities or services needed to deal with the problem, and when he would be able to act on the problem. The seller must participate personally in the vision for the need to be qualified. If the seller finds a buyer for whom some other seller has already created a vision of a solution, and the seller compares his offering to that vision, then the seller is in danger of ending up as "column fodder" (see Figure 3).

Just another sampled seller. The buyer is happy to see you. The buyer will happily gather all of the product or service information you have, but the buyer is already emotionally aligned with another seller.

Some buyers are motivated to act but have no vision of a solution. This, of course, is a seller's delight, especially if the seller is first, because the seller gets to set the buying requirements by creating the initial vision. Unfortunately, except in start-up businesses that may have a "first" product or service, or where businesses operate in monopoly or imperfect markets, in the real world this is seldom the case.

Selling is typically a highly competitive activity, and sellers are forced to compete with a number of other sellers who are contributing to the buyer's vision of a solution.

Buyers are motivated to act once they have a vision of a solution. A second or third seller would have to reengineer that vision before getting in to product or service presentations. We will deal with this common situation later.

Let's recap the three levels of buyer need with one last example. Assume two things: (1) there is a bank where at noon long lines of customers form while they wait for service and (2) the seller's capability is to help banks operate more productively.

At level 1, the bank's need is described this way: The seller drives by the bank, sees people queuing in line during their lunch hour, and says, "Hmm, there is something inefficient in that bank. They appear to have a problem with which I might be able to help them." Here we have a latent need. The seller sees a problem and the solution; the buyer does not.

At level 2, the bank's need is described this way: The seller calls on the bank and gets the vice president of marketing to say (to the seller), "Our bank has been losing a lot of customers to the competition because it takes us too long to get people through our teller line. I know I have a problem, but I don't know how to solve it." The buyer has admitted a problem but doesn't know how to deal with it. The seller sees a solution.

At level 3, the bank's need is described this way: The seller leads the vice president of marketing to say (to the seller), "While the customer is at the teller window, I need some way for our tellers to verify any customer's balance for any account—regardless of the branch at which they bank—within 30 seconds, so we can satisfy our customers and win back some we have lost." Both the seller and the buyer have a vision of solution. The next step for the seller is to *prove* his product or service can match the buyer's vision.

Examine Figure 4. In it you will discover the phrases, "Reference story" and "9-Block Vision Processing Model." It is premature to discuss them; however, I want you to know that we have created bridges for you to construct and use that allow the seller to take a buyer from latent need to pain, from pain to a vision of a solution, from vision back to pain, and then to vision shared mutually by the buyer and the seller. Later we will learn to use reference stories and the 9-Block Vision Processing Model.

In conclusion, it is important at this point to remember that "solution selling" involves a seller finding a buyer with pain, getting a buyer to admit their need/pain to the seller, and mutually developing a satisfactory vision of a solution biased toward the seller's product or service.

FIGURE 4
Three Levels of Need

Level One: Latent

↓ *Reference story*

Level Two: Pain

↑↓ *9-Block vision processing model*

Level Three: Vision of a solution

YOUR CONCEPTUAL SALES TERRITORY

I like to ask salespeople to "tell me about your sales territory." Most salespeople and managers do not look at a sales territory the way I do.

Look at your marketing universe and imagine all of the people who are potential buyers of your product or service. Almost everybody selling something can describe their "universe." It might be parents over the age of 35 with 2.4 children living in southern California. That could be the definition of someone's universe. On the other hand, it might be all of the residential housing units in the United States: something over 100 million units. It might be buyers of carpets, or doctors' offices in Kentucky. Each of you will define the universe of your sales territory in a different way.

I ask my clients, "Right now, today, what percentage of all the potential buyers in your market universe are actively looking to buy something similar to what you sell?" Typically, the answer is overly optimistic.

To be wildly optimistic, let us assume 5 percent of your buyer universe is actively looking, that is, in *pain* or with a *vision*. That means that the 95 percent who are *not* looking are in what we call latent need. Look at Figure 5 and you will see an illustration of what I believe your *conceptual* sales territory resembles—a huge unsold territory of buyers. Does this figure describe your conceptual and actual sales territory?

Some expert sellers know how to step into that huge 95 percent area of latent need and create demand. That is their opportunity to be first. This represents the conceptual and actual opportunity—the part of the market not yet looking. Many sellers think prospecting is finding those buyers already looking to buy something similar to what they are selling. This is an area where *Solution Selling* sales

FIGURE 5
Conceptual Sales Territory

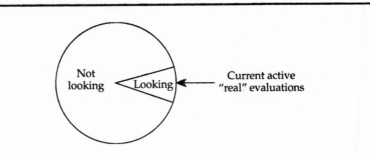

training and sales management training help salespeople lift from mediocre performance to superior performance. Earlier we said that one of the key skills in marketing and selling is to be able to develop buying needs from the latent stage to the active stage. Later on in this book we will talk about the concept of farming. Part of the farmer's job is cultivating the soil. Let's talk about "cultivating" prospects in your territory.

Prospecting

I am continually "underwhelmed" at how salespeople prospect. Many businesses and salespeople with whom I work spend their energy and marketing dollars trying to find the 5 percent of their market that is actively looking.

What's wrong with that picture? If a buyer is already looking for a solution, it's very likely some other salesperson has influenced him, participated in or created his vision. However, because typical corporate rules state that they cannot sole source, such buyers are actively pursuing other vendors when in fact they have already made their selection emotionally. So, in this situation, if you are prospecting for buyers who have already decided to buy, then you are simply helping your competition close business. You are potential "column fodder"—reexamine Figure 3.

I am not telling you that you can't gain control of those situations and turn them around. Actually it is not difficult to do, if you know what you are doing and are selling consciously. However, most salespeople "wing it." Sellers charge ahead oblivious to the buyer's level of need and where in the buying cycle the buyer is. Instead, the seller has his or her "happy ears" on, and the seller only hears the buyer say, "We are going to buy," and "Yes, you look good," and "You've got a really good chance at our business." The seller is mentally ringing up a sale. In the corporate world, every time a seller brings in an order, two or three other sellers must face a loss. *All* the sellers chasing the business had it on their forecasts.

The kind of prospecting we teach answers the question, "How can I develop buyers in the 95 percent latent need area?" "How can I get buyers to initiate a buy cycle?" If a seller can gain mindshare by creating *hope* in the buyer's mind, then the seller is in the lead position to create a vision of a solution biased toward his product or service.

I will show you ways to create hope, to gain attention, to gain mindshare, to give the buyer control, and to help the buyer buy *your* product or service. I will show you how to lead a buyer through the three levels of need.

Strategy 2

Features, Advantages, and Benefits

Feature: *This coffee cup has a handle ...*
Advantage: *that will prevent your fingers from burning ...*
Benefit: *which you said you wanted to avoid.*

FEATURES, ADVANTAGES, AND BENEFITS— OLD TERMINOLOGY, NEW DEFINITIONS

Imagine a beautiful china coffee cup, one with an elegant handle. In this section we will use that coffee cup to learn to distinguish between features, advantages, and benefits.

Feature statement. "This coffee cup has a handle." That is a feature statement. The handle is the feature. Because it is so straightforward, so easy, sellers love feature statements. There is an assumption that everyone wants a handle. Leading with the feature is used extensively by marketing and advertising people, with another assumption: everyone understands how they could use the feature.

Buyers with latent needs are not motivated by features. Features actually invite buyer objections. Most people do not want to feel "sold." In the mind of the buyer, when a seller begins describing the features of his product or service, a red flag goes up. The buyer becomes defensive and defends himself against being "sold" by using objections.

Advantage statement. "This cup has a handle that will enable you to drink your coffee without burning your fingers." An attempt by the seller to explain how the feature works or how it could help a potential buyer turns a feature statement into an advantage statement. *Because of* the handle, *you can* drink hot coffee without burning your fingers. Many sellers have been trained that the *because of . . . you can* format turns a feature into a "benefit." In *Solution Selling* we call it an advantage. It is an advantage if

- The "benefit" is in the mind of the seller, not the buyer.
- The buyer does not have a vision in which the seller participated.

Benefit statement.   "This cup has a handle that will enable you to drink your coffee without burning your fingers, which *you said* you would like to be able to do." That is a benefit statement. It is only a benefit when the buyer expresses a need for it. In this instance, the seller participated in the buyer's vision.

Benefit statements tell the buyer that the seller believes his product or service will be a match for the buyer's vision of a solution.

Solution Selling feature-advantage-benefit statements are different from traditional definitions and statements. Examine the *Solution Selling* benefit statement and compare it to the traditional use.

Old school benefit statement: "We have an on-line sales prompter that will allow your branch personnel to be led through a customer sales situation."

Solution Selling benefit statement: "We have an on-line sales prompter that will allow your branch personnel to be led through a customer sales situation, *which you said you must be able to do to improve branch cross-selling.*"

In the old school benefit statement, the problem is that the seller *assumed* his buyer had the same vision the seller had for him. The impatience of the seller causes him to forget that the buyer may not be able to see the vision yet.

In *Solution Selling*, in order to make a benefit statement, even for a product as ordinary as a coffee cup, you first must get your buyer to a Level 3 buying need—a vision of a solution.

So, *real* benefit statements by *Solution Selling* sellers indicate that the seller's product or service can address a vision of a solution in which the seller and buyer participated. The prospect is enabled. The prospect can see *who* will be doing *what, when* in time *via* a product or service. Once the buyer accepts the benefit by wanting to know more, the seller's next step is to offer proof.

DO NOT ABDICATE INTEREST AROUSAL
TO THE PRODUCT

Many sellers are "feature creatures," especially in this day of electronic media, science, information technology, and information systems. When sellers turn to feature selling, what are they actually doing? They are abdicating buyer interest arousal to the product. The buyer has not even admitted to having a problem. The zealous seller just loves to show buyers his product's or service's amazing, astounding, matchless features—which his equally fervent competition also has, usually.

I believe the role of the product in a sale should be proof—not interest arousal, education, or need development. *Proof.* Proof that the product or service can match the buyer's vision. There are a number of advantages to the seller if he can avoid talking about the product specifically, until the buyer has a vision:

- The buyer does not feel "sold" until the product comes out.
- The buyer will want to see proof if he has a vision.
- The seller will not have to defend product features in which the buyer is not interested.
- The seller will not have to defend the price of the product until the buyer can see its value.

Anybody who has had any sales training has been schooled in features, advantages, and benefits. In *Solution Selling* we are using familiar selling terminology with strong distinctions.

More about Feature Statements

Feature statements are the same as you have always known them. They are statements by the seller describing some characteristic of a product or service:

- We've been in business for 27 years.
- We have 2,000 columns and 2,000 rows on our spreadsheet.
- This sound system has bass and treble.
- We have 14 options on this device.
- Our checking accounts are free.
- Our car has a driver-side air bag.
- This comes in three flavors.

- Our business checking accounts feature direct deposit capabilities.

The distinction I make about features in *Solution Selling* is not whether to use them but *when*. The feature should be used to *prove* a product or service can match the buyer's vision.

Advantage Statements

Advantage statements address *assumed* or undeveloped needs. Advantage statements are attempts by the seller to explain to a buyer *how* the product can be used to help the buyer. The problem? Advantages are usually in the mind of the seller. In my workshops, when someone makes a "because of . . . you can" statement, I ask the question: "In *whose* opinion?"

Most sellers think they are making benefit statements when they are really making advantages. The distinction in *Solution Selling* is that we first have to determine at what level of need the buyer is before we can determine whether we have an advantage or a benefit. If the buyer is at the latent pain or pain level, and the seller is attempting to relate to that buyer, in *Solution Selling* the best he can do is make an advantage.

As an example, if the seller said, "Because our copier makes color copies, you can make better presentations," the seller assumes the buyer *wants* to make better presentations and the use of color copies will achieve that for him. It might be true. The seller is probably *right*. Presentations do look better in color. But if the buyer doesn't see it that way, it doesn't matter how *right* the seller is. Advantage statements assume too much. They assume the buyer has the same vision as the seller. As most experienced sellers know, assumptions can get you into trouble.

Solution Selling *Benefit Statements*

Earlier I said that in *Solution Selling,* to make a benefit statement, we must first have a level 3 need—a vision of a solution that the seller participated in with the buyer—either by creating or reengineering. By participating in the buyer's vision, the seller becomes the person from whom the buyer will want to buy.

The purpose of benefit statements is to confirm to the buyer that the seller believes he can fulfill the vision, so the order of things is important. The seller's strategy must be in alignment with the buyer's level of need. *Where* exactly your buyer is in his buy cycle also dictates what the seller must do.

Yet how many salespeople have you met in your career who have their *routine*? They say, "Here's the way I always do it. First, I do this . . . , then I do this . . . , and then I do that . . . " If you think about it and look at their buyers' buying cycles, perhaps one out of eight times that salesperson is right—when he always does it *that* way. But he's going to be wrong the other seven times.

The *Solution Selling* concept is that, armed with the knowledge of how buyers buy, the seller can usually—within minutes—peg exactly where his buyer is in the buy cycle, and then employ the appropriate selling strategy. Instead of always dragging out a list of features and advantages, *Solution Selling* sellers pause, consider where the buyer is in the buy cycle, then act. One of the things I encourage sellers to do is to stop using the same format when selling. First, recognize where your buyer is and then determine your selling strategy. Neither a feature creature nor an advantage seller be.

Eagles versus Journeymen

It all comes back to a major difference between the best salespeople—the intuitive eagles—and the journeymen. Eagles are able to keep their products and all their amazing features in their pockets. They do not use their product to sell. They use the product to *prove*. Journeymen like to make *presentations*. Eagles have *conversations*.

If you see your competitors doing interest arousal demos or setting up "show and tell" multimedia props on a prospect's desk to illustrate the history of their company and their product's or service's amazing features and advantages, smile to yourself. Those salespeople will be easy for you to beat. They do not know how to create a buyer.

SELF-TEST (FIND OUT IF YOU REALLY UNDERSTAND)

Here are a few exercises from our workshops. Which of the following seller statements is a feature, an advantage, or a benefit statement?

1. Our PBX features both call distribution and voice response capabilities. Feature? Advantage? Benefit?

If you answered Feature, you are correct. Just to get you going I gave you an easy one. If you answered it incorrectly, immediately go back and reread the feature-advantage-benefit definitions.

2. Our network management capability allows terminals on your LAN to communicate with your host. Feature? Advantage? Benefit?

If you answered Advantage, you are correct. In this sales statement, the "your" pronoun indicates the seller is making an attempt to relate (based on assumed need) the product to the buyer. That makes it an advantage statement.

3. Our bank offers no-fee banking for checking accounts with an average daily balance of $2,500 or greater. Feature? Advantage? Benefit?

If you answered Feature, you are correct. Another easy one.

4. I think our experience can help you in this instance. The usual reason for the turmoil you mentioned is the lack of ability to simulate change, which our system allows you to do. Feature? Advantage? Benefit?

If you answered Advantage, you are correct. The seller's expertise and enthusiasm cause him to "prematurely elaborate." All the buyer said was, "This place is in turmoil." The seller is now projecting his vision onto the buyer. A clue—"the usual reason for. . . . "

5. You said you needed immediate on-line status of pending orders, which our system provides. Feature? Advantage? Benefit?

If you answered Benefit, you are correct. In reading the seller's statement, you should see that the buyer has a vision. We will assume that the seller participated in that vision, so it is a benefit statement. The seller is matching his product to the buyer's vision.

6. So you have too many credit losses. I have just the thing for you. Our credit model scoring system will help you reduce your losses and keep your risk exposure low at the same time. Feature? Advantage? Benefit?

If you answered Advantage, you are correct. If you answered Benefit, I encourage you to sign up for one of my seminars. The words "too many credit losses" indicate the buyer is in pain, but has no vision. The seller has prematurely elaborated. "I have just the thing for you" will diminish the seller's trustworthiness.

7. Our methodology features JAD sessions that enable you to ensure a quality design. Feature? Advantage? Benefit?

If you answered Advantage, you are correct. No indication of any buyer vision. The seller is assuming and projecting.

8. Our CASE tool meets the need you gave me of being able to prototype new applications before user approval. Feature? Advantage? Benefit?

If you answered Benefit, you are correct. It's so clear: the buyer has a previously stated vision of a solution. The seller is matching it with his product.

9. You said you needed to be able to staff key projects on an as-needed basis. We can offer you that capability. Feature? Advantage? Benefit?

If you answered Benefit, you are correct.

10. Our on-line inquiry will allow you to quote *accurate* delivery dates to your customers, which you said you must be able to do to improve customer service. Feature? Advantage? Benefit?

If you answered Benefit, you are correct. The tip-off is the seller's statement, ". . . which you said you must be able to do . . . "

A primary difference between eagles and journeymen is patience. If you found yourself thinking benefit when the answer was advantage, you probably have a patience problem. The key in selling is not what you know, but what your buyer sees. The terminology is not new. Sellers have been talking about features, advantages, and benefits for years. The *Solution Selling* difference is making the buyer part of the equation and figuring out at what level of need the buyer is. If the buyer is at latent pain or pain, the best the seller can do is make advantage statements. The buyer must have a vision in which both participated for the seller to be able to make a *Solution Selling* benefit statement.

Participate in the Buyer's Vision

Create a New Vision; Reengineer an Existing Vision

Men are best convinced by reasons that they themselves discover.

Benjamin Franklin

DEVELOP A LATENT PAIN TO AN ACTIVE PAIN

Remember when we compared the human brain to a computer? With computers we talk about backgrounds and foregrounds. I submitted that most people can manage about seven open items—plus or minus two—at one time. More than that and the issue, or concern, is likely to be put in the background, somewhere in the unconscious memory. In our workshops we talk about the importance for the buyer of having an issue addressable by the seller's product or service occupying one of those seven "slots." Although neurosurgeons and psycholoists will probably object, this metaphor allows us as sellers to have a jargon to represent levels of buyer need. Awareness of the buyer's level of need is necessary for sellers to stay aligned.

If the seller's product or service addresses a buyer's *latent need* (seller sees it, buyer doesn't), then the seller is going to have a difficult time selling him anything. So your challenge as a seller is to get an issue that your product or service addresses into the buyer's foreground brain. How are you going to do that? I have heard selling described as a "hurt and rescue" operation. How do we get their attention? Why would a buyer want to bring a pain to his foreground that was comfortably resting in his background? The answer is by offering *hope.*

As human beings, we try to get rid of pain. We can either fix the situation bothering us or stop thinking about it because we conclude we can't do anything about it. The only motivation we have for dealing with a pain in our foreground is hope—hope for a solution.

A Role Play: Developing a Latent Need to an Active Pain

In our workshops we use modeling, also called role play. Role playing provides two main benefits: First, it provides a necessary component of learning—by *doing*. I don't believe you really know something until you can make it come from your brain, out your mouth. Second, role playing allows the dynamics between seller and a buyer to be observed and analyzed. Eagle sellers have conversations rather than make presentations. Many people have told me that they learn as much from playing the role of the buyer as they do playing the role of the seller.

Here is a two-step, "latent need to pain" role play. You first met the buyer as Face #3 in "10 Faces of Buyer Pain." It is a role play adapted from one of our actual seminars, and the role play introduced two key steps—Step 1, rapport, and Step 2, call introduction—and together they form a basic *Solution Selling* call introduction.

The actors are Mike (the "Seller") and Michele (the "Buyer"). Mike is a salesperson with NNC Business Television (fictional), a company that sells communication services to businesses and organizations.

Mike and Michele have already spoken on the telephone. Mike has been invited to visit. The seller must establish rapport with the buyer. Without some basic rapport, it is unlikely Mike will be able to move Michele from latent need to pain. In Strategy 6 we will give you some specifics on rapport and a structure for a call introduction to a new buyer. In this case, we will assume that Mike has rapport; Michele believes he is sincere but is not yet ready to share pain with him. Mike's challenge is to bring a latent pain (for a need he sees, but Michele doesn't yet see) forward to Michele's foreground. He tells Michele a story about a current customer:

Mike: Michele, a particular situation in which you might be interested is another office equipment company with which I have been working. Their VP, sales, was having difficulty meeting sales goals.

The reasons for his difficulty included fast-changing equipment designs and specifications, an inability for sales management to easily communicate price changes and model changes to a large number of field sales reps, and a limited number of experts available to help field salespeople demonstrate changes in the equipment.

What he said he needed was a way, when models or prices change, to easily communicate these changes to all his field reps. He also said he wanted a way to better leverage use of his scarce engineering talent by his salespeople.

NNC Business Television provided him with those capabilities. The results were that sales increased over projected sales by 10 percent, profits improved by 16 percent, and the sales force ran much more smoothly—everyone learned of both the technical and price changes at the same time.

But enough about NNC. Tell me about your business situation.

Michele: Well, Mike, I seem to have pretty much the same problems you just described. I'm having trouble meeting my sales goals.

Intermission

So far, things are on schedule. The buyer *admitted pain*—pain that is aligned with the seller's product.

The reference story helped Michele move her latent need to a recognized active pain because now she has some *hope*—hope that there might be a way for her to make her goal after all. And that is what is supposed to happen. I'm not going to dissect this reference story because we have an entire section on how to write good reference stories in the next chapter. Just be aware that this reference story had all the key components of a *Solution Selling* reference story.

Until the buyer has admitted pain (a level 2 buying need) to the seller personally, the seller cannot take the next step of attempting to create a vision.

DEVELOP AN ADMITTED PAIN TO A VISION OF A SOLUTION

Once the buyer admits pain, the seller can begin to create a vision of a solution for the buyer. The vision should include *who* will be taking *what* action, *when* in time, *via* the seller's product or service.

The seller must diagnose the buyer's pain with a bias toward his product or service. The seller must explore the interdependence of the buyer's organization if the decision will have to be made by more than just the initial buyer. And then the seller must create an action vision for the buyer.

Sound complex? Before we proceed, I want you to become familiar with a powerful tool that facilitates the buyer's transition from pain to a vision of a solution. I call this tool the 9-Block Vision Processing Model.

The 9-Block Vision Processing Model ("the 9 Boxes")

Examine Figure 6. As one keystone of the *Solution Selling* process, it helps sellers do what I call *vision processing*. First, we must learn what the rows and columns mean. The columns represent the need for the seller to diagnose, explore, impact, and create a vision. The rows delineate three forms of questions the seller can ask, that is, they provide a "questioning etiquette" to help the seller stay in alignment with the buyer and for the buyer to feel in control through the process.

Questioning Etiquette

On the left-hand side of the grid box are the words *open, control,* and *confirm.* These signify the types or style of questions the seller will employ. These three words are a variation on the theme of Basic Questioning Etiquette 101, which dates back at least to Socrates. The primary reason for considering questioning etiquette is *buyer comfort.* Lawyers questioning witnesses in a courtroom don't have to worry about "buyer comfort"; salespeople do.

Open questions.   Open questions cannot be answered yes or no or with a number. They usually begin with *who, what, when, why,* or *how.* They invite the buyer to express himself freely: "Tell me about it. What is causing you to have this problem?" "Besides yourself, *who* in your organization is impacted by this problem?" "What is it going to take for *you* to be able to solve this problem?" "How do you do it today?" "Tell me, how do you see yourself using these capabilities?" Your buyer can take these open questions anywhere. Why start with open questions? Because they allow the buyer to feel in control. Of course, most sellers want to be in control as well. In or-

FIGURE 6
Vision Processing: Creation/Participation/Reengineering

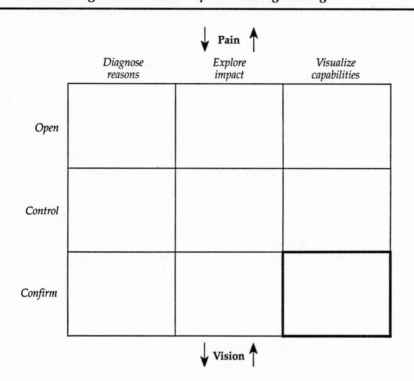

der for the seller to bias the diagnosis and vision to his product or service, he will need to ask *control questions,* not open questions.

Open questions have an advantage and disadvantage to the seller. The advantage is they don't structure the buyer: the buyer feels comfortable and can go anywhere he wants. The disadvantage? The buyer can go anywhere he wants, and 20 minutes later he's still talking about sports or movies or his last vacation. Buyers do not want to be controlled by salespeople. People love to buy, but they hate to be sold.

Lawyers seldom ask open questions. They do not like to let clients and witnesses go wherever they want. They place a higher value on control than they do witness comfort.

Open questions have high value to both seller and buyer. The secret? The *sequence.* The open questions earn the seller the right to ask an almost unlimited number of relevant control questions, but the open question must come first.

Control questions. Control questions allow the seller to keep control of the subject matter being discussed. They might be true "closed-end" questions where the only answer is a yes or a no, or they might *contain* the buyer. "How do your West Coast salespeople get their orders in after you close the office in New York at 5:30 PM?" The buyer can go anywhere he wants within the boundaries of the control question.

Other examples of control questions: "Is it because you do not have the ability to reach all of your salespeople within two hours?" "Is this inability to meet your sales goals hurting dividends?" "Is the chief executive officer impacted?" "What if there were a way for you to communicate a price change to all 1,000 salespeople within 10 minutes, would that help?" Control questions help the seller control the buyer's answers, which enables the seller to position his product and services. But remember, a friendly environment for control questions is established by first asking open questions.

Control questions too have an advantage and a disadvantage. The advantage? The seller is in control. The disadvantage? The buyer might feel controlled and back away. Again, the secret is the sequence.

Confirm questions. Confirm questions summarize the seller's understanding of the buyer's situation. They allow a seller to confirm understanding and content. They allow the seller an opportunity to let the buyer know that he understands her situation. At the highest level, they allow the seller to demonstrate true empathic listening—reflecting back both content and feeling.

Examples of confirm questions: "So, the reasons you have told me for your missing your sales goals are that you lack the ability to easily communicate product and price changes to your 1,000 salespeople, and your technical experts cannot support all your salespeople when needed. Do I understand this correctly?" "From what I just heard, your CEO is concerned because your company is missing its dividend payments." "It sounds like this is not just your problem, but it's a companywide problem, is that right?" "From what I just heard, if you had the ability to communicate product and price changes within 10 minutes of their occurrence to all 1,000 salespeople simultaneously, *could you* solve your inability to meet your sales goals?" Those are all confirm questions and, by asking them, the seller is able to make sure he is in alignment with the buyer—and ultimately confirm that the buyer owns responsibility for solving his own problem.

Reasons, Organizational Impact, Capabilities

You will find those words across the top of the 9-Block Vision Processing Model. Remembering the three types of questions, the seller can comfortably and logically take the buyer through a diagnosis of the reasons for his *pain,* explore the impact of the *pain,* and create a vision of a solution by offering capabilities of his product or service. We will initially take the buyer from admitted pain to vision. Later—when we get good at it—we can start anywhere, depending where the buyer is. A buyer could have pain with no idea of how to deal with it, or he could have a vision created by your competitor. Let's develop a vision for a buyer who knows he has a problem and who has admitted it but does not know how to solve it. Let's walk through the 9-Boxes Model a first time.

Diagnose Reasons Questions

The seller's job is to diagnose the buyer's admitted pain with the bias of his product or service.

Open reasons questions. "Tell me about it. What is causing you to not meet your sales goals?" Answers are usually general, but remember that at this early stage the seller is working only to establish comfort and trust. Once the buyer has had a chance to explain the situation from his viewpoint, the seller has earned the right to ask control questions.

Control reasons questions. Now the seller might use some yes or no control questions. "Is it because you do not have the ability to communicate product and price changes?" [How many answers are possible?] Do you see the product bias—business satellite television—incorporated into the control question? This question will also help the seller find out right away whether some other satellite television vendor is selling to his buyer. In our workshops we use the metaphor of the "bowling pin." We ask sellers to set up the bowling pins with bias control diagnostic questions. When it eventually comes time to create the vision, we will then knock the bowling pins down. Each bowling pin represents an opportunity for the buyer to visualize a product or service capability.

Confirm reasons questions. The seller lets the buyer know he understands her situation. "So, the reasons you have told me for your missing your sales goals are you lack the ability to easily communicate price and product changes, products change frequently, prices also change frequently, and your technical experts cannot support all your salespeople when needed. Is that right? Do I understand you correctly?" The confirmation allows the seller to repeat the diagnosis in "emotional order," not the order in which he gathered the information.

Explore Organizational Impact Questions

Impact questions are powerful because they reveal the buyer's interdependencies with others in his organization. They frequently reveal raw emotions behind and attached to the critical issues and give the sellers clues to where the real political power lies in the organization. Sellers who get good at impact questions frequently make larger sales. Unless you sell to someone who is abolutely solo—someone who does not have to explain it to anyone else—it helps to carefully expore the impact on others.

 Open impact questions. "Besides yourself, *who* in your organization is impacted by your not meeting your sales goals, and *how* are they impacted?" Again the buyer can go anywhere, but the seller is in a transitional box—he is moving from diagnostic questions to exploration of the impact of the buyer's problem on others. The seller is back to earning the right to ask more control questions.

Control impact questions. Now the seller wants to understand organizational impact. The metaphor we use here is a row of dominoes. It's time to line up the dominoes and see where they fall. "Is this inability to meet your sales goals hurting the company's earnings and shareholders' dividends? Are the shareholders impacted? Then is the chief executive officer concerned?" Frequently these questions can lead to a specific question such as, "What's the actual dollar impact of that?" If the seller is able to get answers, then the subsequent vision of a solution can be enhanced with real impact numbers and measurements.

Confirm impact questions. The seller confirms the buyer is not alone with his problem. "From what I just heard, your CEO is concerned because your company's profits are off by 9 percent and your company is missing its shareholder dividend payments. It sounds like this is not just your problem, but it's a companywide problem. Is that right?" When a committee is involved, when the user can't buy, and when the buyer doesn't use the product or service being sold, the impact questions are critical.

Capability Questions

Remember, to make *Solution Selling* benefits, the solution must be in the mind of the buyer, not just the seller. The buyer cannot have a solution in mind without vision. The buyer cannot achieve vision without first accepting responsibility for solving the problem.

Open capability questions. This open question has two purposes: keep the buyer comfortably in control and, more important, put *responsibility* for solving the problem squarely on the buyer's shoulders. "What is it going to take for *you* to be able to meet *your* sales goals?" The buyer may or may not have a vision at this point. The important thing here—regardless of the answer—is that the buyer accepts responsiblity for solving his problem before you ask, "Could I try a few ideas on you?" If you are in alignment, he will answer yes, and you can proceed to the next box and knock down some bowling pins.

Control capability questions. Now it's time for the seller to create a vision of solution through a series of questions that bring the buyer and his product or service capabilities together. The seller might ask: "What if there were a way for *you* to communicate with all 1,000 salespeople within 10 minutes of a product announcement, would that help?" "And what if there were a way for *you* to communicate price changes the same way, would that help?" "If these changes could be communicated to all your field reps at the same time, so no one is left out or gets different information, would that help?" All of these questions are control capability questions. Their purpose is to create a vision. The content for these questions is supplied by the answers the seller received to the biased *control reasons* questions.

In *Solution Selling* workshops we also give the *Enabler* award to the attendee who is best at creating *action* visions. Creating true action visions—where the buyer can "see" himself in control, in action, solving his problem—is difficult.

Confirm capability questions. The seller now confirms that the buyer is enabled. He confirms that the buyer still owns the problem. He confirms that the buyer believes a solution is possible. "From what I just heard, if you had the ability to communicate product and price changes to all field sales reps within 10 minutes, and if those changes could be communicated to all of your field reps at the same time, so no one is left out or gets different information, *could you* meet your sales goals?" "What would that be worth to you?"

If the buyer is truly enabled, he should answer with a specific answer. We will show you how to use that information in a value justification in Strategy 7.

Salespeople, consultants, entrepreneurs, engineers, Ph.D.s, executives, and husbands and wives who study this technique, practice it, and master it are amazed at their results. Buyers love it, too. Because the entire time a seller is going through the nine boxes, he is asking questions, not *selling*. I find it useful to think of the 9-Boxes Model as a "governor" on the seller's expertise and enthusiasm: a governor that helps sellers control their propensity for premature elaboration—the tendency to leap ahead of the buyer and blurt, "We've got just what you need." Many sellers have this problem. Have you ever purchased a PC computer and encountered a saleperson who immediately starts out by reeling off countless features—this PC has a 25 megahertz chip, 4 megabytes of RAM, a 230 megabyte hard drive, and a math co-processing floating point . . . ? That's premature elaboration. The seller has made no attempt to diagnose the buyer's need or create a vision. Instead, he is spewing product features.

The 9-Boxes Model paces and contains enthusiasm and expertise. It acts like a governor on an engine: it limits the seller's RPMs and helps sellers keep themselves under control. Diagnose before you prescribe. If a buyer has confidence in the diagnosis, he will have confidence in the prescription.

A Role Play: Going through the 9 Boxes

Look at Figure 7 the Vision Creation Prompter. This is the one we will use in the following role play. Follow the role play script and see if you recognize where we are in the boxes.

End of Intermission

FIGURE 7
Vision Creation Prompter

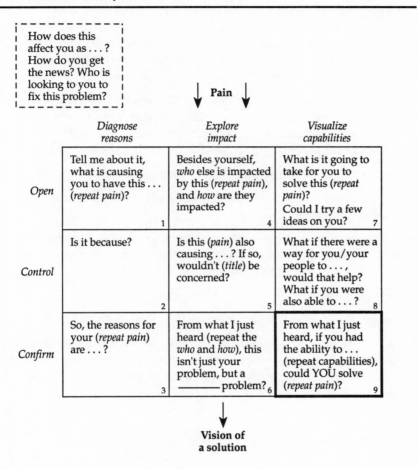

As we go through the 9 Boxes, imagine yourself as the seller. We left the role play when the buyer, Michele, admitted pain to Mike, the seller. Now we will proceed to vision processing.

9-Boxes Role Play:

Pain to Vision

Mike: Tell me about it, Michele. Why do *you* think you're missing your sales goals?

Michele: Mike, we have multiple lines of copiers, and we are constantly introducing new products. We have to stay competitive in the marketplace. The marketplace is changing constantly, and as changes occur, we have to make changes in our product lines—not only in features, but in prices as well. So our sales reps are confused, sales instructions are confused; in fact, the market is confused—our customers are confused.

Mike: All right, let me back up and see if I can catch up with you. You've got many different products you're selling: color copiers, plain paper, different sizes, different volumes. You've got 1,500 salespeople? Do these products change as far as new models?

Michele: More often than you think. Three times a year in some cases.

Mike: And the needs of the markeplace itself change, causing you challenges and difficulties?

Michele: Yes. As our competitors come out with new products, we have to stay equal to or ahead of them, so we are constantly looking for innovative new things to add.

Mike: Is timing critical when that happens?

Michele: Very critical. It can directly affect market share for us.

Mike: Are there instances where you have seen the competition come to market with some innovation and your customers have asked you for those exact competitive capabilities? Is the timing to respond to that important?

Michele: Yes.

Mike: Are your salespeople dispersed all over the country?

Michele: Yes.

Mike: Do you find there is a disparity in their experience? You have some seniors, some middle level, and some juniors?

Michele: Of course.

Mike: With the number of locations you have, the number of people you have, and the number of products you have, do you ever find yourself in a situation where Los Angeles has the new pricing on Product A but Chicago doesn't yet, so you get an "information float" situation of the company selling the same product at two different prices?

Michele: Yes.

Mike: Do you ever get the situation where Chicago has the new model for Product B, but Los Angeles does not? So now we have the same people from the same company selling different products?

Michele: Yes.

Mike: Let me summarize what I've just heard. You are not meeting your sales goals and it sounds like there is quite a bit of confusion in your sales force. They don't always have the right model information. They are not always aligning the right model features with what the market wants. There are frequent product changes and an information float problem. When you do have new product or price information, there is a time lag getting it out to all locations. Bottom line—your sales force is not operating as effectively as you think they might?

Michele: That's correct; that's very correct.

Mike: Besides yourself, Michele, who else is impacted by this problem?

Michele: The VP, finance. We are not meeting our revenue targets and our profitability is being eroded.

Mike: Revenue targets have been missed, profits are off, and the VP, finance, is directly attributing that to the sales force?

Michele: Yes. There might be one more factor here as well. When we introduce new products, I find that I send out product marketing teams from headquarters. When the teams go out, it is very expensive. In addition to the expense, they cannot be everywhere at the same time, causing a lag in product information among our field salespeople.

Mike: So marketing people from headquarters are going out to the field trying to educate the sales reps on new products? Is that right?

Michele: Yes.

Mike: And there is "information float"? Can this cause problems?

Michele: Yes, it is already has.

Mike: All right. So has this also impacted revenue and profits?

Michele: Yes, that's why I talked about the VP, finance.

Mike: It sounds as though, with the product marketing teams getting on airplanes and traveling to the field, with the cost of these rollouts, and with both sales and profits off, the VP, marketing, must also be impacted by this problem.

Michele: Yes, he is.

Mike: Do you think it's at the point where the company's growth has been affected? Have you missed your revenue targets this year?

Michele: Yes, we have.

Mike: Has the stock price been affected?

Michele: Yes, it has.

Mike: So the CEO is impacted as well?

Michele: Yes. As we have had to announce reduced profits, the stock market has reacted negatively and so has the CEO.

Mike: It sounds to me, Michele, as though this problem of your not making your sales goals is not just impacting you, but it is an organizational problem: it's a revenue problem—that impacts the VP, finance. The VP, marketing, is impacted since it's his people who are out educating the field sales reps. The CEO is trying to get your stock price up, but the company's growth has been impacted. Sounds to me like its a company problem.

Michele: It certainly is.

Mike: Michele, what is it going to take for *you* to solve this problem?

Michele: You know, Mike, I'm not sure. I was hoping you could help me.

Mike: Could I try a few ideas on you?

Michele: Certainly.

Mike: What if you had a new product you wanted to tell the field about—a promotional campaign you had to disseminate—and within two hours you could personally introduce the change to all 1,500 salespeople in all locations from your office here at headquarters? Would that help?

Michele: That would help.

Mike: Let me make it a little more specific. They all could see you and they all could hear you and hear each other, so that if a sales rep in L.A. had a question, all 1,500 salespeople would hear the question and hear and see you answer it.

Michele: That would be extremely helpful.

Mike: What if you could also introduce the product expert, so all 1,500 people at the same time would get the new information and they could go out in the next hour making sales calls with current information on promotions, pricing, or technology changes? Would that help?

Michele: It would help eliminate a tremendous amount of confusion in the organization if everyone heard the same information and questions and answers at the same time. That would help us be much more uniform in our message not only to our sales reps but also to our customers. That would help benefit us.

Mike: That would help eliminate the float problem we talked about. Is that right?

Michele: Yes.

Mike: Let me summarize what I've heard. You said you would like to be able to reach all field locations simultaneously, where you could get in front of your people and give them all the same information at the same time. You also said you would like to be able to introduce marketing people so they could disseminate new information, eliminate the information float, and eliminate the airplane trips. If you had those capabilities, *could you* start to make your sales goals again?

Michele: We would be going in the right direction. Yes, I could.

Intermission

We have observed Mike, the seller, go through the 9 Boxes in this example to create a vision. He led Michele from an admitted pain through a biased diagnosis, explored the impact of her problem on other power people in her organization, and led her to a vision of a solution biased with his product—satellite business TV. Michele confirmed that she could increase her sales with these capabilities.

It can take as little as 20 to 30 minutes to take a buyer through the 9 Boxes. In order to do it well, the seller had to have had a vision of a solution for the buyer. The seller would have needed enough expertise and experience to lead the buyer to a specific vision biased to his product. In my client base, the world of information technology, most sellers do not have that level of product knowledge integrated with application knowledge—knowledge of how the product or service is used *situationally*. In Strategy 4, we will introduce you to some tools, some "job aides," that will enable you to dramatically improve your effectiveness in situations where expertise is necessary.

Sometimes, going through the 9 Boxes is overkill. Sometimes we need a scalpel instead of a sledgehammer. If you think about it, taking a buyer through the 9 Boxes is the way we "earn the right" to take our product out. There are selling situations where we need to get our product or service out more quickly than the 9 Boxes allows. I'll give you a couple of examples.

One would be if you are in a *proof* sales call. The buyer has a vision and has given you the opportunity to prove to him that your product or service will be a match for his vision. You could be giving a presentation or a demonstration of your capabilities. Have you even been in such a situation when you had the thought, "I know what he'd like to see!"? "I'll bet he'd like to see our *priority message* feature."

A second example would be if you were reengineering a buyer vision created by a competitor. (We will cover reengineering later in this chapter.) You might ask your buyer an "are you also looking for a way" question. "Are you also looking for a way to have priorities assigned to your voice messages?" There are three potential answers: yes, no, or "What's that?" If the buyer answered, "What's that?" or if you really know what you'd like your buyer to see, the next technique is for you.

ANXIETY CREATION

Anxiety creation is a "mini" need development technique. We want to see if we can take a *specific* latent pain from a buyer's "background" and bring it around to the "foreground"—we want our buyer to go "ouch!" The specific latent need we are pursuing, naturally, is a perfect match for something we are selling! Instead of setting up a row of bowling pins, we are setting up a "spare," a single pin. To do this, we ask an *anxiety question* that is really a *control reason question*.

If our buyer says "ouch," we then ask a *control capability question* to help the buyer relieve his pain. First we hurt; then we rescue. The key is to ask the question in such a way that your product capability can rescue the buyer. Figure 8 demonstrates how we use these two types of questions to move our buyer through the three levels of need for a specific capability.

Let me give you an example. It is taken from a role play in one of our workshops where our client sells voice messaging and

FIGURE 8
Three Levels of Need

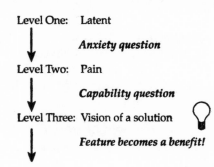

Level One: Latent

        Anxiety question

Level Two: Pain

        Capability question

Level Three: Vision of a solution

        Feature becomes a benefit!

voice response systems. The seller begins by asking his buyer an *anxiety question:*

Seller: Suppose you are at JFK Airport in New York—on your way to Dallas for an important sales meeting. It is after 6 PM and your office in Boston is closed, but you have voice mail so you can retrieve your messages, and your staff is trained to leave messages.

You have only 10 minutes to make your flight connection. You dash to a pay telephone, dial your phone, and listen to your voice mail. After receiving four messages concerning routine matters, the airport loudspeaker announces the final gate call for your flight. You listen to one more message—the gate is closing—then you run for your flight and board your aircraft.

As soon as you arrive in Dallas, you find a vacant telephone booth and check the rest of your telephone messages. The sixth message is from your assistant, "Jim Jones phoned from Dallas and said he couldn't make the meeting—he was called out of town on an emergency. He sent his apologies and said he would phone you tomorrow to reschedule."

How would you feel, having just flown to Dallas for a meeting that had been cancelled?

Most business executives who travel would respond to the *plausible emergency* posed by the seller. If the buyer in the example responded, "I would hate for that to happen to me, but I know it could," the seller was successful in occupying one of the buyer's foreground "slots" with an issue with which he can help the buyer. In our workshops, when we teach this technique, many sellers get pretty good at hurting people, but sometimes they "leave the buyer hanging"—they hurt the buyer but could not rescue him.

In this example, one of my client's features is a *priority* capability in their voice message systems. The seller could then ask the buyer the question:

Seller: What if there was a way to put a higher priority on critical messages? What if your assistant could have given that message about the meeting cancellation a top priority, so when you only had 10 minutes at JFK Airport, you would hear the high priority message first, would that help?

The buyer in this instance would be very likely to respond favorably to this capability question. He might say, "If that were possible, I would find it very useful. I travel quite a bit."

The seller could then turn his priority message *feature* into a *benefit* by saying, "Our priority message feature can give you that capability, and I would like an opportunity to prove it to you."

VISION REENGINEERING

In our first trip through the 9 Boxes, we assumed we had a buyer who had pain but no vision of a solution. This selling situation is most common when the seller is *first*. As many of my clients will tell you, most of the time they are not first. When they meet a new buyer for the first time, in most cases the buyer already has an idea of what he is looking for. Where did the buyer get his vision? It could have come from a competitor. Keeping in mind that we want to make ourselves equal before we make ourselves different in competitive situations, a powerful variation on the theme of the 9 Boxes is what we call *vision reengineering*. Here is another trip through the 9 Boxes. This time, we won't go through them in the same order. Since the buyer wants to discuss his vision, we will discuss his vision. We will stay aligned.

Participate in the existing vision. Your clue that a vision exists is the buyer's language: "We are going to purchase hand-held computers for our entire field sales force." Most sellers would ask the buyer why he needs them. A better starter question in this situation is to ask the buyer, "How do you see yourself using these hand-held computers?" This was an *open capability question*. The buyer might respond with, "We want to eliminate the cumbersome product catalogs they have to carry around."

Add your bias to the existing vision. Once you have the buyer's existing vision on the table, you can now start to add the bias of your product to his vision. The more you know about how your capabilities stack up against specific competitors the better (I will give you some tools in Strategy 4). You can now ask *closed capability questions.* When reengineering visions, they start off with, "Are you also looking for a way to . . . ?" You assume the buyer is smart enough to already have thought of it. "Are you also looking for a way for your field salespeople to be able to verify stock before they commit to their customers?" "Are you also looking for a way to check the customer's credit quickly and unobtrusively?" As we said earlier, there are only three answers: yes, no, or "What's that?" If the buyer answers with "What's that?" branch to an anxiety question. "How would you feel if your salesperson made a commitment to his customer that he couldn't keep?" If the buyer sees the potential problem, he will now respond favorably to the capability question.

Confirm they don't currently have capabilities. A great way to find this out is to ask an *open reason question:* "How do you do it today?" Ideally, the buyer will begin to describe how they operate without the capabilities he is telling you he needs.

Diagnose reasons with bias. Now you can take control of the diagnosis with *control diagnosis questions.* A good lead-in for these questions is the word "today." "Today, are your salespeople quoting from availability information that could be over a week old?" "Today, even if a salesperson knows you are out of an item, do they lack the information to offer a good substitute?" We are back to setting up bowling pins, only in this case, we already know they will go down easily.

Confirm diagnosis and pain. You can now summarize your understanding of the situation with *confirm reason questions.* "So, from what you have told me, today . . . ?" Once the buyer agrees that you now understand the existing situation, you want to discover the business impact. We can't explore impact on others until we get the problem elevated to a true business issue. I like the question, "What is the impact on your business of doing it the way you do it today?" The buyer should answer something like, "We are losing customers to our competition"—a *business* issue.

Explore impact on others. At this point, you could say, "Who else in the organization is impacted by this loss of customers to the competition?" In this case, our buyer, the VP of sales, could say, "The vice president of marketing is impacted directly." With that *open impact question*, I have now earned the right to ask *control impact questions:* "Is the VP, marketing, worried about shelf space?" "If you are losing customers and shelf space, has this impacted your company's revenue?" If the buyer says yes, you could then ask, "Then is your VP, finance, also directly impacted by this situation?" Using the "domino theory," we could spread the pain around the entire organization—morale of salespeople, share price, higher distribution costs, turmoil in production, and so on. We would then summarize the organizational impact with *confirm impact questions.* " . . . this is not just your problem—it is a company problem?"

At this point in our vision reengineering example, we have gone through eight of the nine boxes.

Reconfirm vision. The *confirm capability questions* box should always be *last*. Ideally, we will now be able to confirm a vision that has our product bias added to it. "So, you want to buy hand-held computers for your field sales force so they can . . . " You then make sure the buyer really has a vision with the question, "If you had these capabilities, could you keep your existing customers and win back the ones you have lost?"

State benefit. If the buyer answered yes, we could say, "I am confident that our product will give you those capabilities. I'd like an opportunity to prove it to you. Will you give me that opportunity by taking a serious look at my product?"

Take a look at Figure 9, Vision Reengineering Prompter. What do you think the buyer might be thinking about you at this point in the call? Is he convinced you understand his business situation? Does he have a better understanding himself of how serious his problem really is? Might he be motivated to carry the torch for change to his peers and superiors? People buy from people. People buy from people whom they like, who are sincere and competent, who understand their situation, and who *empower* them.

Think about the process through which we took our buyer. We haven't mentioned our product yet. We haven't done a presentation, survey, or demonstration yet. From the buyer's perspective, because we haven't done those things yet, we haven't been "selling." But we have been selling—selling by the *Solution Selling* defi-

FIGURE 9
Vision Reengineering Prompter

	Diagnose reasons	Explore impact	Visualize capabilities
Open	How do you do it today? ⟨3⟩	Besides yourself, *who* else is impacted by this *(pain)*, and *how* are they impacted? ⟨6⟩	How do you see yourself using . . . ? ⟨1⟩
Control	Today, . . . ? ⟨4⟩	Is this *(pain)* also causing . . . ? ⟨7⟩	Are you also looking for a way . . . ? Would it also help if you had a way . . . ? ⟨2⟩
Confirm	So the way you do it today is . . . ? ⟨5⟩	From what I just heard (repeat the *who* and *how*), this isn't just your problem, but a _____ problem? ⟨8⟩	From what I just heard, if you had the ability to . . . (repeat capabilities), could *you* solve your *(pain)*? ⟨9⟩

What is the impact on your business of doing it the way you are doing it? → **Pain**

↑ **Vision** ↓

nition: helping people buy. I tell my clients they don't need the best product to win; they need a reasonable product. The best sales person, not the best product, will win in most competitive situations. Process will beat product.

What happens when you meet a prospect who already has a vision? He is easily identifiable, because when you meet him for the first time he says, "I need" or "we're going to buy."

Let's say his "I needs" are in perfect alignment with what you have in your product or service. Isn't it tempting to blurt, "Oh boy, I have just the thing for you. It's exactly what you are looking for." If you do that kind of selling, you are prescribing without diagnosing.

The *Solution Selling* discipline calls for a different reaction. The 9 Boxes again serves as a guide and a governor, helping you control your expertise and enthusiasm. Diagnose before you prescribe. The real selling happens in the 9 Boxes.

Solution Selling Tools— Job Aides

These are instruments that Solution Selling *sellers use to help them integrate their product knowledge and knowledge of the buyer's situation with* Solution Selling *skills. They help sellers establish— early in a sales call—rapport, alignment, and competence.*

The primary skill I want you to acquire is the knowledge of how to create a vision of a solution in the mind of a buyer—biased with your product or service. In other words, learn how to align the buyer's vision of problem solving with your product or service. That is a principal value of *Solution Selling*. If *you* can develop such visions, then *you* are far more likely to be in alignment with your buyers. And, in my experience, when a buyer sees that his vision of a solution is matched by your product or service, the buyer actually will push you to close.

Strategic alignment is easier to develop by using three tools: the reference story, the pain sheet, and the telephone script. Each is useful in its own right. The first two tools, the reference story and the pain sheet, are tools a seller needs *before making first contact*.

The reference story and pain sheet are tools that help the seller navigate his buyer through the three levels of need. The reference story has two primary purposes that are highly interdependent: to get the buyer to conclude the seller is competent and to get the buyer to admit pain to the seller. A buyer will not admit pain to a seller he does not deem trustworthy. Stephen Covey defines trustworthy as sincere and competent. We will deal with the sincere decision in Strategy 6. We will deal with the competence issue with the reference story.

THE REFERENCE STORY

Necessity is the mother of invention. The *Solution Selling* reference story format grew out of necessity. Here are some of the situations I faced in 1983 when I started my *Solution Selling* business:

- Salespeople (particularly young salespeople) had difficulty getting buyers to take them seriously—to deem them competent.
- Many salespeople were selling products or services with unlimited applications.
- Many salespeople were having difficulty getting buyers interested in their products and services.
- Many salespeople were selling products and services that were difficult to explain—they were conceptual or intangible.
- Many salespeople were asking people to buy technology they didn't understand to solve problems they didn't know how to solve.
- Many salespeople were in desperate need of something to talk about other than their company, product, or service.
- Most buyers did not want to be the first to try something.

In our workshops we give each participant a first night homework assignment: write a reference story about an existing customer and how they are successfully using their product or service. I am amazed at how difficult this assignment is for some people. Here are the elements of a *Solution Selling* reference story. Try to write one yourself and see if you can see why they are so difficult to prepare.

Reference Story Format

Situation:	The situation must include the customer's job title and industry or vertical market.
Critical issue:	The critical issue is the pain of the person above. (*Anxiety words and phrases are very powerful.*)
Reasons:	The business reasons for the customer's critical issue biased to your product.
Vision:	In the words of your customer, the capabilities he said he needed to solve his problem: "He told me he needed a way to . . . "
We provided:	If the "solution" is described properly in the vision above, all we should have to do here is say that we (our company, product, or service) gave him those capabilities.
Result:	Specific measurement is best.

Throughout this book, I will tell you stories of how people and companies have implemented *Solution Selling.* In Part III—Solution Selling in Action, I will give you multiple reference stories in this same format. It has proven to be extremely powerful in creating interest, allowing young salespeople to establish competence, creating hope, creating peer pressure on potential buyers, and most important, getting buyers to admit pain to sellers. The 9 Boxes is not very useful if a buyer will not admit pain. A buyer will not admit pain until the seller has proven himself competent.

I have learned that buyers will allow sellers to make *intelligent* assumptions *early* in the relationship. Assumptions can be risky, but buyers will allow intelligent assumptions early in the relationship. My definition of an intelligent assumption is one that relates to both a buyer's *industry* and *job title,* and that based on your product's or service's capability, there is a high probability *critical issue* about which that the buyer is likely to be curious. In other words, in a reference story, we are telling a potential buyer a story about how someone in *his* industry, with *his* job title, has already figured out how to solve a difficult problem to which the buyer relates.

Here is an example from the *Solution Selling* workshop manual.

Reference Story Example

Situation:	Vice president sales, F1000 Toy Company with large field sales force.
Critical issue:	The company was only able to fulfill and ship 70 percent of the orders taken by his 1,200 field salespeople. Their competition was "stealing" the other 30 percent. He was selling enough to make quota, but the factory couldn't ship enough.
Reasons:	Every Thursday night, a new product availability report was shipped to all 1,200 salespeople for the following week. Thus, they were all quoting from an inaccurate report by Tuesday of each week.
Vision:	He said he needed some way to get daily product availability information to his salespeople and for his salespeople to be able to confirm their orders from customers before they leave the customer site.
We provided:	We provided him with these capabilities.
Result:	They are now processing orders daily and fulfilling 96 percent of all orders taken by his field salespeople. He is on track to make his quota.

If you were a seller and told that story to a Fortune 1000 sales executive with a large sales force, what do you think the reaction would be? Particularly if he is shipping less than 96 percent of all orders taken? Even if you were in your twenties and he was in his forties? What is the likelihood that your buyer might respond, "I have the exact same problem!"—reasonable? He might also say, "I don't have that problem, but I am having a problem in this other area."

What did the buyer just do? He admitted pain. What did we do? We went "fishing" with an assumption—we assumed he would be interested in a story about a peer. Early in the relationship, we can get away with intelligent assumptions. Once the buyer admits pain to you, further assumptions will hurt your credibility. Why? Because once a buyer trusts you enough to admit a problem to you, you can get straight answers to all future questions. You don't have to go fishing anymore, and, if you do, he might be insulted.

Our reference story is really an advantage statement. We are telling our buyer via a story how our product could be used or could help someone very much like our buyer. Advantage statements have their highest value early in the sell cycle. Once they serve their purpose, it should be benefits from then on out.

THE PAIN SHEET

*"A principle of Solution Selling, 'No **pain**, no change,' is a variation on what you might hear at your health club. The only thing that is going to motivate somebody to spend money is an unsatisfied need."*

Once a buyer admits pain to a seller, the real selling begins—the real selling for eagles, that is. Journeymen sellers have a difficult time diagnosing pain. Diagnosing, by definition, is an interactive process. It requires conversation—situational fluency—questions, and answers. Journeymen sellers are most comfortable making presentations—giving slide shows and demonstrations. Why? It is much easier. Every gesture can be memorized.

The 9-Block Vision Processing Model is an interactive model. It involves questions, answers, and listening. It is an interactive model designed to allow journeymen sellers to sell the way eagles do—conversationally.

When I began my *Solution Selling* business in 1983, I showed the 9 Boxes to approximately 40 sales executives of information technology companies in my first six months. They unanimously agreed that "it is the way it should be done." A couple of them went even further by saying, "Mike, that's the way I do it." Within five minutes, however, most of them also told me that it wouldn't work in their company. The reason? Those *control* questions. Those control questions worried them. They didn't think most of their sellers could do them. They knew their support people could ask them, their application consultants and industry marketing people could ask them, but their salespeople couldn't. Why?

The answer did not come right away. It took me six months of wrestling with this issue before I came up with a solution to the problem. The problem? The control questions require situational fluency of the capabilities the company sells—not product knowledge, not industry knowledge, but situational fluency. They require knowledge of which specific product capability a financial executive would need on the 15th of the month to plan his cash for the remainder of the month.

When sales executives look at the 9 Block Vision Processing Model, they see the *open* and *confirm* questions as being easy—a little training and drill and most sellers should be able to execute them quite well. The *control* questions are quite another matter.

The breakthrough for me came after six months of hearing concerns from sales executives about the control questions. Typically, when a seller is going to attempt to take a buyer through the 9 Boxes, it involves what we call a *situation*. A situation is a combination of *job title* (a vice president of finance, for instance) and a *pain* (too much obsolete inventory impacting profits, for example).

What if we were able to make a list of the most probable situations a seller would face selling a particular product or service? Could we then get the most qualified person in the organization to tell us the control questions he would ask in that particular situation? Could we write those situation questions down for sellers to use? These situation-specific control question prompters are what we call in *Solution Selling* Pain Sheets™—situational fluency prompters.

Pain Sheets (see Figure 10) have three columns: Column 1 is a list of *control reason questions* for a situation, column 2 is a list of *control impact questions* for that same situation, and column 3 is a list of *control capability questions* for that situation.

Recall the narrative in Face #3 ("10 Faces of Buyer Pain") between Michele, a vice president of sales of an office equipment supplier, and Mike, a sales rep for a satellite business television company. Mike used a Pain Sheet (see Figure 11) that prompted his control

FIGURE 10
Pain Sheet—Situational Fluency Prompter

Pain:
Situation:
Our Capability:

Reasons	*Impact*	*Capabilities*
Is it because . . . ; Today . . . ?	*Is this (pain) causing . . . ?*	*What if . . . ; Would it help if . . . ?*

FIGURE 11
Pain Sheet—Situational Fluency Prompter

Pain:	Not meeting sales goals	
Situation:	VP, sales, Large field sales organization	
Our Capability:	Satellite business television	

Reasons	Impact	Capabilities
Is it because . . . ; Today . . . ?	*Is this (pain) causing . . . ?*	*What if . . . ; Would it help if . . . ?*
Field salespeople need more "face time" with company leadership, product experts, and so forth	Missed revenue targets Increased travel expenses Lower profits	You were able to reach *all* field locations simultaneously where *you* could:
Lack of product knowledge in the field due to:	*Is the VP, finance, concerned?*	Personally position the product? Introduce the product/market expert?
Do you have: A complex product?	Product managers living on airplanes Costly product rollouts Eroding market share	Demonstrate the product? Receive immediate live feedback?
Frequent product changes? How many?	*Is the VP, marketing, impacted?*	You could select any/all field locations that you need access to within two hours?
A dynamic marketplace? A large number of salespeople? How many?	Does he feel the sales force is not properly executing product strategy?	You could continue to train your new employees without travel?
Salespeople that are geographically dispersed?	Impact on company's growth Impact on future product strategy Impact on stock price	You could eliminate "information float" by reaching all field people simultaneously?
A disparity in sales experience? A finite number of product experts? How many?	*Is the CEO affected?*	
Have you found the cost of training escalating? What percent?	Frustration, morale problems, turnover	You could increase the product knowledge of your people while reducing the cost of training?
	Are customers, salespeople, and HQ staff impacted?	

questions to establish the reasons, impact, and vision of a solution for Michele to be able to solve her problem. The Pain Sheet enabled Mike to demonstrate situational fluency to his buyer.

Mike did not have to be an expert running an office equipment sales force, because with his Pain Sheet and Michele's admission of a problem (not meeting her sales goals), he was able to effectively establish the reasons for her pain (framed by his product's capabilities), explore the impact of the problem, and bias her vision of a solution with his satellite business television product. All of the control reason questions he asked came *from* the left column of the Pain Sheet.

The middle column, the control impact questions, illustrates how Mike got and used that information to link Michele's problem to the vice president of finance and to the vice president of marketing and up to the chief executive officer.

If you look at the right-hand column of the Pain Sheet, you will see Mike's control capability questions—questions that enable Michele to become a mental user of NNC satellite business television. Thus, the Pain Sheet allows salespeople to carry more products to more vertical markets, and it allows new salespeople trying to learn complex markets and products to be more productive more quickly.

Create a Pain Sheet for your own products and practice it two or three times and you will be amazed at the difference. The first time many salespeople try using a Pain Sheet to navigate through the 9 Boxes, they compare it to the first time they tried to drive a stickshift car. They were so busy trying to figure out which pedal their foot should be on, they drove off the road. In our workshops, it typically takes two or three role play practice sessions before sellers get comfortable with the *rhythm* of the 9 Boxes.

The Pain Sheet is the kind of "product knowledge" that most salespeople need. Many businesses, in my opinion, spend needless training dollars training salespeople on product or service features and advantages. They just become another sales robot who "spews" features at hapless buyers. Salespeople do not need to know the thousands and thousands of features of your products or services. It only confuses things. As matter of fact, one of the greatest dangers with salespeople is that the selling organization fills their brains with vast detailed knowledge of the product. Then sellers are tempted to share that vast knowledge with their prospects.

Situation

Critical issue

Reasons

Vision

Capability

Results with measurement

Most of our clients revamp their product training curriculum for their salespeople once they understand the power of the Pain Sheet. Some clients have added fourth and fifth columns to the Pain Sheet so they can align specific products and features with the capabilities and reasons. They can then follow a *Solution Selling* workshop with product training that directly integrates with the sales training. Those clients who have integrated their product training with *Solution Selling* have experienced dramatically reduced "start-up" times for new hires. You can read about these successes in Part III—*Solution Selling* in Action.

THE SOLUTION SELLING TELEPHONE SCRIPT

I "broke the code" to prospecting in 1987. Prospecting is something almost every seller hates and on which he tends to procrastinate. The telephone script holds the "code," and, as you would guess, *Solution Selling* phone scripts are based on a foundation knowledge of the three levels of needs and buyer alignment, among other *Solution Selling* principles. Because the phone script is so critical to the prospecting success of the seller, we spend quite a bit of time practicing it in our workshops.

But first, why do most salespeople hate cold phone call prospecting? Because the chance for success is so small. Many salespeople have a miserable 1 to 2 percent hit rate. At that rate, even strong sellers with an enormous emotional capacity for rejection avoid telephone prospecting. It is the first thing sellers stop doing as soon as they get busy, causing performance to go up and down like a roller coaster. Even eagles are not immune to the roller coaster. And today, with travel so expensive, businesses should make better use of the telephone. But how?

What if there were a way to increase the hit rate to 50 to 70 percent? Would sellers scramble for telephone time? Yes, and more telephone time means a lot more prospecting. In the technique I am going to show you, many of my customers report an 80 percent hit rate. You might be asking yourself, "What is a *hit*?" My definition of a *hit* is when, after 20 seconds on the phone, the potential buyer says, "Tell me more," or something similar. So, let us explore the *Solution Selling* phone script.

The first thing on which we need to focus is writing a script aimed at a power person. Remember, *power buys from power*. Assume for now we are able to get past the "gatekeeper," and, after we dial our telephone, the power person answers.

You have only a 20-second window of opportunity. The first order of business is to reduce the prospect's anxiety over being called. I believe the primary problem salespeople have with prospecting—the reason phone prospecting success rates are so low—is that sellers are creating *tension* rather than *interest.* How many of you have come home after a long day and you get a telephone cold call from a salesperson? It may be about telephone services or a newspaper or magazine subscription, or it may be about financial planning, or house siding, or gardening services, whatever. Most people I know, including salespeople who should be the most tolerant of all, are intolerant of such an intrusion. From the moment they pick up the phone and hear an unfamiliar voice call them by name, their tension rises. Because of this tension, you have only 20 seconds to alleviate the tension and create interest.

Important Components to a Good Phone Script

Good scripting—I call it "wordsmithing"—and planning can lead you to many successful phone prospecting calls. When creating phone scripts, here are a few things to remember:

- Make sure you can get through the script at a reasonable pace in approximately 20 seconds. That's the window of opportunity.
- Think of a problem the buyer is *likely* to have. Do not bore the buyer with your company history. Do not ask the buyer to admit pain. Do not ask the buyer for an appointment.
- Seek only to gain one thing: *curiosity.* Establish curiosity about how another person in the same situation as the buyer, with the same job title, has already figured out the solution to a problem the buyer is likely to have.
- Be prepared for a positive response—to continue selling on the phone or to book an appointment. We will address selling on the phone in Strategy 6.

The foundation for a telephone prospecting script is a reference story. It would be impossible to read most reference stories in 20 seconds, but we don't use all of it. We only use the situation and critical issue sections.

I believe in focused, *situation specific* prospecting. That is why the reference story format starts from the base of a real situation and a critical issue. By *situation* I mean, if I want to call doctors, I tell doctors of a *critical issue* of another doctor. If I call entrepreneurs, I tell them of another entrepreneur's critical issue and how I helped that entrepreneur. If I want to call vice presidents of finance, I tell them how I have helped another vice president of finance solve a problem. In other words, intelligent assumptions are needed in order to put together a phone script. Intelligent assumptions focus in on a person's situation.

Telephone Script (20 seconds)

"This is *[name]* with *[company]* . We have been working with *[industry]* for the past *[#]* years. One of the chief concerns we are hearing from other *[job title]* is their frustration with *["wordsmithed" critical issue]* . We have been able to help our customers deal with this issue and I would like an opportunity to share with you how."

Here is an example of an effective phone script to the VP of sales for a toy company:

Seller: Tom, my name is Mike Jones with the ABC Computer System Company. We have been working with the toy industry for the past four years. One of the chief concerns we are hearing from other sales executives is their frustration because manufacturing is unable to fulfill all the sales orders written by their salespeople, causing them to lose valuable shelf space to their competition. We have been able to help our customers deal with this issue and I would like an opportunity to share with you how.

Buyer: Tell me more.

That script does exactly what I want. Tom, the prospect, responds with, "Tell me more." That is *curiosity*. My clients confirm that when their phone scripts are crafted well, they get spectacular results. Such scripts have to be wordsmithed and practiced. No extra "uhs" or "ums." Each telephone script has to be smooth and tight, and, when they are, try—which is why as I have stated I have clients who report up to an 80 percent curiosity rate. That means 80 percent of the time they are hearing, "Tell me more." That is an appreciable improvement from 2 percent! The key is the critical issue and how you wordsmith the critical issue. Put some anxiety in it. Accent the *frustration* you are hearing from his peers.

Here is a shorter but still effective phone script that I or my distributors could use with the CEO of a computer hardware company:

Mr. Jones, my name is Mike Bosworth. I do sales training for computer companies. Some of my clients include the ABC Company and the XYZ Company. One of the chief concerns I am hearing from other CEOs is their frustration over the inability of their salespeople to make effective calls on non-MIS executives. I've been able to help my clients deal with this issue, and I'd like an opportunity to share with you how.

In other words, in 20 seconds with the phone script, a seller is asking a buyer, are *you* curious how someone with *your* job title in *your* industry has already figured out how to solve a problem that *you* might also have? That's the secret to prospecting.

When I prepare a phone script, I like to start with four critical issues. I pick the one that is more probable for the initial script. Then I have the others in reserve. Why? Because as you may have already figured out, buyers don't always say, "Tell me more." Sometimes they say, "I don't have that problem." I can then say, "Other problems we have also helped our customers address are . . . (critical issues, B, C, and D). *Are you curious* how we have helped our customers deal with those issues?" Now it is down to a yes or a no. If it is a no, say, "Thank you for your time" and move on to the next phone call.

How much time have you spent on this prospect? Less than a minute (once your script is prepared). And what is your job as a salesperson? To go through your conceptual sales territory—see Strategy 1—and turn latent need into active need. When the prospect is curious, it is the beginning of a buy cycle. If you are the salesperson who initiates the buy cycle, your competition will have to compare their products and services to the buyer vision created by you.

If, after your best efforts, the answer is still no, and you had to say, "Thank you for your time," and then hung up the phone, you've done your job. You did not waste money sending sales literature, no postage was wasted, no travel expenses were wasted, no costly demonstrations were employed. Sales always has been and always will be a numbers game—no matter how good you become, not everyone will buy from you.

Ask yourself, if a prospect is not curious about how you helped someone with the *same* job title at another company in the *same* industry with four critical issues related to his situation, would that have been a tough sales call had you gone out in person?

Phone Prospect High

Another possibility when you cold call is that you get delegated down a level. If you do, you will have a much easier time getting access to power than if you begin low. Most sellers have had the experience of getting "locked in" at a low level in an organization. By calling high, you can avoid this problem, but if you call high, the "critical issue" and your conversation must be *appropriate* for that level. If you find yourself getting delegated on a regular basis, you might be talking to a high-level buyer about low-level issues.

Sometimes we get leads. I have learned the hard way that most "hot" leads aren't quite as hot as I initially thought they were. Most leads come from low levels in an organization. It might be from a person who is simply researching your product or service—perhaps they are evaluating similar products or services. What I recommend is to send that low-level buyer some sales information via third-class mail. But the piece I would send out would be reference story oriented, and it would have no detailed product information, no pricing, no features, no specifications. It would simply be a story (*Solution Selling* reference story format) of how another company like the buyer's was successful using my product or service. I would then prepare a phone script for that situation, pick up the phone, and cold call the line vice presidents of that organization. If there is a legitimate evaluation going on, he will say something like, "You know, Mike, funny you should call. I think we're looking into something like that right now. Here's the person you should talk to." Now you have access to power. You can talk to the "delegee" and copy the power person on all correspondence.

Most sellers admit to me that there are not enough active evaluations going on in their territory for them to achieve their goals. I poll any territory of mine twice a year to find active evaluations. When I discover one, I cold call high and get delegated down to the project leader. I then attempt to re-engineer the existing vision—Strategy 3—and qualify the buying process—Strategy 6.

Most of your territory, though, is that huge, *latent needs* area. The advantage here is, if you are first, you will get to write the buying requirements. And if you continue to challenge your prospects with further anxiety questions, further visions, every time you talk with them, your buyer will "see it" a little more each time. Yes, they will look at other alternatives. That is the way corporations buy. But no other competitor can easily march in and take that buyer from you.

Phone Scripts for Startup or Young Businesses

What if you are in a situation where your business, product, service or idea is new. If the foundation of a good phone script is a good reference story, what do you do? Well, the secret to prospecting still applies. It is still possible to ask buyers the question, *are you curious?* Here is an example.

Seller: Dave, this is John Doe and I am with the ABC Startup Company. For the past four years, we have been doing research into the operational problems of toy companies. A problem we encounter again and again is their difficulty filling many of the orders taken by their field salespeople. We have developed a new approach to dealing with this issue, and I would like the opportunity to share with you how we have begun to help the toy industry deal with this issue.

What makes it go? The critical issue. If your buyer becomes curious about how somebody has figured out how to solve his problem, he will see you. He will say, "Tell me more." The keys are the critical issue and curiosity. Are they curious how someone else has solved a problem?

Again asking, "Are you curious?"

Keep Statistics

I encourage my customers to keep hit rate statistics. You might discover that only half the time with critical issue A you get interest, but you get curiosity 80 percent of the time with critical issue B. Your hit rates will vary by situation and by critical issue. I had a client who was experimenting with different versions of a phone script. They found that by changing *one* word in the phone script, the hit rate went from 40 percent to 80 percent. Try many approaches, many scripts, and keep statistics.

In Strategy 10, we are going to give you some ideas on pipeline management. In order to manage a pipeline, we must first have a pipeline. The *Solution Selling* telephone script is a proven way to dramatically reduce the rejection of traditional prospecting. The "are you curious?" theme can be carried to a number of other prospecting areas: direct mail, seminars, and trade shows. There is an old saying in sales—I don't know who originated it—always be prospecting. If you are a farmer and you want a crop in August, you must do some critical things in April. In selling, every month should be April.

Align with the Buyer's Shifting Concerns

There are a series of steps every buyer goes through as they buy.

One of the most useful pieces of knowledge I have acquired is an understanding of how people buy. If you can understand the psychological steps a buyer goes through to buy, you can predict the buyer's behavior. When you can predict your buyer's behavior, you will be a lot less likely to overreact to behaviors to which less knowledgeable sellers might react negatively.

THE BUYER'S SHIFTING CONCERNS

While I was at Xerox Computer Services, I learned from some researchers Xerox had hired to study the selling process that buyers go through phases of shifting concerns as they buy.

The buyer typically expresses four main concerns:

- Do I have a *need?*
- Do I have a *solution* to my need?
- What will be the *cost?*
- What is the *risk* of buying, or not buying?

As a buyer progresses through the cycle, her priorities change. The primary concerns shift over time. For example, at the beginning of a buy cycle, the buyer is primarily concerned with need, cost, or pain. By the end of the buy cycle, the buyer's concern is going to shift to risk and price.

Examine carefully each of these four concerns as they peak or wane over time (see Figure 12).

FIGURE 12
Shifting Buyer Concerns

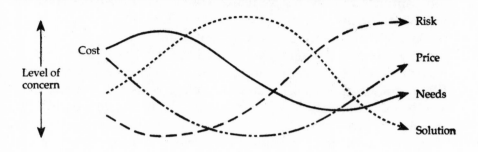

THE THREE PHASES OF SHIFTING
BUYER CONCERNS

Let's talk about each of the four concerns. The first is *needs*. People don't even start a buy cycle until they have a perceived need in one of their foreground slots. As an example, let's say that your spouse is driving your small children around on bald tires. You have been meaning to buy new tires but haven't done it yet. At home one night, you pick up a magazine and see the Michelin Tire ad with the baby in the tire. You are now in a buy cycle. Your primary concern is buying tires for your spouse's car.

The next concern is *cost*. You know tires can be expensive, but you know that you need them. You decide to stop at the tire store on your way to work the next morning.

Now look at the *solution* curve. You have pain, you have a vision, you now want a solution to match your vision. The tire salesperson shows you many alternative brands. You select the tire that you believe offers you the best value—not the most expensive.

Now you are in the *risk* phase. Notice that the *cost* line has now become the *price* line. Risk and price are your final concerns. Risk: You didn't select the top of the line tire; you selected the "economy" tire. Is this one as safe? What about wet weather? Will it wear out sooner? And price: Am I getting the best deal? What if I buy these tires and they run a sale this weekend, 30 percent off?

The researchers I worked with at Xerox™ believe that you go through a buy cycle like this for all major and minor purchases even when you buy a Snickers™ at the store. (There is some risk to a Snickers, right?—sugar, fat, and calories?)

Recall for a moment Face #8, where the buyer was in a state of panic. The seller thought the buyer had agreed to purchase a $400,000 life insurance annuity, but for reasons unknown the buyer appeared to be backing away from the agreement. Then the seller began to panic. Both buyer and seller are in panic mode.

How should the seller have handled this dilemma? Drop the annuity amount, thereby lowering the buyer's monthly payments? What options did that seller have to close a win—win transaction? This is a scary situation for most sellers. The wrong move can ruin months of hard work.

When I see a buyer in panic, I believe it is almost always a good sign. Why? Because that buyer is in Phase III of the buying cycle—risk analysis. If that's true, I am going to get this business, unless I do something stupid. When buyers hit the risk phase of their buy cycle, in most cases they have narrowed their selection to *one* alternative. If I am that one alternative, this is good. Right?

In most cases, when a buyer enters the risk phase, she needs comfort and reassurance, not answers. The problem most sellers face is their own panic when they see a buyer that loves them one day and avoids them the next.

When I first looked at the Shifting Buyer Concerns chart (Figure 12), I felt something was missing. It seemed to divide nicely into three phases. In the *Solution Selling* process, we continually refer to the three phases of the buy cycle so that we, as sellers, are always in tune or in alignment with our buyer's concerns. Figure 13 illustrates the three buying phases.

It is with this tool that sellers can gain understanding of the buyer that will give them a conceptual "leg up" on their competition. The

FIGURE 13
Buying Phases: Shifting Buyer Concerns

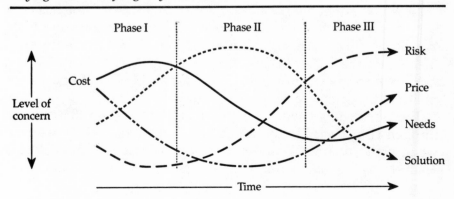

seller can begin to *anticipate* how the buyer will act according to what phase the buyer is in. By having the ability to anticipate buyer behavior, a seller will be far less likely to overreact to a shift in buyer behavior. As we will see later, numerous sales have been lost by sellers who overreacted to their buyers.

The buying cycle divides very easily into three phases:

Phase I—Need definition
The buyer is concerned with questions such as: Do I need to change? What do I need? (Vision of a solution.) What are the reasons for my problem? Does this need impact others? How much does it cost?

Phase II—Evaluation of alternatives
The buyer evaluates alternatives with questions such as: Is there really a solution? What are my alternatives? Which one best meets my needs? Can I afford it?

Phase III—Taking action within risk considerations
Having made a mental selection, the buyer advances to risk–reward questions: Should I do it? What if I don't? What are the consequences? Is it the right price?

From Pain Back to Latent Need

I have learned that "need" concerns can shift dramatically as one buys. For instance, go back to that story in Face #1 about baldness, mentioned earlier in the "10 Faces of Buyer Pain." When Buyer #1 read the *Wall Street Journal* article about a new genetic discovery that would eradicate the problem of baldness, he immediately went from latent need to need (pain). He went squarely into Phase I of the buying cycle. Notice that in Phase I a need concern is at an intense level: it is an immediate concern—the buyer might be able to solve his problem of baldness. Also his concern for cost is great. Anytime a buyer has a hope for a solution, one of the first questions asked is, "How much is it?" If in that article the buyer read the cost and thought it was exorbitant, the hope would disappear, the need would leave his foreground and go back into his background (latent need area), and he would go no further. End of buy cycle. The need is now rationalized as "too expensive."

Dramatic Changes in Buyer Behavior

Often buyers can go with great speed from Phase II to Phase III, and this transition can confuse and throw sellers off balance. If the seller anticipates the risk behavior and can view it as a positive buying sign, she can help the buyer face the risk he perceives.

For example, assume the seller sells an expensive software system, one that means a large sales commission. Let's price this system at $400,000 and assume a sale will put a $30,000 commission check into the seller's pocket. Let's also assume that our seller got in early and gained access to power. All of the decision makers share the same vision of a solution. The seller is in control of the buying process. She has done it by the book.

Assume now that those executives are in Phase II of their buy cycle. They need proof. They come to the seller's place of business for a demonstration. The demonstration goes *very well*. How do we know it went very well? What did the buyer do to let the seller know it went very well? The buyer said to the seller something like, "You know Michele, not only will I be able to fix my scheduling problem with your software, *I'll also be able to solve* my budgeting problem as well. I didn't even realize that until just now. This software is fabulous!"

Haven't you had calls like that? You were on; everything you did turned out well. What happened in this example? Prior to this demonstration, the seller's vision *exceeded* the buyers'. Why? Because the seller knows more of what her product is capable than do the buyers. On this call, however, the buyers finally *got it*. They finally realized conceptually how powerful the product really is. Now, because they understand their business better than does the seller, their vision has *surpassed* the seller's. What happens to the excitement level of a seller when the buyers' vision now exceeds the one he created? The seller sees their heads nodding and can see that they understand. Most salespeople I know think they have it "in the bag" at that point. They get very excited.

So let's say we have a session like that. It is 3:30 PM on a Thursday, and the prospects leave. The seller goes back into the bull pen on "cloud 9" and says to her peers, "I own them. They're mine. It's going to be a done deal next week." A little premature bragging, maybe?

What really happened that afternoon is that those buyers, in their minds, completed Phase II. They concluded that the product fits and that it is cost justified. Major victory for the seller. However, all four of them woke up at 3:00 AM Friday thinking about risk. They also woke up early Saturday morning, Sunday morning, and Monday morning thinking about risk. They were thinking about the financial viability of the seller's company. They were thinking about the economy. They thought about whether or not they should get an outside consultant to come in and help them make this decision. They thought about the resistance to change in their organization. They thought about the timing of the payback. They also thought about the consequences if it does not work.

First thing Monday at 8:00 AM, the seller phones the buyers. After all, when the buyers left last Thursday, they were "ready to buy." When she calls, however, the executive buyer happens to be in a meeting. When the executive comes out of the meeting and sees the little pink phone message from the seller, does he want to return the call? No, because he is still going through his risk analysis and he knows if he returns the call, the seller is going to say, "OK, let's go. Let's get started." The buyer does not want that pressure. Is it possible that the executive might avoid returning the seller's call all day Monday? About 4:30 PM on the same Monday, our seller is not bragging anymore. Our seller is *pacing* back and forth. "Why didn't he return my call? What happened? Who got to him?"

On Tuesday morning, even though the prospect is 83 miles away, the seller *just happens* to be in the buyer's area and she thought she would drop by and see how things are going. Because the seller is there physically, and because everyone has been working together for four months, the buyer sees her. They go into the buyer's office. Remember, this is the same human being who only last Thursday was verbalizing his vision. Now the *same* buyer is leaning back into his chair, his arms are folded, and he is bringing up all sorts of negative thoughts. "Well, we're not sure about timing." "We're not sure about the economy." "We're not sure about the support service." "We're not sure we studied this one area closely enough." "We're not sure if the sequence of implementation is right." "What if this fails?" "We need some contingency plans."

The seller looks at what she perceives to be negative behavior and thinks the worst. She's sure somebody got to him. She thinks, "Between last Thursday and today, somehow the competition got to him and I'm losing this deal."

The Death Spiral

Once the seller starts that kind of thinking it is highly likely that she will panic. If the seller panics, the *death spiral* begins. Do you think that the seller is going to be able to disguise the fact that she has panicked? Do you think the buyer will be able to sense that the seller is panicking? The buyer will be like a shark smelling blood in the water, and the problem is that *the buyer's perception of risk is real*. If the buyer sees the seller panic, it will validate his fear. It is like throwing gasoline on a fire. The seller is ready to beg. She goes back to her office and into her boss's office and pleads, "Boss, we're losing it. We're going to have to drop the price or we're going to lose it." This happens frequently. Or the seller may go back to her office and say, "Somehow the competition got to them. They don't have the vision of ours anymore. Let's give them another slide presentation." Or, worst of all, the seller might just lose her temper and become angry and combative.

Do you think it's possible for you to be winning a potential contract for two, three, or four months, and then, near the end, panic, get combative, and shoot yourself in the foot and blow the deal? Is that possible? It happens to sellers every day.

Over the years, I have had a number of clients who competed with IBM. In order to compete with IBM, most had to be able to claim superior technology at a lower cost. There have been hundreds of companies making those claims. Smaller companies are typically closer to the market and do a better job of getting buyers' pains identified and their business issues identified. Smaller, leaner companies can sometimes do a better job of proving that their product is a better fit. However, what's the probability that their buyers will eventually consider risk? Virtually 100 percent. If the seller's management is pressuring the seller to *get the business* in order to make the payroll or to achieve some corporate quarterly goal, or if the company is putting heavy pressure on its sellers to *get the business*, this is an accident waiting to happen. The buyer will most likely see his sales rep panic (because the seller misread the buyer's behavior). What if the seller gets angry? Then the buyer gets angry, and the sales rep panics even more. Who was waiting in the wings? IBM. Wasn't the cheapest. Wasn't the latest technology. Was the *safest*.

Buyer Panic is Usually Good News

In Phase II the buyer will try to match the vision achieved at the end of Phase I with someone's product or service; then the buyer will go into value justification. Once the buyer concludes the option he is evaluating *fits* and is *cost justified*, he then moves to Phase III. Now he has to overcome his fear of risk and justify the price before action can be taken. This means—assuming the seller and the buyer have been through all of the need development stages—that when a buyer becomes negative with a seller, this is a good sign, not a bad one. Ask yourself: if a buyer is looking at four alternative sellers, did the buyer become negative with all four or did the buyer only become negative with one seller? A buyer only goes negative with the seller with whom the buyer can see himself signing. When a buyer begins to verbalize his concerns to the seller, the buyer is actually saying, "I can see myself signing your contract but I have to work through all the fears I have." It is actually one of the most positive—if not the number one—buying signs a seller will see.

Watch Those "Happy Ears"

"Happy Ears" are what many great salespeople and leaders have. They listen for the good news, the stimulating news, the promising news. What a great source of energy! However, "happy ears" are simultaneously a friend and an enemy. People with "happy ears" have a tendency to miss the warnings, the cautions, and the bad news and may go on to make unnecessary mistakes.

What is that same buyer telling sellers B, C, and D at the exact same time the buyer is complaining (appears to be panicking) to seller A? When those sellers call the buyer, the buyer is returning their calls and saying, "Oh, yes, Sally, it still looks good. We still have a little more work to do, but we're almost there." Why? Because the buyer wants to keep the other two or three or four sellers around just in case something happens *and*, if the winning seller knows the other sellers are still around, that seller will be more likely to drop price. This is because most buyers are learning in "buying school" that the best way to price negotiate is to have multiple vendor alternatives.

In this example, Sally will go back to her boss and say, "We are real close. I'd give it a 90 percent chance of closing." Sally has her "happy ears" on.

Beware of False Price Negotiations

A word of warning. If you have a buyer who suddenly starts to negotiate price with you *without having shown you any fear of risk*, you could have a serious problem. Because another thing buyers learn in "buying school" is to price negotiate with multiple vendors in *reverse preference order*. I call it a *false price negotiation* when a buyer is negotiating price with a seller from whom he does not intend to buy. If a buyer gets sellers D, C, and B to drop price, then, when the buyer goes to price negotiate with seller A, the favored vendor, the buyer already has quoted discounts from the others. Now it's easier to scare seller A into dropping price.

So, whether or not a buyer demonstrates concern over risk is a very telltale buying signal. If a buyer talks price with a seller *without having shown any fear of risk,* the odds are high that the buyer is simply using that seller for price leveraging—a false price negotiation. Therefore, the next time a buyer starts giving risk objections, smile to yourself, because you are being told by the buyer that you are "Column A." The buyer has simply got to work through his buying risk. You are *not* being told you have lost it, that the competition beat you. Try not to overreact! Stay cool and help the buyer deal with his risk.

Another Buy Cycle Example: Moving Homes

I want you to think about the last time you had to *move.* Few people view moving as a pleasant experience: packing boxes, carrying furniture, changing your address, making new friends, and so on.

What type of pain would cause you to move? You may have received a job transfer or your kids are outgrowing the house, you are on a busy street, and you may be fearful that your children will be hurt. That is pain. Or perhaps your house is old, the plumbing has come unglued, and repair costs are too high. Or possibly you are in a school system without good schools. All are types of reasons. All are examples of pain.

At this point you are in Phase I, need definition. The primary concerns are need to move and the costs associated with moving. The last time you moved, did you decide early in the process that you could not spend more than X dollars? Did you set a budget? Did you start off within your budget? Did you end up on budget? By the time you get to the end of Phase I, you have a vision of a solution. You can describe it. For example, you must have at least a 3,000-square-foot house; it has to cost under $300,000; it has to be within a 20-minute commute to work, and so on. Once you have a vision of a solution, you enter into Phase II: evaluation of alternatives. You begin looking at properties. You compare each piece of property with your vision of a solution. What are the odds you are going to find 100 percent of your needs within budget? So, in Phase II, most buyers examine and compare all of their potential alternatives; then they come back and reexamine the alternatives, narrowing them to two or three or four choices. Buyers then make a final review and narrow their choices down to one or two. When you reach this point—the point where you believe that about 87 percent of your needs will be met within budget, you make a selection: you move on to Phase III.

Note the rise in two concerns: the risk concern and the price concern. You will begin to be concerned about the risks of buying the home you selected. Should you hire an inspector? Does the house have termites? Does it have electrical problems? Is the school system as good as they say it is? Have you personally sat in a classroom? Have you tested the commute during rush hour? (You only drove it during the middle of the day.) There are potential risks of buying the house. Because you exceeded your original budget, will you be able to afford the payments? But risk goes both ways. What is the risk of *not* making the move? Do you have to move? Your pain says you have to move, so you have to act. Should you act on *this* house? It might be the best one for the money. Somebody might come along a day later and buy it right out from under you, and then you will have to settle for less.

The Buyer's Risk is Real

When a buyer is in risk analysis—Phase III—in the buyer's mind that risk is tangible, real, active. How would you feel if a real estate salesperson came up to you and said, "You know, this is a hot piece of property. It's only been on the market six days; the market's hot, and it's going to go soon. If you want it, you had better make an offer." How do you feel when the seller pressures you? On whose agenda is the seller working? His own or yours? He may have a quota problem. He may have a month-end goal. Possibly he is in a contest. Sellers who push their buyers immediately create an alignment problem, especially if the seller is pressuring the buyer to buy before the buyer has completed his risk analysis. *Don't close before it is closeable.*

Price Considerations

The other Phase III consideration is price. "Am I getting the best price?" is a question we have all asked ourselves when making a major purchase. We wouldn't be in Phase III if the home were not cost justified: we believe we can afford it. The price justification is another matter. As a buyer, we won't sign on the line until we believe we are getting the best possible price. We will discuss price negotiations in Strategy 9.

Buying Committees

What if you are selling to a committee where you have multiple buyers going through a buy cycle? There is a real potential for a seller to lose control in this situation. A classic case of being out of control that I have seen is when a seller's buying sponsor was in Phase III, risk, and two buying beneficiaries were in Phase II, still evaluating the product. Further, the chief financial officer, whom the seller had not even met yet, had no buying pain and did not even know about the pending buying transaction. If you are in a situation like that, it is not going to get signed at the time you think it will be completed. In our workshops, we teach people to identify all members of the buying committee, link them together via their inherent interdependence, and "herd" them through each phase of the buy cycle as a group.

ALIGNMENT OF BUYING AND SELLING PHASES

What should the seller be doing at each phase of the buy cycle? Let's talk about each phase from the seller's perspective.

Phase I: Qualify Needs and the Buying Process

In Phase I, our mission is to help define a buyer's need with our product bias. We either create a vision where none existed or re-engineer an existing vision. Once we have "qualified" the need, the second part of our Phase I mission is to qualify the buying process: how will this person and this organization buy? I will give you the specifics on qualifying the buying process in Strategy 6.

Phase II: Prove and Help Buyer Cost Justify

In Phase II, our mission is to prove and help the buyer justify the cost. The proof can be done in many ways: testimonials, presentations, benchmarks, demonstrations. If we are in control, we will not think about proving unless we have influenced the vision. If we attempt to align our product or service with a vision created by a competitor, we will end up as column fodder.

Cost or value justification is a step many sellers skip. Primary reason: They don't know how to do a good one. I will give you a model in Appendix B. When your buyer tells you, "We know what it's worth," don't believe him. He doesn't know how to do a value justification either.

Phase III: Close the Sale

Phase III is where you have to close the sale. We know the buyer's concerns in Phase III: risk and price. We also know that if the buyer makes it into Phase III and shows us his fear of risk, it is ours to lose. The buyer only gets into Phase III when it fits and is cost justified. If the buyer has a strong action vision and a value justification he owns, his risk will be minimal, but he will still need comfort. I will discuss creating the "perfect time to close" in Strategy 8.

I have consulted for many kinds of companies: some big, some small. I've had many battles with salespeople who work for self-proclaimed "industry leaders." One I remember in particular—when I think about shifting buyer concerns—involved a particular salesman who depended blindly on the fact he worked for the *industry leader:* his company was the biggest, had been in business longest, had the greatest number of customers, and had the most support centers. Therefore, what did that sales rep find himself talking about within two minutes of a first sales call with a buyer? Things with which most buyers are more concerned near the *end* of their buy cycle, not the beginning.

Be more sensitive to where your buyer is: develop his needs and his vision of a solution, and then dig into your arsenal of features to present and prove your product. Ideally, the longer you can keep back your product and arouse interest, getting your buyer to admit problems, diagnose reasons, and create visions—without using the product—the greater the odds are that you will make the sale.

Eagles use product to prove, not to create interest, educate, entertain, or develop needs.

Many new salespeople go on calls and after 10 to 20 minutes see their buyer is clearly uninterested. The new salesperson panics and says, "Would you like to see the product? Would you like a presentation? What if I arrange a demonstration? What if I take you out to one of my customers?" What is happening here? The seller is abdicating interest arousal to the product, because he is unable to create interest. If salespeople cannot create interest, for what are they good? To buy lunch?

FEATURES, ADVANTAGES, AND BENEFITS OVER TIME

In Strategy 2 I discussed seller "selling statements"—features, advantages, and benefits. At Xerox I was exposed to some very interesting information regarding selling statements. Research showed that feature statements had little or no value at *any* point in the buy cycle—neither at the beginning nor in the middle nor at the end. I believe that features actually put the seller in a negative position, because they so easily invite buyer objections.

Buyers defend themselves from salespeople with objections. When a salesperson gets *too close*, the simplest way for a buyer to create distance is to say, "I would need more than that," or "I don't want to pay those fees," or "Would I have to pay for that particular feature, since I know I would never use it?" *Objections are used by buyers to keep salespeople at bay. Objections are used by buyers to control salespeople.*

Avoid Buyer Objections

Rather than teach sellers to *handle* buyer objections, my philosophy is to *avoid* buyer objections in the first place. Early in Phase I of the buy cycle, there is no vision of a solution. Therefore, if the seller begins to throw product features at the buyer, objections are going to fly left and right—and those objections will *not* be serious product objections. The buyer is really saying, "Get away from me" or "You're getting too close" or "Why would I need that?" Their purpose is to increase the distance between themselves and the seller.

However, if your buyer is in Phase II or Phase III, the objections are different. Objections become serious. When the buyer is trying seriously to match the seller's product to his vision in Phase II and objects to the seller's product or service, the seller has a serious problem. The buyer's vision and the seller's product or service are out of alignment. The seller will have to correct a misunderstanding, reengineer the buyer's vision, or change the product. But he must deal with it.

Objections at the End of the Buy Cycle

I have been asked to review hundreds of loss reports. After two, three, four, or six months of work, the seller finally realizes the sale is not going to be completed. Such bad news is conveyed rather uniformly by buyers. Typically, the buyer says, "Ralph, I have some bad news for you. We've decided to go with your competition. We want you to know *we liked you the best.* You gave the best presentation, but the other people just had this one feature in their product that you don't have. Therefore, we had to go with them. Sorry."

Sounds like another product objection, doesn't it? And it gives the seller an excuse that is beyond his control. So what is the likelihood that the seller will go back to his office, see a senior executive, and say, "I just lost another opportunity for us because our competition has this particular feature that our product lacks." What's the likelihood of that excuse? Very high. I've seen many development schedules disrupted because sellers have blamed lost sales on the product or service. The truth frequently is something else.

How many buying prospects have the courage to look the seller in the eye and say, "Ralph, I have bad news for you. I'm going with your competition and the reasons are (1) she knew our business better, (2) she only showed us product features that were meaningful to us, (3) she was sensitive to our timing, (4) she helped us prepare a value justification, and (5) I think my probability of success is higher with her than with you"? How many prospects have the courage to look the seller straight in the eye and say that? I've never met one. In many cases, the seller has developed a relationship over a period of time and the buyer does not want to hurt the seller. And since smart buyers play by corporate rules that prescribe multiple vendors, they will have to say no to several vendors. How do buyers let sellers down easy? "We like you the best." "We liked your presentation the best, *but this one thing missing in your product . . . the other people have.*" They blame it on the product. Then sellers use this easy excuse, and development schedules are rearranged—because improper intelligence is coming in from field salespeople.

One year when I was at Xerox I redesigned our loss report form. As an experiment, I added a check box called *poor salesmanship.* Guess how many times that box was checked in the four years I was monitoring losses? Never. Salespeople, when they lose, typically blame someone else: their boss would not discount, the product was uncompetitive, the consultant blew the demo, and so on. I've seen few salespeople who could say, "Mike, I blew it. I got outsold."

When a salesperson is outsold, I believe that most of the time it's because they are out of alignment with the buyer. The seller did the wrong thing at the right time, or the right thing at the wrong time, and the buyer is not comfortable. People buy from people. Time and time and time again, I see eagle salespeople (who can intuitively align with their buyers) with inferior products beating journeymen with superior products.

I also have had the opportunity to see top salespeople jump from company to company in the same industry. If a salesperson in the top 10 percent of the sales force in Company A goes to Company B, then within a year that salesperson will be in the top 10 percent of Company B. And if they leave again and go to Company C, within a year they will be in the top 10 percent of Company C. It happens over and over. The best salespeople win regardless of what company or product they represent.

My advice to my clients is to face the loss and investigate it honestly. I tell sellers: "If you choose to go the distance and lose, then *you got outsold*." If it is the product's fault, the seller should get out early. Many of my clients now tell their salespeople, "If you work on an opportunity for more than 60 days and lose, you cannot blame the product." In Strategy 8, we will show you how to decide on which prospects you can go the distance.

Advantage Statements over Time

Advantage statements have high value early in the buy cycle, in a narrow window of time. However, this high value declines rapidly as the buyer moves through the buy cycle. This is because advantage statements are based on *assumptions*. Buyers will allow sellers to make intelligent assumptions early in the relationship. My definition of intelligent assumptions is those that relate to both a buyer's industry and function.

The primary reason a seller must make assumptions is because of lack of knowledge about a buyer's specific situation. Intelligent assumptions by the seller can help build competence. A buyer demonstrates belief of competence to a seller by admitting pain. From that point on, further assumptions by the seller will diminish his credibility.

In Strategy 3 we showed you how to take reference stories and turn them into powerful advantages that establish your competence, which is a critical component of trust. Development of that trust will encourage buyers to admit their pain to you. Once they do, you can then offer benefits, not advantages.

Benefit Statements over Time

A *Solution Selling* benefit statement has high value to both the seller and the buyer all the way through the buy cycle. In other words, *any time* the seller can make a true benefit by the new definition—meaning the seller specifically relates his product or service to a buyer's vision in which he has participated—it will have high value to both parties.

By my definition of a benefit statement, however, a seller cannot make a benefit statement initially with a buyer. The prerequisite for a benefit is a buyer vision in which the seller has participated. The prerequisite for that vision is that the prospect trusts the seller enough to admit a problem—and that the seller has the patience to avoid premature elaboration and can diagnose the problem. The prerequisites for a buyer to admit a problem to the seller are trust, sincerity, and competence. And the prerequisite for that trust is for that buyer to conclude the seller is different from most other salespeople.

Once a seller has established rapport, sincerity, and competence and created a vision from an admitted pain, he can then take out his product or service and say, "I believe my product or service will fill that need for you. I believe we can give you that capability." He can then make benefit statements. A seller might be able to make a benefit statement 20 to 30 minutes after he meets a buyer, but he cannot, by my definition, make a benefit at the initial handshake.

Risk Objections

As I discussed earlier, when buyers express risk objections at the end of their buy cycle, many salespeople panic. The reason? The buyer has changed his behavior radically "overnight." The seller views the change in behavior as negative—as opposed to the true buying sign the risk objection is—and panics.

The seller's tool for dealing with risk objections is the benefit statement: reminding the buyer of his pain, his vision, and the proof provided. The *delivery* of the benefit statement is important.

First, empathize. "You're right, it is a big decision." Then answer the objection if it's answerable. In many cases, though, the buyer just wants to vent. Objecting buyers want validation of their discomfort.

I believe that two-thirds to three-fourths of buyer risk objections are about the need for validation of their risk evaluations—objections that do not even require specific answers.

It is best to respond to risk objections with benefit statements. Benefit statements have particularly high value when a buyer is evaluating risk. How would I make a benefit statement? I would take my buyer back to his pain, "Yes, Tom, insurance is a big decision, but why have we spent the past three months together? Your family is seriously exposed. Your business is exposed too. You told me the only way you were going to be able to sleep better at night in the years ahead is if—if you die or become disabled—your family and business were financially safe: your wife's needs, the children's education, your business, the household debts. I have demonstrated that my product meets these needs. Yes, it's a big decision, but it is the right thing to do—for you, for your family, and for your business."

Buyers in risk evaluation are uncomfortable. They want a comforting arm around them, figuratively, and benefit statements are useful. "Yes, sure it is a big decision, but we're in this thing together. We've gone this far together. We're partners. We're going to be here for you." That is what buyers frequently want to hear.

Risk objections are positive because they show that the buyer is in Phase III and very close to buying. If sellers don't understand that such risk objections are positive, then bad things can happen. Sellers can become afraid that the competition has influenced their buyer—after all, the last time they saw the buyer he was friendly and nice. Now the buyer is objecting, defensive, fearful. Sellers can easily panic. They can become combative. They often drop price unnecessarily. And they scramble to schedule another feature presentation.

Can you see how many sales have been lost at the end? The buyer's fear of risk is legitimate. But, if the buyer sees his seller panic, it can reinforce the buyer's fear.

RFPs AND SHIFTING BUYER CONCERNS

Many workshop attendees ask me, "Can (we) talk about a situation in my career. Frequently I enter into a selling situation where an RFP has been created. I meet the buying committee and I am presented with a document that represents their vision, and I have not had the benefit of being able to create their vision with a bias of my product. In my experience, I seldom have the luxury of being able to process their need development and reengineer their vision. I cannot take them through the process again, so that I can achieve that alignment. And I'm not . . . I don't have a solution for that. On occasion I win, but most of the time I lose. What can I do?"

Frequently the question of RFPs comes up. If you look at the buying phases in Figure 13, where would a buyer be if an RFP is on the street? Go back and take a look. An RFP is a *request for a proposal*. Basically, it is a company buying request. The buyer knows what it needs in great detail, and the buyer mails its RFP to a number of appropriate vendors saying implicitly, "Please respond and tell us if your product or service meets our needs." The RFP buyer is at least in Phase II, evaluation of alternatives, if not in Phase III, risk. What is the best way to align with your buyer? I have found that with RFPs, in most cases, if you follow the rules you will lose.

The way many companies buy things is that typically some good salesperson (or an outside consultant) gets into the buying company at the middle management level and finds a middle manager with a problem. And the first person in is good enough to get that middle manager to see that there is a potential solution his company should consider. Since the middle manager cannot buy, he goes in to his boss and says, "Boss, you know that quality problem you have been concerned about for the last six months? I have found a solution. There is a company that has exactly what we need to solve our problem. I want to buy it." Well, in corporate America, his boss says, "Who else have you looked at?" The middle manager says, "No one." The boss says, "Well, I want you to look at a couple of other alternatives and, by the way, I don't want to see any salesmen." So now what we have is an evaluation delegated to a lower-level person, a "project leader" who has been instructed by his superior that he does not want to see any salespeople. This person does not have any expertise to put out a specification, so he goes to the first seller and says, "You know, Ralph, I have got to go and look at some others. Who should I look at?" Would the seller tell a buyer names of organizations who can beat him? Of course not. He will pick sellers he can beat. So, being the first seller is a wonderful advantage when the buyer says, "Could you help me put together an RFP specification?" Therefore, the specification that the first seller dictated is the one mailed to all other vendors for their response, so, when sellers B, C, D, and so on, say they would like to meet the buyer's top management, the project leader says, "This selection has been delegated to me. They told me it's my decision. I'm supposed to look at the alternatives. They are going to rubber stamp whatever I pick." Get your "happy ears" out.

An RFP Answer, Finally

It's a tough situation—a very tough situation. To make a long story short, you have got to do some negotiating right up front. Some RFPs take 20, 30, 40 hours to do properly. Here is what I recommend when you receive an RFP you did not write:

Call the sender and say, "Mr. Jones, I have received your RFP. It looks very interesting and we want to respond. In order to do the kind of job I know you want me to do, it will take me 30 to 40 hours of support person time. Before I invest that time on it, I would like the opportunity to have three one-hour interviews: one with the head of the finance department, one with the head of marketing, and one with the head of MIS." You can tell which departments are affected based on the content of the RFP. In some cases they will say no. You then have to be willing to say, "Well, if you are unwilling to give me three hours so I can get a clear picture for myself of the important issues at stake, then I am unwilling to put 40 hours into it. I cannot in good conscience respond, because I do not want to submit a shabby proposal that may not meet your needs." Somewhere from 10 to 33 percent of the time (when the RFP comes from a consultant) and about 80 percent when it is internally generated, my customers tell me that if the seller is willing to say no up front, within a week to 10 days sincere buyers come back and grant the seller the interviews. I recommend this approach, unless, of course, you are in the free RFP business.

If the buyer is willing to grant the interview at a high level, the seller now has the opportunity to use the 9 Boxes to gain control of the vision.

However, if you fail to get the access—that eyeball-to-eyeball contact with the power person—you did yourself a favor by not responding. If you play by the rules, you will most likely lose.

In Conclusion

Alignment is both a vertical and horizontal concept: Vertical when we align with the buyer's level of need and horizontal when we align with the buyer's position in a buy cycle over time. If our definition of selling—helping people buy our product or service—is to become true for our buyers, we, as sellers, will have to learn to consciously align constantly with our buyers.

Lead the Buyer and Stay Strategically Aligned

If you find yourself out of alignment with your buyer, go back to the point where you were last in alignment and pick up from that place.

I know you have heard it before, but let's think about precall preparation. If you have an appointment, do you know the person's position ahead of time? His type of business ahead of time? Could you research existing customers to see if you have any reference stories that are a potential match? Could you make a copy of each pain sheet in your library that matches the buyer's situation. Could you role play the 9 Boxes with an office mate prior to the call?

Too many sellers "wing it." The primary reason? They lack a process to follow and they don't have tools. In *Solution Selling* we are offering you solutions to both of those problems. We talked about tools or "job aides" in Strategy 4, "Solution Selling Tools—Job Aides." In this strategy—"Lead the Buyer and Stay Strategically Aligned"—I will take the theory and tools we have discussed so far and put them into a logical process.

We will assume, for the majority of the time we spend in Strategy 6, that we have an expensive, conceptual, intangible product or service that is sold to a Fortune 1000 company. There will be a committee involved. We will have to start "below the line." They will look at the competition. A value justification will be necessary. It will be a multiple-month sell cycle with multiple steps. Some of our calls will be multi-legged sales calls. The buyer's company has no active evaluation in place. They have no prior knowledge of our company or products and services.

There are eight basic steps to follow for this initial call:

1. Establish rapport.

2. Make the call introduction.
3. Make the transition to need development and vision processing.
4. State benefits.
5. Close for agreement to explore further.
6. Qualify the buying process.
7. Find power.
8. Bargain proof for access to power.

We will go through these logical steps and I will explain how each step works and where the buyer should be at each step.

THE FIRST CALL OF A MULTIPLE CALL SALE

Throughout the following role play, the seller is a sales rep with NNC Business Television, a company that sells communication services to businesses and organizations. The seller's purpose is to sell private business television network services.

Some assumptions are required: the seller has already made his first telephone prospecting call on the CEO but was delegated to the vice president of sales. Her employer, AAA Copiers Inc., is a large company that sells copiers, fax, and office equipment. Her company employs about 1,500 sales reps, and her pain is that she is not meeting her sales goals. His telephone call to her aroused her curiosity. She said, "Tell me more," and the seller booked an appointment. AAA is not looking at any other providers of business television services.

Step 1: Establish Rapport

Is it possible to lose a major sales opportunity because in the first 30 to 60 seconds your buyer concluded that you are a person with whom he would not do business. Is that possible? It's extremely possible. So the first decision the buyer makes is his decision to listen to you.

The first 30 to 60 seconds with your prospect are very critical. *Insincerity* is the number one negative decision prospects make about salespeople in the first 30 to 60 seconds. And that decision kills more salespeople than any other prospect decision. Unfortunately, many salespeople are *taught* insincerity. For instance, I have trained numerous salespeople who had been taught that when they enter a prospect's office for the first time, they are supposed to scan the office for pictures, trophies, and so on—things to which they can relate—so that, if they see a picture of a horse on the wall, they can say, "Oh, you ride?" or, about a bowling trophy on the shelf, "Oh, I see you bowl." They've been taught to scan the office and look for something to which they can relate in order to establish rapport.

Think about it. What if the seller is not a bowler, yet, because he wants to establish rapport, he decides to talk about bowling? How long will it take a serious bowler to figure out that he's faking it? Less than 10 to 20 seconds. And his very next conclusion will be: This person is insincere. The seller has just dug a deep hole and jumped into it. The problem in selling to corporations is that in many cases they won't tell you when you're in that hole, because they want you to participate in their buying evaluation for the next six months. Therefore, they will smile at you and pretend that everything is perfect, because they want your product information, your pricing information, and your proposal for their decision matrix. A big advantage to being first, when there are no columns yet, is that you will get a much more honest reaction from the buyer. But don't assume you are first.

A few years ago, the *Boston Globe* printed an article on the "halo effect," which was about the effect of first impressions. The article asserted that first impressions are extremely powerful in both directions—for you and for your buyer. If the first impression is positive, your buyer will think you're better than you are; on the other hand, if it's negative, he'll think you're worse than you are. In an experiment, they took a personable young man who was about to graduate from Harvard Business School in the top 5 percent of his class. He held an undergraduate degree in engineering from MIT and had five years of work experience. He was sent to a job interview for a job that perfectly fit his ability and experience. However, because he had been in college for a couple of years, he had grown a beard, his hair was a little long, and he went dressed in a sports coat, casual shirt, no tie, casual pants, and casual shoes. He didn't get past the first interview, which lasted less than 10 minutes.

Three weeks later they sent the same human being—this time with a haircut and shave, white shirt, tie, suit—to the same company. They used the same résumé but changed the name. He was interviewed by the *same* interviewer and was offered the job—on the spot. What was the interviewer unable to do the first time? He could not get past his negative first impression, formed in the first 30 seconds.

Who carries the conversation in early rapport building? Many salespeople think it's their responsibility as the seller to carry the conversation. As a seller, if you think it is your responsibility, that can get you into trouble. There are vast cultural differences between America's states. If you're from the deep South or from parts of the Midwest, it's culturally appropriate to talk about where you grew up, where you went to school, what you thought of yesterday's game, and kids. And unless you take a sufficient amount of time in that kind of rapport talk, your buyer can't decide whether or not you're the type of person with whom they want to do business.

Then there's the opposite end of the spectrum. If you're in Clifton, New Jersey, or New York City, there is virtually no—as in zero—rapport time. When you first meet your buyer, he is likely to say, "So, what are you going to try to sell me? What've you got?" And you're immediately forced to get into your business call. In that case, you'll have to build rapport as the call proceeds.

It would be wonderful if we had a handy pocket guide that we could take out and read. It would say, in Atlanta, Georgia, take 12 minutes for rapport and talk about family and sports. In New York City, get right to it. It would be nice if we had a rapport guideline city by city. But we don't. What I teach salespeople to do is to *put the responsibility for carrying the conversation on the host.* Imagine if they came to your office. What would you do? You might offer to take their coat, direct them to a chair, get them a cup of coffee, give directions to the restroom, ask if they had trouble finding the office, make small talk, and arrange for an appropriate moment to talk business. Why do you do that? To explore the salesperson's personality, to see if a basis for rapport exists. Therefore, because you're in your buyer's office, put that responsibility on your buyer.

The routine for meeting a prospect for the first time, whether it's in the lobby or in your prospect's office, is to look him straight in the eye, extend your hand first—beat him to the draw (remember the Wild West)—and say your first name and last name. When I walk up to a prospect, I always extend my hand first and say, "Mike Bosworth." In this way my prospect will usually follow suit with his first name and last name. Now I am on a first name basis with my buyer.

I'll give you an example of this first name issue and why it's important. I was asked to train salespeople who sold software systems to doctors. They had severe power problems with their doctor prospects. Because most of the company's salespeople were female, the salespeople found themselves in the position of having to call their prospect, "Doctor": but the doctors were addressing them by their first names. Doctors would not volunteer their own names, Jim or Janet or Tom, and so on. What's the power relationship between "Doctor" and Mary? Not equal! Once I taught them to beat the doctor to the draw, extend their hand first, and say their name—first name, last name—they reported that better than 80 percent of the time, they got doctors on a first name basis: Jim or Janet or Tom—not just Doctor.

In rapport establishment, extend your hand quickly and say your first name, last name. Then follow with. "I appreciate the opportunity to meet with you today," not, "Thank you for your time," in order to maintain your power. Then shut up for a full four seconds. This can be the longest four seconds in your life. During this time, don't stare at your buyer; look around and find a place to sit. Start thinking: one thousand and one, one thousand and two, one thousand and three, one thousand and four. And by one thousand and four your prospect will let you know clearly whether or not he wants to talk about football or kite flying, or get right down to business. He'll let you know both verbally and with his body language.

Try to mirror your prospect's body language, speaking volume, and pace. If the prospect leans back in his chair and you lean forward onto his desk, he could feel pressure from you. If he leans back, you lean back. If he's a fast talker, try to speak as fast as you comfortably can. If he's a slow talker and you're a fast talker, consciously put a governor on your speech or you will make your prospect uncomfortable. This can be a challenge, but try your best to reasonably mirror your prospect.

Get your buyer to decide that you are different from other salespeople. You want to be in the 5 percent of salespeople who are sincere, not the 95 percent who are perceived to be insincere and who will try to take advantage. Use the common perception of our profession to your own advantage. Instead of doing the predictable things that most salespeople do, be different. As an example, instead of being immediately familiar with your buyer, try to align with the buyer's "warm up" rate.

I had a customer once who played games with salespeople. They always used a specific office for their meetings with salespeople. In that office was a tall bowling trophy, a large marlin mounted on a wall, pictures of an attractive family, a golfing trophy, and so on. They kept statistics on first call salespeople. Their statistics tracked how many salespeople fell for the bowling or golf trophies versus the marlin versus the family pictures. Unfortunately, the salespeople who fell for those traps were not going to be taken seriously. They messed up in the first 30 to 60 seconds and never knew it. Though I don't approve of this, the story makes my point.

Once you complete the rapport step, you still have to convince your buyer that you are trustworthy—both sincere and competent—different from your sales competitors. The hard work is yet to come.

Role Play

Establish Rapport

"Beat 'em to the draw!"

Seller: Mike Seller, NNC Business Television.

Buyer: Michele Buyer. I'm vice president of sales.

Do not "thank" buyer for time that has not yet been given.

Seller: Michele. I appreciate the opportunity to meet with you.

[They walk to her office. On the way, in a friendly manner, she points out the board of director's room and some executive offices, and asks Mike if he wants coffee. Then they enter her office. She complains how busy her day is, half apologizing. Mike is motioned to a chair. He sits and waits a full four seconds, taking out a note pad on which to write, then he looks up at the buyer.]

Intermission

Once in her office, she pauses to see if the seller wants to talk. Michele then lets Mike know that she wants to get right to business.

Step 2: Call Introduction

The purpose of the call introduction is to tell your buyer why you are there, state your company's mission, and provide a general introduction about who you are. Then you're going to make an advantage statement via the *Solution Selling* reference story format.

In this case, with no active evaluation going on, we will assume the seller has to earn the right to question the buyer. In the next four minutes, the seller's objective is to get the buyer to talk freely and, better yet, admit pain.

In this role play, the buyer jumps straight into the business of the meeting. Even during the walk from the receptionist to her office, there is little small talk. The seller decides to skip the small talk and get down to business.

Role Play

Call Introduction

Buyer: I have a full schedule this morning, Mike, so, if you don't mind, I'd like to hear about your product. OK?

Seller: OK. What I'd like to do this morning, Michele, is introduce you to NNC Business Television and tell you about another office equipment company with which we have worked. I would then like to learn about you and your situation. At that point, the two of us will be able to make a mutual decision as to whether or not we should proceed any further. Is that all right with you?

Purpose of the call

Buyer: Yes, I like that approach.

Seller: NNC Business Television is in the business of helping companies with large field sales forces operate more productively and profitably through the service we sell.

Position company

NNC Business Television was founded in 1983. We have a base of 600 business companies, many in the Fortune 500 listing. NNC has projected revenues of $75 million, and we're a public company listed on the NASDAQ. Our customers are in virtually every industry domestically and internationally. Customer satisfaction is important to us—each year we ask an independent firm to sample our customers and assess their overall satisfaction with our services.

Introduce the company

A particular situation in which you might be interested is another office equipment company with which I have been working. Their VP, sales, was having difficulty meeting sales goals. The reasons for his difficulty included an inability for sales management to easily communicate price and model changes to the field sales reps and the high costs of sending experts out to the field to support the sales force. What he told me he needed was some way to easily and

Reference story

Critical issue with reasons

Vision

We provided help

Results with measurement

efficiently communicate model and price changes to all 1,000 field reps, and to be able to cut back on the costs of flying expensive engineering talent around the country. NNC Business Television provided him with those capabilities. The results were that sales increased over projected sales by about 10 percent, profits improved by 16 percent, and the sales force ran much more smoothly. It also stopped a lot of price arguments when everyone learned of both the technical and price changes at the same time.

But enough about NNC. Tell me about your business situation.

Buyer admits pain!

Buyer: Well, Mike, I seem to have pretty much the same problems you just described. I am having trouble meeting my sales goals, and I have a large sales force, 1,500 reps.

Intermission

The call introduction objective is to get the buyer to admit pain. So far, things are on schedule. Michele found Mike's company introduction credible and his reference story spoke directly to her difficulties. She trusted Mike enough to admit pain. This is a signal to Mike that she believes he is both sincere and competent. Mike's pre-call planning involved the reference story he just told. It looks as though that planning has paid off.

Step 3: Transition to Need Development/Vision Creation

This step involves the 9 Boxes we discussed in Strategy 3, "Participate in the Buyer's Vision." In this case, Michele had no previous vision, so Mike will try to create a vision for her. You can only go to the next step if the buyer has admitted pain. Admitting pain is a crucial milestone. Mike is going to take Michele "through the boxes." In real life selling, a typical first call vision creation exercise—Step 3—can take anywhere from 10 to 20 minutes.

This is where the seller needs a pain sheet—a pain sheet in this case for a sales executive with a large number of field sales reps who are missing her goals.

Going through the 9 Boxes. Therefore, Step 3 is about going through the 9 Boxes. Imagine yourself taking your buyer through each of the 9 Boxes. Remember, we already know the buyer's admitted pain: inability to meet her sales goals.

Role Play

Going through the Boxes

Seller: Tell me about it: why do *you* think you are missing your sales goals?

Buyer: We are constantly introducing new products. We have to stay competitive in the marketplace, which is changing constantly, and as changes occur, we have to make changes in our product lines— not only in features, but in prices as well. So our sales reps are confused and sales instructions are confused; in fact, the market is confused—our customers are confused.

Seller: All right, let me back up and see if I can catch up with you. You've got many different products you're selling: color copiers, plain paper, different sizes, different volumes. You've got 1,500 salespeople? Do these products change as far as new models?

Buyer: More often than you think. Three times a year in some cases.

Seller: And the needs of the marketplace itself change, causing you problems?

Buyer: Yes. As our competitors come out with new products, we have to stay equal to or ahead of our competitors, so we are constantly looking for innovative new things to add.

Seller: Is timing critical when that happens?

Buyer: Very critical. It can directly affect market share for us.

Seller: Are there instances where you have seen the competition come to market with some innovation and your customers have asked you for those exact competitive capabilities, and the timing to respond to that is important?

Buyer: Yes.

Seller: Are your salespeople dispersed all over the country?

Buyer: Yes.

Seller: Do you find there is a disparity in their experience? You have some seniors, some middle level, and some juniors?

Buyer: Of course.

Seller: With the number of locations you have, the number of people you have, and the number of products you have, do you ever find

yourself in a situation where Los Angeles has the new pricing on
Product A but Chicago doesn't yet, so you have the company selling
the same product at two different prices?

Buyer: Yes.

Seller: Do you ever get the situation where Chicago has the new model
for Product B, but Los Angeles does not? So now we have the same
people from the same company selling different products?

Buyer: Yes.

Seller: Let me summarize what I've just heard. You're not meeting
your sales goals and there is quite a bit of confusion in your sales
force. They don't always have the right model information and
they are not always aligning the right model features with what
the market wants. There are frequent product changes and an
information float problem in that when you do have the new
product information, there's a time lag getting it out to all locations.
Bottom line, your sales force is not operating as effectively as
they might.

Buyer: That's correct, that's exactly correct.

Seller: Besides yourself, Michele, who else is impacted by this
problem?

Buyer: The VP, finance. We are not meeting our revenue targets and
our profitability is being eroded.

Seller: Okay, so revenue targets have been missed, profits are off, and
the VP, finance, is directly attributing that to the sales force?

Buyer: Yes. There's another factor here as well. When we introduce
new products, I find that I send out marketing teams from
headquarters, and when the teams go out it is very expensive. In
particular, we have one critical group that cannot be everywhere
at the same time, causing a lag in product information from one
territory to the next.

Seller: So marketing people from headquarters are going out to the
field trying to educate them on new products. Is that right?

Buyer: Yes.

Seller: And there is a time lag? Is that expensive?

Buyer: Yes, it is expensive.

Seller: All right. So that expense also impacts profits?

Buyer: Yes, that's why I talked about the VP, finance.

Seller: It sounds as though, with the marketing people getting on airplanes and traveling to the field and the cost of these rollouts and with sales off and profits off, couldn't the VP, marketing, also be impacted by this problem?

Buyer: Yes, he is.

Seller: Do you think it's at the point where the company's growth has been affected? Have you missed your revenue targets this year?

Buyer: Yes, we have.

Seller: Has the stock price been affected?

Buyer: Yes, it has.

Seller: So the CEO is impacted as well?

Buyer: Yes. As we have had to announce increasing costs and reduced profits, the stock market has reacted negatively, and so has the CEO.

Seller: Well, it sounds to me, Michele, as though this problem of not making your sales goal, is not just impacting you, but it is an organizational problem: it's a revenue problem that impacts the VP, finance; the VP, marketing, is impacted since its his people who go out on the airplanes educating the field; the CEO is trying to get your stock price up; the company's growth has been impacted. Sounds to me like it's a companywide problem. Is that correct?

Buyer: It certainly is.

Seller: Michele, what is it going to take for *you* to solve this problem?

Buyer: You know, Mike, I'm not sure. I was hoping you could help me.

Seller: Could I try a few ideas on you?

Buyer: Certainly.

Seller: What if there were a way, when you had a new product about which you want to tell the field or a promotional campaign you had to announce, that within two hours you could be face to face with all of your 1,500 salespeople. What if that were possible?

Buyer: That would be great.

Seller: Let me make it more specific. What if they all could see and hear you and hear each other at the same time? If a sales rep in L.A. had a question, all 1,500 salespeople could hear the question and hear and see you answer it, would that help?

Buyer: That would be extremely helpful.

Seller: What if you could put the product expert on the television network, so all 1,500 people would get the new information at the same time so they could go out the very next hour making sales calls with current pricing, technology, and promotional information? Would that capability also help?

Buyer: That would really help eliminate a tremendous amount of confusion in the organization if everyone heard the same information and questions and answers at the same time. That would help us not only be much more uniform in our communications with our sales reps, but also with our customers. That would benefit us greatly.

Seller: Would that eliminate the float problem we talked about?

Buyer: Yes.

Seller: Let me summarize what I've heard. You said you'd like to reach all field locations simultaneously so you could give your people new information at the same time. With this same capability, you also said you would like to be able to introduce product experts so they could disseminate new product information, eliminate the information float, and eliminate the airplane trips. If this were possible, *could you* start to make your sales goals again?

Buyer: We would certainly be going in the right direction. Yes, I think I could.

Intermission

At this point, Mike has completed the 9 Boxes. He has taken the buyer through need development to a vision of a solution biased with his service. Michele has agreed she could now solve *her* problem. The 9 Boxes let Mike do it in a friendly and natural way.

I said earlier that typically, in real life, it takes 10 to 20 minutes to take a prospect through a vision creation. Some situations allow a much shorter period of time—for example, a bank financial services rep (FSR). An FSR can do this in 4 to 10 minutes, depending on the buyer's need and vision.

After the seller has completed the need development part of the call and created a vision, he is ready to state the benefit and ask for a firm commitment from the buyer to explore further.

Steps 4 and 5: State Benefits and Close

Now the seller must move the buyer to commitment. The seller can, for the first time, make a *Solution Selling* benefit because he is now able to match his service with the buyer's vision. In this example, we are not asking the buyer to buy anything today; we are only asking for a commitment to explore further. We will blend the benefit statement and close together in one smooth motion. I teach two versions of the benefit statement:

Option 1:   Michele, I'm 95 percent sure my company can give you those capabilities. I want to go back and check on a couple of things with my experts. If they bear me out, would you take a serious look at my company?

This is a conservative option. You give yourself an out. When you say that you are 95 percent sure, you give yourself the ability to go back and check. And if your company or supplier bears you out, then you are asking your buyer to seriously look at what you have to offer. This close is to get your buyer to agree to look seriously at your product or service.

Option 2:   Michele, I am confident that we can give you both of those capabilities, and I would like the opportunity to prove it to you. Would you give me that opportunity by taking a serious look at my company?

In this option, we are more aggressive. But it is too early to forget our job title—salesperson. Our job title requires that we *offer* proof early in the relationship.

Salespeople have to offer proof.   Why do you have to offer proof? *Because you are a salesperson.* Your job title requires that you offer proof early in the relationship with your buyer. Any time you as a salesperson say, "I am confident we can give you those capabilities," and you do not offer proof, you are saying, "Trust me." Most people have learned not to trust salespeople. It will take time for you to establish trust.

Get in the habit of offering proof. My experience is that once you offer proof and deliver on it, your buyer will then believe everything you tell him from then on, but still, the first time, and maybe even the second time, you have to earn his trust. Earn your way into the 5 percent of salespeople who are trustworthy, not into the 95 percent who are perceived as untrustworthy. The majority of the sellers with whom you compete will not offer proof; they will ask their buyers to trust them implicitly.

Buyer skepticism.   When do you use "I'm 95 percent sure" versus "I'm 100 percent sure"? The logical answer is any time you are less than 100 percent sure, use the first alternative. Your future credibility might be at stake. Can you think of an instance where you are 100 percent sure that your product or service has got exactly what he needs to solve his problem, but you might *choose* tactically to say, "I'm 95 percent sure"? The answer is any time you sense your buyer is skeptical. Most experienced salespeople can sense skepticism. Even though their buyer is saying the right things and nodding his head, an expert seller knows. In that case, it's better to say, "You know, I'm 95 percent sure my company can give you those capabilities, but I want to go back and check with my experts before I make a commitment to you." Why? Because too many salespeople say, "Hey, no problem. We've got it. We can solve your problem."
Differentiate yourself by the way you sell.

Role Play

State Benefits and Agree to Explore Further

The seller has just completed taking his prospect through the 9 Boxes.

Seller: Michele, I am 95 percent sure we can give you those capabilities. There are a couple of things I want to check with my resources. If they bear me out, will you take a serious look at what we have to offer?

Buyer: Yes, Mike, I will. I want to see what you have.

Intermission

Only when the buyer agrees to take a serious look at your capabilities have you earned the right to go further in this call.

Step 6: Qualify the Buying Process

So far the seller has just been qualifying the buyer's need. Now it is time to qualify the buying process.

The imaginary neck brace.   Once your buyer agrees to look further, you can ask, "How would you like to evaluate my company and product?" Buyers have a variety of answers: We'd like to talk to some of your customers. We'd like to go see where it's operating and try it. We want financials on your company. We'd like a demonstration. When you ask this question, an important point is that you wear an imaginary neck brace.

Without the imaginary neck brace installed, most sellers will be bobbing their head up and down with each buyer's request. From the buyer's side of the desk, the seller is thereby *agreeing* to each request. If the buyer thinks you have committed yourself to a demonstration, ask yourself, "What did I get in return for this demonstration?" Nothing!

The objective at this step is to gather information from the buyer about how they would see their organization evaluating yours. Don't agree or disagree with anything the buyer requests. In our workshops, we teach people to repeat what was requested as they write it down. In this way, you acknowledge to the buyer that you heard him, but you didn't agree to do any of it.

Proposal process definition. The three topics discussed below are designed to allow you to keep control at the end of a long buy cycle, which is when many salespeople lose control. Once your buyer has responded to your Step 6 questions, you then cover each of these three topics, which help you to keep control down the road.

Proposal. Following your buyer's evaluation instructions, you can ask, "Michele, if we do get down the road and it looks like we might do business, will you want a proposal from me?" Ninety-nine percent of all buyers respond, "Yes, I'll want a proposal."

No new information. Then you can say, "If we do get that far and I prepare a proposal, I want you to know it will contain no *new* information. It will simply document and confirm the business arrangements we will have already discussed. OK?"

Preproposal review. That is followed up with, "What I would like to suggest, if we get that far, is that I come out a week in advance of the final proposal with a rough draft. We call this a preproposal review. There are two benefits: The benefit to you is that there are no surprises in the final proposal. The benefit to me is that I can get the proposal correct the first time. Is that all right with you?"

Most buyers will accept this proposal definition because you are in alignment, they have a vision with an idea of its value, the process is logical, it is not threatening, and it passes the reasonable man test.

[Throughout this step, write everything down and *do not agree or disagree.* All the seller is doing is finding out what the ground rules are.]

Role Play

Buyer Qualification

Seller: Michele, how would you like to evaluate NNC?

Buyer: I will require a demonstration at some point, a presentation to our buying committee, and your company would have to commit to training our staff.

Seller: Anything else?

Buyer: Yes, information on NNC, such as financial statements and the names of two customers who have already bought the kind of product and services about which we are talking.

Seller: Anything more?

Buyer: No, that's it. If something else comes up, I'll let you know.

Seller: If we do get down the road and it looks as if we might do business, will you want a proposal from me?

Buyer: Yes.

Get buyer to agree that a proposal will be necessary.

Seller: If we do get that far, and I prepare a proposal, I want you to know that it will contain no new information. It will simply document and confirm the business arrangements we have already discussed.

Buyer agrees to proposal definition.

Buyer: OK.

Seller: What I would like to suggest, if we get that far, is that I come out a week in advance of the final proposal with a rough draft. We call this a preproposal review. There are two benefits: one, you get no surprises, and, two, I get it right the first time. Is that all right with you?

Buyer agrees to rough-draft review of proposal content one week before final proposal.

Buyer: Sure. That sounds reasonable.

Intermission

The seller did two important things during this buyer qualification: first, he set up the ground rules for the proposal process, and, second, he set up a *preproposal* review meeting that, as you will learn later, will allow the seller a "perfect time to close." By having a preproposal review, the seller can assure himself that he does not have to go to press until the buyer has bought it entirely in draft form.

Now the seller will move to find out where the real power is in the organization. Although he has a sense of it from the impact questions he asked in the 9 Boxes, the buyer has not yet explicitly identified who, in her opinion, is the real power person.

Step 7: Find the Power

The seller must find out who has the power and must get access to that person. My customers—and I keep good statistics on them—tell me that once they have switched on their buyer's light bulbs, created visions of solutions in their mind, 70 percent of the time those buyers *volunteer* to take them to see the power person in their organizations. If you think about it, that makes sense. The odds are that the buyer's pain comes from above her in the organization. If the seller helps a buyer see (perhaps for the first time) how she can now solve a problem with which she's been wrestling, who is the first person she would like the seller to meet? With her light bulb switched on, I find in many cases, she will eagerly take you upstairs and introduce you to the person who is applying the pressure.

It is not always that easy. If that does not happen, we will need to work harder. The strategy here is to get the buyer to mentally project the solution into the future—past the point of proof. The seller could say, "Michele, let's say you become convinced that it really is possible to get face-to-face with your 1,500 salespeople in less than two hours, and you *want* our service—once you say yes, what has to happen?

There are only two answers:

First answer: I'll buy it. It's my decision and I will sign for it.

Second answer: I would have to take it to [*name of specific person*]

At this point, all the seller wants the buyer to do is reveal *who* (in the buyer's opinion) has the power to buy. The *power person*—as I have learned to define it—is that person within the organization, *regardless of title*, who has so much influence that if she wants it, she can get it. I refer to this person as the "vice president of change."

Most buyers understand their own informal organization and who their "vice president of change" is.

When you say, "Once you want it, what happens?" typically the first person the enabled buyer names is the vice president of change. I usually then ask, "Since I am here, may I meet her today?" About 90 percent of the time the buyer will object and say, "Oh, no, no—it's too early. I want to make sure that this is viable and that it really works before I take it upstairs." If your buyer wasn't willing to volunteer it, she probably wasn't going to give access anyway. But it is good to ask, because if the buyer denies you, he will "owe you one."

Role Play

Find Power

We are looking for
the identity of the
"vice president of
change."

Seller: Michele, if you become convinced that this product will give you the capabilities you need and you decide you *want* it, what has to happen? What will you do?

Buyer: I would take it to Harry Steele, our EVP. He would make the final decision. Joan Robinson, our CFO, would sign the check.

We ask, even though
the odds are we
will be denied.

Seller: Could you set up a meeting with them for me today?

Buyer: No, it is too early. Mike, I want to first be convinced that what you say is really feasible.

Intermission

The buyer refused to let the seller have access to her company's power (i.e., the main decision makers) so the seller must go to the final step, Step 8, to negotiate access to power.

Step 8: Bargain Undefined Proof *for* Access *to Power*

Now it's necessary to strike a bargain. You can say, "Would you be willing to make a bargain with me? I am not yet sure of the best way for us to prove these capabilities to you. Whatever method we use to prove these capabilities to you, it's going to cost my company money, resources, and time. We are willing to make that commitment today. If we succeed in proving to you that you will be able

to . . . (*restate buyer's vision*), in return will you introduce me to . . .
(*power person*)? Is that fair?" Most of the time the buyer will agree
that it is fair and you will get a conditional promise of access to the
power person. A small percent will not bargain, but they almost
always agree that the proposed bargain is *fair*.

When buyer refuses access to power.   Let's talk about that
small percentage of people who—despite an enabling vision—will
not be willing to risk taking you upstairs. The primary reason?
Political fear. The risks vary: a reorganization, a new boss, the last
time they took a new idea upstairs they got refused. Political fear
exists in many organizations.

When your bargain is rejected, since the "light bulb" is turned on,
empathize. You might say, "I understand the situation. It sounds
like this would not be a good thing for you to do at this time. Since
you have something to gain personally by these capabilities, could
you suggest someone else on whom I could call who, if they see the
same value that you do, would be willing to take this upstairs?"
Your fallback position is that you get yourself a lateral appointment
in the company.

Since you are not getting what you want—access to power—the
buyer is not getting a demonstration or a presentation. Best case:
your initial buyer will personally take you to meet someone more
assertive. Worst case: she will say, "Don't use my name, but if
you can convince John Doe that this has value, I know he will take
it upstairs."

Step 8 involves negotiating access to a power person and ending the call. Our mission is to bargain *undefined* proof for access
to power.

Role Play

Bargain Undefined Proof for Access to Power

Seller: Would you be willing to make a bargain with me?

Buyer: I'm not sure. What do you have in mind?

Seller: I'm not yet sure of the best way for us to prove these capabilities   Bargain undefined
to you. I first want to consult with my resources. Whichever method   proof for access to
we end up using will take some of my company's resources and we   power.

are willing to make that commitment today. If we *succeed*, through that effort, in proving to you that it is possible to get face-to-face with 1,500 sales reps in less than two hours, in return will you introduce me to Harry Steele and Joan Robinson? *Is that fair?*

When the buyer agrees to the fairness of the proposition, he also agrees to grant access to power if he sees proof of capabilities.

Buyer: Yes, I agree, that would be fair, and I would introduce you.

[Having achieved access to power, the seller ends the call.]

Seller: Thank you for your time. I am going to write you a letter confirming my understanding of your situation. In that letter I will summarize my understanding of your situation and I will propose a *specific* way for NNC to prove these capabilities to you. You should receive a letter in a day or so.

End of role play

Let's examine the bargain again. Why is the seller bargaining *undefined* proof for access to power? Most sellers are paid on revenue, regardless of what it cost their company to make the sale. Most of the executives who hire me to train their salespeople are paid on *profit*. Those executives are not comfortable giving their salespeople carte blanche access to expensive resources without someone who is paid on profit to make sure the opportunity is worthy of company resources.

What was the final question the seller asked the buyer? Is that fair? When the buyer agrees that it is fair (it *is* fair), the buyer is also agreeing to the terms of the bargain. Most Americans have a strong need to be perceived as a fair person by others. It is a powerful selling word if used sparingly. In Strategy 8, "Control the Process, Not the Buyer" I will give you the rest of the building blocks of the qualification model.

THE ONE-CALL CLOSE

Many of our clients sell things that can be sold in one call. It might be voice mailboxes, flexible staffing, training, financial or banking services, or a consulting engagement.

In most cases, a one-call close is made on an individual rather than a group, but if the entire buying group is assembled together, a one-call close can still be accomplished without high pressure.

Our one-call close is a variation on the theme of our first call. There are nine steps to a one-call close.

1. Establish rapport.
2. Call introduction.
3. Transition to need development and vision creation.
4. State benefits and offer proof.
5. Ask the buyer if he would like you to return with a decision vehicle.
6. Ask the buyer what he would like to see in the decision vehicle.
7. Sketch out a "draft" of the decision vehicle.
8. Ask the buyer if he is satisfied with the content of the decision vehicle.
9. Ask for commitment to begin today.

We will go through these logical steps and explain how each step works.

A One-Call Close Example

In 1989, an independent PR consultant for high-tech start-up firms in San Diego attended one of my open workshops. She objected when I was giving my preproposal review logic and said, "Mike, you are making this too complicated. I want to go out and make *one call* on an executive and do business." So together we reengineered her strategy. She approaches her prospect with the same initial steps we discussed earlier for the first call. She establishes rapport, does her four-minute introduction with a reference story, and asks her buyer to tell her about his business. She gets pain on the table and takes her buyer through the 9 Boxes. Once she gets to the benefit statement, things are different. She must be able to offer immediate proof if she is going to close in one call.

Once she has given the buyer some proof—samples of work she has done for other start-up companies—she asks the buyer if he would like her to come back in a few days with a proposal. If he is enabled and has seen proof, he says yes. She then takes out a blank tablet and says, "Let's sketch out what will be in that proposal." The buyer is relaxed—this is a "working session." Once she lays out the estimated number of hours, the work plan, her rates, and so on, she asks the buyer, "Is this what you are looking for?" If he says yes, she then asks, "Is there any reason we can't get started right now?"

Let's take a look at a role play example of this approach.

Seller: I am confident I can give you those capabilities. Would you take a serious look at my services?

Buyer: Yes, I will.

Seller: Let me show you some examples of work I have done for other clients.

[She reaches into her briefcase.]

Seller: Here's a campaign I did for the ABC company. Here's some press I got for that executive I told you about in that reference story.

[She and her buyer examine the proof and she explains the special PR points and benefits. The buyer is relaxed and curious.]

Seller: Would you like me to come back next week with a proposal?

Buyer: Yes, I would.

[She takes out a blank piece of paper and a pen and continues.]

Seller: Let's sketch out what should be in that proposal.

[The buyer believes he's going to be closed next week, because they are mutually working on a proposal she will make next week. Once she can understand the extent of her buyer's needs, her talk becomes more pointed and she moves into costs.]

Seller: Typically, up front, I spend 8 to 16 hours on a media study. Then we'll have an approval meeting—a go/no-go point. The next step would be for me to . . . . and so on. My hourly rate is $60/hour and it looks like this project will take between 60 and 80 hours to complete—between $3,600 and $4,800. Is that about what you're looking for?

Buyer: Yes. We thought it would cost about that.

Seller: Is there any reason we can't start right now?

[Note: Her buyer is relaxed and he's not thinking about risk because he *thought* he was going to be closed next week. And he let her close him.]

Buyer: No. There's no reason to waste time. I feel comfortable. Let's go.

That consultant wastes little effort, and because she has a business that lends itself to a one-call close, she does not hesitate; she keeps control, qualifies her buyer, evaluates his proposal request, negotiates price, confirms or finds the power, and closes. It only works this well when the buyer has a strong action vision.

Key point: *Separate when a buyer thinks he's going to be closed from when it's closable.* It allows the buyer to focus on his satisfying his needs without obsessing on risk.

Advance the Buyer's Vision with Value Justification

People will spend money when they know they can make money.

A value justification can be a key element in causing a buyer to *volunteer* to buy. People will spend money if they can *see* that they can make money. Making money happens in a variety of ways: increasing sales, decreasing costs, avoiding costs, managing taxes, and complying with the government.

Salespeople have been preparing value justification calculations for their buyers for years. This is not a new idea. A situation I have observed numerous times is a frustrated seller saying, "Look at the payback here! I can't believe they haven't signed yet!" Sound familiar? If the payback is so good, why hasn't the buyer taken action? I believe the reason is that the payback is in the mind of the *seller*, not the buyer.

The only way the payback can be in the mind of the buyer is if the buyer has a vision. The only way the buyer can have a vision is if the buyer has ownership of the problem. As long as sellers are telling buyers, "We can solve your problem," they are disabling the buyer's ability to see payback.

The beauty of the 9 Boxes diagnosis process is that we end up not only with an enabled buyer, but with four of the five value measurement elements as well:

- ☑ What will be measured?
- ☑ Who is responsible?
- ☑ How much is possible?
- ☑ What capabilities will be needed?
- ☐ When will this investment pay for itself?

We can't answer the last question until we have an understanding of how long it will take to implement the capabilities being purchased.

MEASUREMENT PLUS ACTION VISION EQUALS VALUE JUSTIFICATION

When a buyer is in Phase II of the buy cycle, he is going to ask the question, "Is this really cost justified?" In my workshops we deal with how to get the answer to this question. Most attendees are surprised to realize that their buyer will have, in a manner of speaking, already provided the measurements. This is because, if the seller took the buyer through the 9 Boxes, he was able to *measure* the problem as he diagnosed it. In both the control reasons box and the control impact box, there was a wealth of information available. Those measurements can now be assembled into a value justification presentation that allows the seller to advance the buyer's vision. The stronger the justification, the easier the price negotiation will be.

I contend that a good value justification will get you through even the toughest price negotiations in the toughest competitions. I am always rewarded when the light bulbs turn on over the heads of attendees and they exclaim, "I love this. This is *the* tool that will increase my sales." Because this is true. They leave the workshop, include value justification in their sales repertoire, and close more sales.

THE BUYER DISCLOSES WHAT WILL BE MEASURED

If you ask the right questions—and you have rapport and alignment—your buyer will give you the measurements. If your buyer does not have the facts or numbers, he will be willing to arrange for you to get them from the right people. If your buyer cannot give you the right information, you may be selling to the wrong buyer: it's time to politely find out to whom you should be talking and to arrange to meet the other buyer. Know to whom you are selling: a power sponsor, a sponsor, a beneficiary, or a technocrat.

Control reasons questions. When you were exploring the reasons for your buyer's pain, did you get measurements? The right ones? Did you ask the right questions and did your buyer give you answers with real measurements, not guesses or estimates, and did you write them down so you can factually recall them? Most reasons explored can be measured.

Control impact questions. While you were taking your buyer "through the boxes," you had the perfect opportunity to diagnose the impact of the buyer's pain throughout his organization—and the opportunity to measure the impact on others in the buyer's organization.

Measuring can get emotional. If you want active emotional visions, get measurements that hit the emotions—below quota sales results hurt salespeople, shrinking retail deposit balances impair banks, falling sales scare sales managers, rising administrative expenses upset controllers, reduced state funding threatens civil servant jobs, declining dividends agitate shareholders and sometimes cause CEOs to lose their jobs—after they have fired their own share of blamable management and workers. You can learn who is responsible, who hurts, how they hurt, and what capabilities they require with a little digging.

Dig for those measurements: cross-examine, inquire, pump, squeeze, flail, root out, uproot, unearth, probe. Do it with a win-win attitude and your buyer will appreciate it. When your buyer shows signs of tiring, move on—come back to more measurement questions after the buyer is rested. Remember that your buyer is discovering the real issues and the full impact, too. Do not rest until you *and your buyer* have all the measurements that will allow your buyer to own a strong value justification.

The buyer decides what will be measured and discloses the measurements. You get to ask the questions and to bias those questions with your product or service, but the buyer must be part of the equation. If you can get your buyer to give the measurements, *your buyer will own them.* That's because everything being diagnosed, explored, and solved belongs to the buyer.

FIVE ELEMENTS OF VALUE JUSTIFICATION

The key to a successful value justification is helping the buyer answer five questions.

- What will be measured?
- Who is responsible?
- How much is possible?
- What capabilities will be needed?
- When will this investment pay for itself?

If the buyer owns the problem, has an action vision of a solution, and can answer the above five questions, you should have very little difficulty closing the business if *you* were the seller who helped get the answers.

Element 1: What Will Be Measured?

Many measurements are superfluous. You can clutter your buyer's vision if you choose measurements that subtract from the real issue and the real measurements. Find out what few things really make your buyer's business or organization work, remembering Pareto's Law: 20 percent of the resources produce 80 percent of the result. When two to four reasons account for the problem, and those reasons align with your product or service, stick to those reasons.

A few recommended yardsticks follow.

Revenues. Try to financially measure the reasons for your buyer's pain and their impact both above the line and below the line: gross sales, net sales, profit margin, and net profits. If you are unfamiliar with financial statements, ask your controller to teach you what financial questions to ask in order to get vital and emotional measurements. For example, if your buyer's sales quotas are not being met, then why, by whom, and by how much? Because if your service or product can enable your buyer's sales reps to gain the ability to make two extra calls per day, while holding expenses down, then how much additional sales revenue will result? How much extra profit?

Revenues are powerful because businesses and organizations depend on them to pay staff, vendors, and shareholders or voters, so revenues tend to have direct action, emotional, consequential meaning. Revenue measurement can focus great buying attention on your product's or service's capabilities, because isn't that what you're selling—capabilities?

There are a number of business factors that can impact revenue: sales productivity, market share, time to market, inventory availability, cycle times, and so on. I look for revenue reasons early, because they produce the focus and emotions with which buyers are struggling—not forgetting that *eventually*, in all probability, you are going to have to get the CFO's signature—and it is revenue problems that tend to produce the most pressure on the buyer from the rest of the organization.

Costs. Whether absolute or relative, we are talking about *cost reduction* or *containment.* I have seen more sales won tactically using this measurement—cost savings—than all other measurements combined. This is a big opportunity area. Every part of every organization is in one way or another a "cost center," and smart buyers have detailed budgets and accounting procedures that track their expenditures. Even "profit centers" such as sales departments and retail stores have costs that are watched carefully by bookkeepers, accountants, controllers, and IRS agents; and smart sellers use cost reduction as a part of their product's or service's capabilities.

There are two kinds of cost reduction for which salespeople are taught to dig: displaced costs and avoided costs.

Displaced costs. If your product or service can displace, or get rid of, an existing cost, then you want your buyer telling you how and by how much. Your school testing and report computer system will replace a manual system, and the buyer can displace the costs of 10 school clerks, 8 district level clerks, and 2,000 overtime hours. Such displaced costs certainly reduce costs. Costs are measurable, and they can be included in an effective value justification presentation.

Avoided costs. If by purchasing your product or service I can avoid spending $90,000 to upgrade my old equipment, that is an avoided cost. It is money I will not have to spend tomorrow for today's problem. By buying your school testing and report computer system, the school district will also avoid the costs of three district report clerks and 500 overtime hours spent in collating reports for the state educational office. Again, costs are reduced. Costs are measurable, and they can be included in an effective value justification presentation.

Intangible. Although you and your buyer are likely to discuss employee morale, customer satisfaction, reduced stress, and public goodwill, these are hard to measure. You should only include them in your proposal if your buyer *owns* them. Intangible benefits can be your best friend or worst enemy. Assume, for instance, you were at a preproposal review meeting with a high-level buying committee. You mention how their morale will improve with your service. The CEO asks, "Who said we have bad morale?" If the morale issue is your opinion—even if it is based on past experience—you are in trouble. If I bring up morale, it is because one of my buyers had previously told me that he thought morale would improve. I can then say to the CEO, "John Doe told me he thought morale would improve. John, would you share your thoughts?" Ownership is key.

Element 2: Who Is Responsible?

Speaking of ownership, who is responsible for achieving the savings and/or the revenues? The "who" needs to be on the prospect's side of the desk, not your side. For example, if I say to the buyer, "You said your inability to provide accurate and timely testing scores to the state is causing your school district to get reduced state funding. Does this impact your superintendent of administration?" The buyer says yes. Then I ask, "How much in reduced revenues this year?" "How much next year?" And if the buyer did not know, I would ask to meet with the person who did know—that superintendent—because the answer will powerfully add to the buyer's value justification and, possibly, to an early close.

Again, ownership is key. Responsibility cannot come without control. Control cannot come without a vision. At this point, we still have a few pieces missing from our value justification equation.

Element 3: How Much Is Possible?

How much can revenues increase? How far can costs be reduced—either displaced or avoided? How much is possible? The answers depend on two things: the strength of the vision and the measurement of the problem. We get the answer in the confirm capabilities box or "Box C3," as my workshop attendees like to call it. Once the buyer says yes, if I had those capabilities, I could solve my problem. The seller can then ask, "What would those capabilities be worth to you?" The answer goes into the value justification.

Element 4: What Capabilities Will Be Needed?

When the seller asks control capability questions, he finds the answer to this question. What if you could enter the attendance information directly from the teachers' attendance sheets without keying the data? Would that help? And what if you could transmit the attendance data to the district office and eliminate the rekeying of those data at the district level, saving them those 500 overtime hours each month? Would that help? And what if that would allow the school and the district staffs to share the same attendance files and eliminate the overtime needed to reconcile the two present file sets because of your present manual systems? Would that also help? And what if you were able to produce those state and local reports required for your district and schools to get proper funding? Would these help? When the buyer says, "Yes, that would help," those capabilities will be part of the value justification.

So far, the answers to the first four value justification questions have come from the 9 Boxes. The only answer we still need to complete our equation is the next one: When will this investment pay for itself?

Element 5: When Will This Investment Pay for Itself?

In my client base, most of my clients sell products and services that offer high payback, but they don't return that payback from Day 1. When you first present the price of your product or service to your buyer, his natural reaction will be to mentally compute whether or not it is worth it. You can then point out the potential value based on what we know so far, but true payback cannot be calculated until we know how long it will take our buyer to (1) acquire the capabilities needed and (2) use them to achieve the payback.

When we build value justification models for our clients, we typically set up spreadsheets. With a spreadsheet we can separately plot increased profit, reduced costs, avoided costs, one-time product costs, and on-going product costs. What we will see is a point in time at which the cumulative savings begin to exceed the cumulative costs. That point in time is what we want to know: When will this investment pay for itself?

A SAMPLE VALUE JUSTIFICATION: SEE APPENDIX B

A sample value justification presentation is provided in Appendix B. It was prepared by Mike "Mac" McLoughlin, a licensed *Solution Selling* affiliate. Sometimes a picture is worth a thousand words.

Control the Process, Not the Buyer

Let the buyer direct himself.
Let the buyer buy.

Keeping control of the selling process and letting the buyer buy without pressure appear to be mutually exclusive, but they are not. *Solution Selling* is about keeping control while letting the buyer direct himself. I believe the seller should be a *buying facilitator*. People love to buy, but hate to feel sold. When people buy, they are taking action to satisfy one of their own needs. That feels good! The best salespeople seldom have to close—their buyers *volunteer* to buy. This does not mean you will escape the tension of price negotiation, but it does mean a positive foundation for that negotiation.

Respect for the buyer is the foundation of *Solution Selling*. A wrong move, particularly near the end when tension is high, can destroy your buyer's trust in you. Many sellers lose their buyer's trust when they attempt to "overcontrol" the buyer by closing too aggressively. Too many sales have been lost at the eleventh hour because the seller lost the buyer's trust. In most of these cases, the seller lost the buyer's trust because he lost control of himself and the process. Try to remember that buyers also want to keep control of the situation. Both the buyer and seller should feel in control. In this chapter, I will show you some techniques for mutual control—where you stay in control of your sell cycle by *facilitating* the buyer's buy cycle.

When we empower our buyers, we give them a feeling of control. The buyer owns the value justification. The foundation of the value justification is pain and an action vision—measured factually and emotionally. The buyer has the power to buy. The buyer believes that by taking action, he will be able to solve his own problem. If your buyer feels that good about a situation, why wouldn't he ask you to get started? This occurs frequently when sellers practice *Solution Selling* principles and strategies. Your buyer is in control and you are in control. You are prepared to close—but only if you have to.

DON'T CLOSE BEFORE IT IS CLOSEABLE

Have you ever gone out to a buyer's office, convinced in your own mind that you were going to get a contract *that day*, but you didn't get it? What are the warning signs that clue sellers that the deal won't close today? Do buyers become aloof and distant? Do they give vague explanations why today might not be the best time to start, such as "Well, it hasn't been through legal" and "The board has to look at it" and "A new requirement has come up"? Think back to when you have been in this situation. Is it possible that you were *closing before it is closeable?*

Ideally, as a buying facilitator, you should never have to close again. In reality, you have to be prepared to close the sale in a way that shows respect for the buyer. You will know when your sale is closeable. If you have properly facilitated each stage of the buy cycle, the buyer will have given you every indication through dialogue. *You will know.* It's a feeling, and also a shared conviction with the buyer that the time is right. Both you and your buyer know it's the right thing to do.

I encourage sellers to deal with the legal, technical, and administrative issues in parallel rather than in series. This strategy can eliminate a big percentage of the excuses I typically hear from sellers about why the buyer would not buy today. My philosophy is, if I as the seller can think of a reason why the buyer won't buy today, the buyer can also. I recommend you live by this rule: *Never ask for the business until you cannot think of a single reason why the buyer cannot or will not buy today.*

What happens to your relationship with your buyers when you do ask for their business *before* they have reached the comfort level to buy? Your relationship starts to deteriorate. Once a "death spiral" begins, it is extremely difficult to recover. If you do not sense the time is right, be careful. Don't close before it is closeable.

PROCESS CONTROL LETTERS

After the first meeting with a buyer, control is very difficult for most sellers to establish and maintain. A key strategy in keeping control of the sell/buy cycle is to focus on control from the very beginning. Keep in mind that the buyer also wants to be in control. A key premise of *Solution Selling*, to borrow from Stephen Covey's *The Seven Habits of Highly Effective People,* is win-win or no deal. My customers give me enthusiastic feedback that they are successful using two *Solution Selling* process control letters: the sponsor letter and the plan letter with its schedule of events. When sellers use these letters, their sales increase. The letters are neither manipulative nor pushy, but they do incorporate key *Solution Selling* strategies, so they enable both sellers and buyers to feel in control—as they progress through the buy cycle together.

The Sponsor Letter

Sponsor letters are written when sellers have to negotiate access to a power person. This letter helps both the buyer and the seller. It helps the buyer by confirming the qualified needs and the qualified buying process (documenting the bargain for access). The sponsor letter helps the buyer by giving him a "script" for his own internal selling. This last point is significant because a buyer whose "lights are on" will want to share his action vision of using your product or service with others in his organization. Without a script, he will find it difficult to do so. He could even wreck your sale.

A sample sponsor letter is shown on the next page.

Key Components of Process Control Letters

We ask managers to edit the process control letters their salespeople write. We find it is the best way to reinforce the *Solution Selling* process, particularly during the first critical weeks after the workshop when habits can be formed. The only people present at a sales call, in most cases, are the seller and the buyer. Any significant sales call (for which a seller would like credit) deserves a follow-up letter. Once managers have coached at least one *Solution Selling* workshop, they are typically able, in one minute or less, to understand exactly how effective their salesperson was on a particular sales call, by reviewing the follow-up letter.

January 9, 1994

Mr. Steve Jones
VP Sales
ABC Technology Company
Ashland Parkway
Richmond, VA 33065

Dear Steve:

Thank you for your time and interest in Solution Selling®. The purpose of this letter is to summarize my understanding of our meeting and our action plan.

Pain

In our discussion, you told me your primary critical issue is your difficulty predicting company revenue. The reasons we discussed are your long sell cycle and the varied backgrounds of your field managers, which prevent you from being able to view your pipeline through a consistent grading system.

Reasons

You said your salespeople need a way to gain early access to senior executives and you need to view your entire company pipeline via a consistent grading system that will reflect both quantity and quality of the opportunities. You also said that you needed a company sales process that would allow you to monitor progress and easily audit the pipeline from your desk.

Vision

You agreed to take a serious look at Solution Selling®. You also said that if we succeed in proving to you that we can give you these capabilities, you would introduce me to Jim Smith, your president. You mentioned that Jim is not happy about reporting to the board that profitability goals are not being achieved for the third consecutive quarter.

Agreement to explore

Bargain for access

I have arranged for you to speak with John Doe, the VP of sales at the XYZ Software Company. He is expecting your call on the 13th. I am confident you will like what you hear, and help us introduce Solution Selling® to the rest of your organization.

Proof proposal

Sincerely,

Bill Hart
BH/de

Many of our clients now have an "edit stamp" for their process control letters. Sales managers use the edit stamp when reviewing the follow-up letters of their salespeople. I have an example of that stamp for you in Strategy 10. Here are the elements for which we look:

1. Pain.

2. Reasons.

3. Vision.

4. Agreement to explore.

5. Bargain/hooks.

6. Proof/plan proposal.

The first element is *pain*. You did not see the word *pain* in the sponsor letter. Pain is an internal word useful for training and qualifying, but not a great selling word. In our letters to prospects, we use phrases like "primary critical issue." In our sponsor letter example, the buyer's pain was his inability to predict his company's future revenue. As a VP of sales, that is *pain!*

The reasons for the buyer's pain are the next items we like managers to evaluate. The reasons should be biased toward whatever the seller is selling. These reasons came from the *control diagnosis* questions the seller asked when taking his buyer through the 9 Boxes. It doesn't take long for most sellers to know which reasons commonly lead to sales for their products and services.

The buyer's vision is the next key component of the sponsor letter. There is a big difference between a *goal* and a *capability*. A goal might be to "improve forecasting ability." Goals don't answer the question *how?* In the sample letter, the *capabilities* the buyer said he wanted were a way for his salespeople to gain early access to senior executives, a way to view his pipeline through a consistent grading system, and a way to audit his pipeline and a company sales process from his desk. These *capabilities* will allow the sales executive to better predict *his* future revenue. Remember, at this point the buyer has not yet seen proof. He is only saying that if he had these capabilities, he could solve his problem. Proof comes later.

Documenting the agreement to explore is a great qualifier. If the buyer was just being polite at the time, this restatement should "smoke out" those not really committed to seriously evaluating a new approach.

It is also important to document the bargain for access to power. Again, if the buyer is not serious, documenting the verbal agreement in a letter smokes out the nonserious. The "hooks" are the logical links between the primary buyer and others in his organization impacted by his critical issue. We typically look for the "hooks" in the plan letter, which I will cover later this chapter.

The final component we ask managers to evaluate is either a proof proposal or a plan proposal. If we are "below the line" and had to bargain for access, we submit a proof proposal. If we are dealing with a power person, we submit a plan proposal, of which you will see an example in the plan letter.

Now go back and review the sponsor letter example and locate the six points. Sponsor letters contain *Solution Selling* basic components: pain, reasons for the pain, vision, an agreement to explore, the bargain for access to power, and a proof proposal. Why a proof proposal? Remember that when we struck the bargain, we were bargaining with *undefined* proof. Once the seller's manager deems an opportunity qualified, she can choose to invest *specific* resources to prove the capabilities to the buyer.

Ideally, when you restate the pain, reasons, and vision, you had a tape recorder in your pocket. The closer you can come to the exact words and phrases you used face-to-face, the better. Why? Because after your buyer receives your sponsor letter, he can use it as a "script" when he attempts to share his vision with others in his organization.

How well does the sponsor letter work? As I mentioned, the reason we write a sponsor letter is we are "below the line," and our buyer did not volunteer to take us to power. We had to bargain. The sponsor letter restates the vision that is the foundation of the bargain. We find that this letter works so well that about 50 percent of the time, when the sponsor shows up for the proof session, he brings the power person along. This tells me that sponsors are frequently able to use their written "scripts" to share their visions with power buyers.

The Plan Letter

Once our sponsor keeps his bargain and introduces us to a power person, plan letters are written to document a successful call with the power sponsor. Their primary purpose is to *negotiate a sell/buy cycle* with the buyer's organization. Note that the sample plan letter is addressed to the sponsor, but it was actually written for the power sponsor, Jim Smith. The sponsor is important because he is our primary relationship with ABC Technology Co. and we have no intention of losing him. However, because Jim Smith is the power person, we copy Jim to keep control of events and to keep him informed. Jim is ultimately going to be the person who will make the buying decision.

Plan letters do the same things as the sponsor letter: confirm the qualified needs and qualify the buying process, but at a *power* level. The proposed sequence of events will eventually be the seller's control vehicle during the buying cycle—once the power sponsor assumes ownership for the plan. The seller is now proposing a sequence of events that will eventually lead to a decision to buy or not to buy. The buyer can change it as many times as he wants—there are several go/no-go decisions along the way—so it keeps the buyer in control, yet it keeps the seller in control also. Win-win. Because we are breaking a large decision into smaller "bite-sized chunks," the buyer feels in control. The buyer looks at each go/no-go point and says to himself, "I can get out here if I want to." In order for the buyer to comfortably plan this far into the future, he must believe that he can stop the process at any time.

An example of a plan letter is on the following page.

After the seller's meeting with Jim Smith, the power sponsor, the seller has been able to link their pains, reasons, and visions. What remains is for him to find a way to control the rest of the events so he can get to a signed agreement. He does that by including and attaching a *proposed* sequence of events as page 2. A sample proposed sequence of events appears on page 142.

Remember in Strategy 6 when the seller put on the "imaginary neck brace" and asked the buyer, "How do you want to evaluate my service?" The seller then wrote down everything the buyer requested, neither agreeing nor disagreeing. That list is the foundation for the proposed sequence of events. In the spirit of quid pro quo, the seller constructs the initial proposed sequence of events interspersing items he wants with items the buyer wants. It does not become *the* sequence of the events until the buyer accepts it. The buyer accepts the plan by *changing* it. I tell my workshops, "If he doesn't change it, he doesn't own it."

Think about the go/no-go points. Yes, they break a big decision up into multiple little ones. They also

- Give the seller the opportunity to "close" at each of them.
- Give the seller the ability to stop early if the buyer is not meeting him half-way.
- Give the seller the opportunity to close on major items incrementally: needs, implementation plan, value justification, success criteria, legal, and schedule.
- Give the seller's management the ability to calculate a "percent complete" to help with forecasting.
- Make the final close a nonevent.

January 16, 1994

Mr. Steve Jones
VP Sales
ABC Technology Co.
Ashland Parkway
Richmond, VA 33065

Dear Steve:

Thank you for arranging yesterday's conference call with Jim Smith. I believe it was time well spent for both ABC and Solution Selling®.

Jim confirmed that his primary critical issue is having to explain not achieving the company's profit target to the board of directors. In addition to your forecasting problem and the impact on the company's cash position, Jim also said he is concerned with the sales force's increasing reliance on technical support resources. — Pain

He said he needed to be able to rely on the forecast you give him. He also said he would like your salespeople to manage the sell cycle with minimal involvement of the company's technical resources. He said if these two things are possible, he could report to the board that he would meet his profitability goals. He also said that improved predictability would enable him to improve the company's share price. — Reasons (hooks) / Vision (hooks)

We told Jim we are confident that Solution Selling® can give him these capabilities. I am as pleased as you that he is also interested in exploring Solution Selling®. — Agreement to explore

Based on my knowledge to date, I would like to propose a sequence of events for your further exploration of Solution Selling®. Look it over with Jim, and I will call you on January 19 to get your thoughts. — Plan proposal

Sincerely,

Bill Hart
Attachment
BH/de
cc: Jim Smith, ABC

ORCHESTRATE THE "PERFECT TIME" TO CLOSE

You can't close a sale until it's closeable. I teach salespeople to orchestrate the *perfect time to close*. A seller's management must also support this strategy, or it won't work.

Mr. Steve Jones
Page 2

*Proposed Sequence of Events**

Event	Week of	Go/No-Go
Interview Jack Berman (CFO) Interview Bill Watkins (VP Support) Interview Jane Doe (Director of Training)	1/22	
Summarize findings to top management team via fax and conference call	1/22	*
Top management team to see proof of capabilities via attendance at Solution Selling® open workshop	1/29	*
Implementation plan approval by Training Dept.	1/29	*
Solution Selling® cost estimate	2/5	*
Determine success criteria and value justification	2/5	*
Send SS® Confidentiality Agreement to legal	2/5	*
Review final schedule "rough draft"	2/12	*
Final schedule approval	2/17	*
Begin customization	2/17	
First custom Solution Selling® workshop for ABC marketing and field management (ABC executives to coach)	3/17	
Final review of custom material	3/24	
First workshop for ABC field personnel (ABC managers to coach)	3/31	

As you will notice, we will stop and mutually decide to proceed eight times
(at each *) in this proposed sequence of events. Again, this is my first cut.
I'll call you to discuss.

The Unexpected Time Is Frequently a Perfect Time

I have found that the perfect time to close is when it is closeable, but
the buyer doesn't think he is going to be closed. For example, if you
are at a point where you have agreement on needs, fit, cost, value,
technical issues, legal issues, and implementation, and the buyer
was not expecting to be closed that day, wouldn't that be the perfect
time to close? That is why I am a proponent of the *preproposal review*

technique, which is really designed to be a *proposal avoidance* technique. The word proposal is not sacred. Some of my clients use "prerecommendation review" or "predecision review." The word you use will depend on the name of your *decision vehicle*. Your "decision vehicle" could be a work plan, a service agreement, a purchase order, a contract, a sales order, or a proposal. In the proposed sequence of events example, the "Review final schedule rough draft" is really the preproposal review. We just didn't use the word *proposal* in this case.

Proposal Avoidance

I preach to my audiences that proposals don't sell: *salespeople* sell. I teach *proposal avoidance*. Once you hand a buyer a proposal with product/service details, pricing, support, training, and so on *how much control* do you have over that situation at that point? Zip! All you can do is call or drop by once a week and ask, "How's it going? Have you reviewed my proposal yet?" Your buyer might say, "Hang in there, Mike. We are giving it *serious consideration*. We'll let you know as soon as we are ready." As most experienced sellers know, sales is not fun when you are in this position.

To avoid this problem, we say to a buyer, "If we get down the road, to a point where it looks like we're going to want to do business together, will you want a proposal from me?" The buyer almost always says yes to that. Then we say, "I want you to know that *if we do get that far*, the proposal I give you will contain nothing that you don't already know. The purpose of a proposal is simply to *document and confirm* whatever business arrangement we have come to—*if* we come to that point in time where we'd like to do business together." Buyers usually say, "That makes sense." You then say, "And I'd like to suggest that if we get that far, that I come out a week in advance of the final proposal with a draft. This will allow us to go through the content ahead of time, so you won't have any surprises, and I can do it right the first time. We call this a *preproposal review*." Most buyers agree to this logic. The phrase "if we get that far" is important in letting the buyer know that he is in control and can stop the process at any time.

We have now established some ground rules that will allow you much more control at the end of the sell cycle. The buyer has agreed that the only reason you will be preparing a proposal is to document and confirm your business arrangement, *if* you both decide you want to do business. The buyer also understands that he will not learn anything new from the proposal and has even agreed to review the content in draft form a week in advance of delivery. This means that if there are any unanticipated surprises, you have a chance to resolve them before you finalize your proposal.

The key to creating the perfect time to close is to have a "closeable situation" before the buyer thinks he will be closed. If you build the *preproposal review* into the buyer's plan as the step before the final approval step, then the buyer *thinks* he's going to be closed at the "final approval" step in the plan, but is *closeable* at the preproposal meeting. As I demonstrated in Strategy 6, you can even use this technique on a one-call meeting.

Let me emphasize one more time: *separate when a buyer thinks he's going to be closed from when it's closeable.* It allows the buyer to focus on satisfying his needs without obsessing on risk. The buyer is in control of the buying; the seller is in control of the process. The seller is a *buying facilitator.*

Draw the Line in Price Negotiations

A smart buyer will not stop wringing the washcloth until water stops dripping. The seller is the washcloth.

Price negotiations are emotional. At their beginning, the outcome is uncertain and, dramatically, the actors—the ardent seller and the suspicious buyer—are at once protagonist and antagonist, depending on which role they perform.

Price negotiations require planning. In Strategies 1 through 8 you learned how to facilitate each point in the buy cycle. You now have a lot of knowledge, but you have more than knowledge. You have a buyer with whom you are aligned and share a strong vision. Too many sellers squander those strengths with poor price negotiating skills.

You have heard the adage, "buyer beware." Well, at price negotiation time, seller beware! Seller beware of negotiating pitfalls: cost justification versus price justification, the buyer's emotional hurdle, the seller's emotional hurdle, buyer take-aways, the ritual "wringing of the washcloth," and price negotiation in reverse preference order, to mention only a few of the immediate contingent pitfalls. I have learned that preparation is half the battle.

Anticipation of negotiating problems gets the seller halfway there; *practice* of negotiating alternatives often gets the seller the rest of the way. "There" in this instance means getting a win-win, profitable, signed contract.

DO NOT CONFUSE PRICE NEGOTIATION WITH COST JUSTIFICATION

Many salespeople take wrong turns on the winding road to a signed contract. They think a buyer's previous acceptance of the cost justification constitutes price agreement. Not so. Acceptance of the cost justification meant only that—it was viable enough to move from Phase II to Phase III.

Cost justification means simply that: the buyer accepts his own measurements, cost estimates, payback calculations, and implementation schedule. Remember the confirm capabilities box in Strategy 3? The buyer agreed he could solve his problem if he had specified capabilities and verbalized the value. In Phase II, the buyer convinced himself your product or service meets his needs, and he confirms that it is in fact cost justified.

Price justification is another matter entirely. Let's use a car example. Most of us have purchased a car for ourselves. Most of us knew ahead of time which car we wanted to buy. We came to the conclusion via car magazines, friends, road tests, and so on. Most of us also knew ahead of time how much the car we wanted costs. *With that knowledge,* we went out to a car dealer with serious intent to buy that car. At that point it was *cost justified.* When you got to the dealer, did you want to pay sticker price? No? What did you want? I'll bet you wanted to be convinced in your own mind that you were getting the *best possible deal* on that car. Am I right? That's price justification. Am I getting the best deal?

At negotiation time, a strong cost justification helps. A strong cost justification should result in the buyer believing he will make money with the purchase. *Buyers will spend money when they see they can make money.* Thus, if the cost justification is accurate, promising, and probable, then the buyer should be less inclined to grind the seller over price. In spite of that strong cost justification, don't be surprised if all of a sudden your buyer is telling you *your price is too high.* Cost justification is cost justification, and price negotiation is price negotiation. They are different and separate.

Before the ink hits the contract, two emotional hurdles must be overcome. One of them belongs to the seller, the other to the buyer.

BUYERS WRING THE WASHCLOTH; THE SELLER *IS* THE WASHCLOTH

Do you use a washcloth when you bathe? Most people do. When your washcloth gets full of water, what do you do? Do you wring it out? When do you stop wringing? When the water stops dripping. Just to make sure, do you give it an extra squeeze? Maybe a squeeze and a shake just to make sure? Most people do.

At negotiation time, in the buyer's mind, the seller is a washcloth. I repeat: the seller *is* a washcloth. And if that buyer has an IQ over 80, he's going to take at least one wrenching squeeze to see what happens. Am I right? And the squeezing will continue until the seller stops dripping. As long as the seller drips, the buyer squeezes.

How does a seller stop the squeezing? By resolving to stop dripping, by resolving to walk out if the business is not right, and by resolving to walk away from the business. So what is the seller's emotional hurdle? The seller's emotional hurdle is his *resolve* to draw the line, to walk away. When the price negotiation may cost the trip to Hawaii, some sellers can withstand a squeeze or two. But when the price negotiations reach a point where the deal is threatened or a job loss is threatened, then that is tough. Sellers must have the stomach to resist dripping, because as long as the seller continues to give things away, the buyer will keep squeezing. The seller must take his stand with conviction—enough conviction to convince the buyer he is getting the best possible deal.

THE BUYER'S EMOTIONAL HURDLE

What is the buyer's emotional hurdle? The most frequent answer I hear is *risk*. No, it's not risk. The correct answer is, "Am I getting the best deal?" Buyers normally will not buy until they believe they are getting the best possible price.

Think about the last time you bought a car. Were you face to face with the car salesman? As a buyer, what did you do with that salesperson to convince yourself you were getting the best deal? Did you walk out? Yes, walk out. Could you walk out on another salesperson? (Were *you* wringing the washcloth?) A salesperson with four children to feed and patches on his sleeve? Why did you walk out? Because if that car salesman was willing to let you leave the car lot, you became convinced you had the best deal you could make. He could not drop (or "drip") any further. However, if he said, "Wait, don't leave. Maybe I can do a little better." What did you just learn? You learned you did not yet have the best deal. So, the smart buyer you are, what do you do to convince yourself you have the best deal? You *take it away* from that car salesman— figuratively—*just to see*. To see what? To see how bad he wants it, and your measurement is the best price possible. Of course, your buyers *aren't smart enough* to do that to you. Are they? Do you believe that? Many sellers naively do.

Have your buyers ever thought of taking the sale away from you— at least once? No? Have you ever noticed how sales bookings look in many industries? Most sales, shipments, or bookings come in during the last 10 days of the quarter. By March *40th*, June *40th*, September *40th*, and December *40th?* Why is this? Is it because buyers are stupid? I don't think so. What have sellers taught their buyers over the past 25 years? What has the information technology industry, for instance, taught its buyers? Buyers of information technology systems have learned December 40th is a great time to buy. Why is December 40th an ideal time to buy? Because buyers have learned through experience that the pressure is on everyone's sales department to produce the best possible year-end financial results; so these smart buyers wait to negotiate their purchasing on December 38th, a date that reflects the seller's stress.

Sellers openly telegraph their deadlines: our quarter is ending, the Hawaii trip competition is in full swing, marketing's promotions blatantly announce amazing features, *discounted*. Why? Because most sellers know, deep in their gut, that they don't have very much control over when the buyer will buy. Buyers love pressured sellers. The comic book character, Pogo, has said it already, "I sees the enemy and the enemy is us."

THE SELLER'S EMOTIONAL HURDLE

Sellers have an emotional hurdle too. The emotional hurdle for the seller is having the intestinal fortitude to *withstand* the wringing by the buyer—in other words, the ability to "branch to door" (see Figure 14) if necessary. Part of a seller's power comes from having the fortitude to walk away from a buyer who is not meeting him halfway. This strength of character is necessary from the first call on.

Examine Figure 14. We use this picture repeatedly in our workshops. We put it up each time a seller faces a situation where he has to have the strength to walk away if necessary. In this example, we are back on the very first call. The "decision points" are buyer decisions:

- Should I listen to this salesperson? Y or N?
- Is this person sincere? Y or N?
- Is this person competent? Y or N?

What if one of these decisions is a *no*? Should the seller persist anyway? Should he overcome these objections? Should he try to

FIGURE 14
Branch to Door

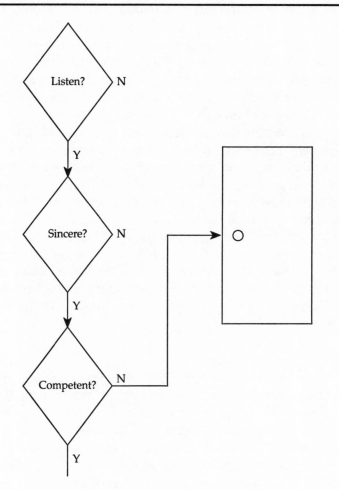

ram a square peg in a round hole? My point is, if things are not working, at some point, the seller has to make the tough decision to leave. He must "branch to door." If he is a good prospector, he knows he can go back to the office, pick up the phone, and find another opportunity.

Sellers need even more intestinal fortitude at negotiation time. Now the seller has invested weeks or months of hard work. Now he has other people in his organization pressuring him to close this business. What if he is 30 percent of quota? What if the trip to Hawaii is on the line? How well will he do with a tough buyer who *will not buy* until he is *convinced* he is getting the best deal? How does the buyer become convinced? The seller must convince him!

The seller convinces the buyer with courage: the courage to draw the line on price and then withstand one or more "squeezes" by the buyer. Who has to overcome the emotional hurdle first? *The seller*, because the buyer cannot overcome his emotional hurdle without taking a couple of squeezes and coming up dry. The seller has to demonstrate to the buyer that he is willing to "branch to door" if the buyer is not willing to meet him halfway.

This decision is very difficult to make. I recommend to my clients that sellers who are less than 100 percent of quota, year-to-date, always bring their manager along to negotiation sessions. The manager is the "bad guy"; the seller is still the "good guy." The decision to draw the line can be difficult for the manager as well. What if the manager is 30 percent of quota?

I have learned the hard way, playing the role of the "bad guy" in many negotiations, that as the seller *I have to draw the line first*. It didn't take me long to learn to draw the line while I still had some profit in the deal! The seller must overcome his emotional hurdle first. It is a *prerequisite* for the buyer being able to overcome his. It is part of the process.

SMART BUYERS

I believe that buyers today are much smarter than many sellers give them credit for. They did not just fall off the turnip truck. Many have attended courses in buying, or they have attended one or more negotiating seminars. Smart buyers use expert skills and tactics to get the best possible price from unprepared sellers. Sometimes, these skills are devastating even to prepared sellers who are well-trained in negotiation.

Here are things smart buyers do.

Smart buyers never sole source. Smart buyers compare products and services, features, advantages, benefits, warranties, and such things. Most of all, they compare prices. Smart buyers, particularly if an evaluation is complex, will put at least three vendors through their paces.

Smart buyers assign a sponsor to each alternative. Smart buyers assign a sponsor to each vendor. The "sponsor's" assigned role is to keep her assigned vendor actively participating through the entire evaluation process. "Four months from now, I want the ABC Company here at the table, thinking they can win our business." Similar instructions are given to the sponsors for the DEF Company and the XYZ Company.

Smart buyers never let you know you are winning. Why? Because, if they do, they know they will have to pay full price. And paying full price is about losing. As long as two or more vendors are willing to slash each other's throats, the chance a buyer will pay full price is minimal to nonexistent.

Smart buyers never let you know you are losing. When a seller knows all is lost, the seller leaves. When unwanted sellers leave, the buyer cannot use the unwanted seller to negotiate against the preferred seller.

Smart buyers price negotiate in reverse preference order. Smart buyers first use the vendor of least choice, extract a price, and negotiate that price against the next least-preferred vendor's price. This insidious tactic stops only after the buyer settles the price with the most favored vendor. Uncompetitive sellers and other "bridesmaids" find themselves reduced to price haggling in the leavings of the marketplace.

Smart buyers take it away from you at least once. Any buyer who has taken Negotiating 101 has learned to take it way from the vendor at least once to see how badly the seller wants it (to see how far the seller will "drip"). In some areas of the country, buyers tend to take it away two or three times.

Smart buyers are aware of your deadlines. Smart buyers know a seller's sales performance deadlines. They know about that Hawaii trip and when qualification ends. In 1986, I provided consulting to a large, New Jersey–based company that flew its salespeople long distances to potential buyers: in many instances to Arkansas, Tennessee, Georgia, and Alabama. More often than not, a buyer scheduled the closing meetings—that is, price negotiations—for a *Friday afternoon*. That is what happened to the seller in the Face #2 story. Did the buyers call their local airport to plot the time of the last airplane flight to New Jersey? Why? Because they knew that most salespeople are eager to get back home and to their families for the weekend. The buyer knew right to the minute when the seller had to leave, barely allowing time for the seller to make her flight connection. And those buyers waited right up to the frantic end, because they knew *that* was the moment they could get the best deal.

LESSONS FROM TWO PRICE NEGOTIATIONS

Here are two stories I present from my point of view, because I was part of both negotiations. I tell these stories in my workshops because they illustrate important lessons about price negotiations. You may disagree over how good they are, but they work for us and for many of our participants.

Story #1: The Saga of Dave Crabtree

This is the unabridged version of the story in Face #10.

In 1972, after I left Xerox Computer Services, I joined a venture capital-financed startup company that sold manufacturing productivity systems for Prime Computers. My company was unknown and its product was unknown. I was hired to open southern California's lucrative aerospace markets.

I established two offices: one in the San Fernando Valley and one in Orange County. It was a "ground up" operation, and one of the first things I did was to hire four salespeople, a couple of administration people, and a couple of manufacturing consultants. In May 1982, we opened for business. One of the salespeople I hired was my younger brother, Dick, and another was a talented salesperson named Dave Crabtree. Dave is a former Navy fighter pilot who saw action in Vietnam. He graduated from the Naval Academy at Annapolis and, after he mustered out of the Navy, he went to graduate school, earning an MBA.

Dave was working on a large opportunity—in those days, large for us. Our typical sale was $150,000, including all hardware and software components. Then, thanks to Dave's farming efforts, a large Los Angeles–based defense contractor, a $40 million company, sent us a request for a proposal (RFP). It was aimed primarily at our competition, but we were included in the mailing. Dave successfully negotiated interviews with the buyer prior to exchange of our RFP response. Getting those interviews was crucial to our small company for the competition against large, well-financed competitors.

We were able to get their senior people to admit pain, and we were able to reengineer their original vision to include our product.

We held a high opinion of ourselves as salespeople, and we had a *hot* product. We had the ability to create visions for the line vice presidents on which our competition just couldn't match us. Dave and I had a classic "solution selling" buyer situation with a critical issue. Our energy levels ran high, because this opportunity was not the usual $150,000 contract size: Phase I was $450,000, and Phase II was $150,000, totaling $600,000.

A $600,000 opportunity! Dave lived and breathed this big opportunity and, because he was a senior sales rep, I did not ride him about keeping his sales pipeline full, nor did I push him to do more prospecting. I let him go at his own pace.

But a couple of problems arose. First, the original four-month evaluation plan (with go/no-go steps) ended up stretching to seven. Delays caused it to drag out to seven months. Dave thought he would achieve his annual sales quota in the fourth month of the transaction, so he had stopped prospecting. All of his eggs were in this one basket. I call salespeople like that, "elephant hunters." Dave had an elephant in his sights. He had giant dollar signs—six digits, that is 000,000—in his brain. He was chasing the big one.

Second, since this sale had dragged into its seventh month, Dave was having cash flow problems. He was down two payments on his Jaguar, and other household bills were unpaid. (In our young company, compensation was based on a low monthly base salary but offset by a high commission schedule.) By the seventh month, Dave was noticeably threatened, because the "repo man" was calling him repeatedly. They intimidated him saying, "Dave, if we don't get some money, you're never even going to hear us. One morning you're going to get up and that car will be gone." Dave and, more important, Dave's wife loved that British racing-green Jaguar. Because bill collectors were hounding him, he was screening all incoming telephone calls with his answering machine. If I called him at night, the answering machine would activate, and, after his message, "This is Dave Crabtree, I'm not in, please leave your . . . ," I would have to say, "Dave, I know you're there. Pick up the phone. It's Mike. Here's the rest of the story (with my margin notes):

Red flag!

[Seven months into a four month plan—finally, Dave scurries into my office. He's excited. I know *they* have called. It's price negotiation time.]

Dave: They've phoned. They're *finally* ready to do business.

[Dave and I drove out to the aerospace company in his Jaguar. It was raining and the wipers didn't work. At least the car started, but the wipers did not work. The inoperative windshield wipers did not faze Dave. It may have been because he was a former fighter pilot. Dave drove through the pelting rain without wipers better than I could drive with wipers.

As soon as we arrived and were met in their reception lobby, a red flag went up. We thought the meeting would involve all of four members of the buying committee: the VP of manufacturing, the VP of purchasing, the VP of engineering, and the VP of finance. Instead, only one executive, "Frank Johnson," the vice president, finance, met us.

Until that point, we had always dealt with the senior level buying committee as a group. Now there was just one person: the VP of finance, *solo*. Red flag! Why? Why was Frank alone? (With 20/20 hindsight, the reason was that Frank was the best negotiator, and Frank knew he would be a far stronger negotiator *without* the other members of the buying committee saying, "Come on, Frank, we need this thing." Frank knew he could be tougher alone. At the time, we did not know this.) Dave and I looked at each other with that look surprised people

More red flags.   have: Gee, something's wrong here, because we've been meeting with four people every time. Now all of a sudden Frank is alone. I was 35 years old and Dave was 37. The VP of finance was 59 years old, slim, 6'3, white hair, and tanned, and he had cold, gray eyes. We had never seen Frank smile. But this time he was smiling. He was warm and friendly, which was another red flag. Frank spoke first.]

Frank: Sit down, guys. Let me get you a cup of coffee.

[We sat in Frank's office at a round table. Despite his thin attempt to create an illusion of corporate democracy, I always felt he preferred a financial dictatorship. Frank began immediately to apologize.]

Frank: Mike, first of all, let me apologize for the delays. You guys hit all your deadlines; all the delays are our fault. I apologize. However, I'm really glad we found you guys. We think you're a much better alternative than XYZ Corporation. I've got one problem left, then I'm ready to do business.

Mike: What's that, Frank?

[Frank paused for a moment, looking us in the eyes, then answered.]

Buyer's washcloth   **Frank:**   Your price is totally unacceptable.
squeeze #1.
[Dave was struck dumb, paralyzed. I laughed, then I went into Stand #1, a deflection.]

Seller's stand #1.   **Mike:**   This is a joke, right?

Frank: You think this is funny? There's the door.

Buyer's washcloth squeeze #2.

[Frank pointed to the door. It was not funny. I wiped the smile off my face. I could not understand what had gone wrong. We had done a formal value justification with this guy back in month 3 or 4. Frank had signed off on a less-than-nine-month payback. So I used Stand #2, a more determined stand.]

Mike: Frank, I don't understand. I was there the day we did the cost justification. You, yourself, said the payback was shorter than nine months. You've known the price for four months. I don't understand what's going on.

Seller's stand #2.

Frank: Mike, I have a friend at Prime Computer. I found out how much you're paying for that hardware. I see what you're charging me. I think you guys are being greedy on that. Take the software. I know how much it costs to duplicate a tape. I know you've got some development costs, but I look at what you are making on this and it exceeds my "reasonable man" test. I think you guys are making way too much money on this. It's obscene, and I'm not going to pay it. The price is unacceptable.

Buyer's washcloth squeeze #3.

[I resort directly to more resistance.]

Mike: Frank, you're a businessman and I'm a businessman. You're in business to make a profit; I'm in business to make a profit. I don't resent your profit. The profit I make is going to enable me to build a strong support organization to support you down the road.

Seller's stand #3.

Frank: Mike, you're not listening. Your price is unacceptable. I'm not going to pay it.

Buyer's washcloth squeeze #4.

[I looked over at Dave. His armpits were wet *down to his belt*. I could almost feel his heart beat. Beads of sweat oozed down his forehead. Perspiration covered his upper lip. Have you ever seen somebody come back from Mexico and their skin is a pallid shade of green? He looked ill. And this is a guy who flew combat jets over Vietnam. Now what job is tougher? (Matter of fact, I had Dave coach a workshop just last February, and, while I repeated this story, Dave broke out into another sweat.) I flashed Dave a don't-say-*anything* look, and I faced Frank and vaulted into Negotiation 102.]

Mike: Frank, the price of my system is a small portion of the money you're putting into your company to turn it more toward commercial markets. Five years from now, will they remember you for changing the direction of the company or for squeezing Mike Bosworth out of a few thousand dollars? Let's get our priorities straight.

Seller's stand #4.

[*I thought this approach was pretty good.*]

Buyer's washcloth
squeeze #5.

Frank: Mike, you're not listening. Your price is unacceptable to me. I'm
   not going to pay it.

[Frank is tough! What should Dave and I do now? Had I been alone, I
was willing to walk out. I considered using the briefcase tactic. I always
lay my briefcase open on the table in front of me, because then I can
close it, indicating that I will not drip further, while I am still at the table.
I decided against using this tactic. Again, because I thought we had
earned the business, I thought we might have to leave without a signed
contract, in order to convince Frank the deal was as good as it was
going to get. My problem was that I would have had to carry Dave, who
was nearly comatose. Dave is bigger than I, and he was wet—from
sweat and perspiration. I didn't want to touch him and I didn't think I
could carry him. I decided to try to get the contract today. But Frank had
convinced me that, if I wanted it today, I would have to drip more.]

Seller's stand #5

Mike: Frank, the only possible way I could do anything for you is—

[I saw his eyelids flicker, probably visualizing more water dripping.]

Mike: —if you could do something in return for me.

Frank: Like what?

Mike: Well, (when I need time to gather my wits, I talk like that,
   with "wells") the only two things I can think of are . . . if there was
   some way—

[I spoke slowly, hurt. I wanted Frank to appreciate my dripping.]

Seller's
condition "drip."

Mike: —to combine Phase I and Phase II into a *single* order, and if
   you could make the decision quickly enough so that I could get the
   hardware shipped this quarter so I could get the revenue credit this
   quarter. If those two things were possible, I could do something
   for you.

[When I negotiate price, I talk in long, unbroken sentences with phrases
run together. This allows me to gather my wits.]

Frank: Both of those things are possible.

[I knew Frank had been to negotiating school. Now I had to put something I knew Frank wanted on the table. I knew Frank and his buying
committee highly valued my manufacturing consultant, Ralph. They
thought he "walked on water."]

Seller's
conditional offer.

Mike: *If those two things are possible*, I'm willing to put on the table an
   extra *200 hours* on-site of Ralph's time. I know you have concerns
   about this new system's proper installation and implementation.

[Frank stared at Dave and me for what seemed to be hours.]

Frank: Deal. Let's do it.

Buyer accepts
condition.

[Frank signed and pushed the contract over to me for my signature. Frank's job would be safe with Ralph around. Incidentally, we had those hours in our price list at $135/hour. Ralph cost me $30 an hour, so it was not a "break the bank" giveaway. To be fair to Frank, *value* to Frank included a risk-free installation, because a faulty manufacturing system would have been extremely costly—much more than the $27,000. Dave and I walked out with a $600,000 order. At the car, Dave tried to give me a jubilant victory hug. I didn't want to touch him—all that sweat.]

Story #2: Three Plumbers Wring the Washcloth

In my last year at Xerox Computer Services, the management became convinced that we needed to get into the "turnkey" system business. Although we were based in Marina Del Rey, California, XCS acquired a New Jersey company that sold distribution systems on DEC computers.

My assignment was to integrate the acquisition product into our field sales force, which consisted of 100 salespeople. They had been eagerly waiting for something "state-of-the-art" to sell. I felt we had to develop a sales model before we turned 100 salespeople loose with a new product on a new platform. My sales strategy was to form a team of five sales eagles, five support eagles, an administration eagle, and me—twelve people in all. Our mission the first year was to agressively sell the new product for a year and, by doing so, develop our selling model and stimulate the "greed gland" of the field sales force to the point where they all would want to sell it.

One of my salespeople, Michele Wrzesinski, now one of my *Solution Selling* affiliates, was working on a large opportunity—a prospective sale that totaled $500,000. The buyer was a privately held plumbing and pipe distribution business with $180 million in annual sales.

If you are one of three owners of a business selling $180 million annually, how are you doing? Get the picture? I do not know if you have ever looked at the plumbing and pipe business, but at that time there was not a standard order entry system on the planet capable of doing pipe order entry. This was because the plumbing pipe business has to account for inside diameters, outside diameters, and custom threads, plus there were special prices for special customers.

Of the $500,000 potential sale, $150,000 was allocated for a custom order entry system.

Again, I tell this story from my perspective.

[Michele entered my office. She was getting nervous about this large opportunity with the end of the quarter near.]

Michele: Mike, their VP of finance, Joe, is getting real nervous.

Mike: Good, what's his problem?

[I am happy that he is nervous because that means he has entered Phase III. A buyer only goes into Phase III with one alternative. I know it is ours to lose.]

Michele: He's really nervous that with all this custom code we've got built into this thing—he's worried that we don't have enough on-site hand-holding built in to the price to make it work properly.

Mike: Michele, what does he want? What do you think it will take to make Joe comfortable?

Michele: I don't know.

Mike: Well, call him up and talk with him. See if you can come up with some number.

[Michele came back into my office about 30 minutes later.]

Michele: Mike, I've got Joe on the phone. He says that if we'll bundle an extra 200 hours of hand-holding, he's ready to do business.

[Two hundred hours seems to be a standard buying ploy, but this is a true story. Joe, whom I had never met, wanted 200 hours.]

Mike: Are you sure, he's ready to do business?

Michele: Absolutely.

Mike: Give it to him.

[Michele rushed out and a few minutes later returned, very excited.]

Michele: We have an appointment for tomorrow morning at 11:00. It's contract signing time!

[Her eyes had the look of the hunter appraising its prey—in her case, a well-earned commission. A few minutes before 11 AM the next morning, Michele and I pull into their parking lot. Again, a red flag went up. Occupying the first three parking stalls are three Mercedes Benz "flagships!" One, two, three.]

As things unfolded, we are not going to meet *just* with Joe, the vice president, finance, but also with Jim, the chairman, and Roger, the president. They're in their mid-50s. Although everyone now worked and lived in Los Angeles, Joe, Jim, and Roger are originally from New York. Having worked on the East Coast for a number of years, I had immediate memories of previous negotiation sessions in which I had participated in New York and New Jersey. Each is wearing a thick gold chain on one wrist and a solid gold "max" Rolex watch on the other. These Rolex watches began their lives as solid gold watches, but you could not see the gold. They were completely covered by diamonds inlaid everywhere. There were diamonds on the watch face, diamonds all the way around the band—diamonds, diamonds everywhere! They are also wearing three carat pinkie rings. They are not wearing ties.

We shake hands with Joe, Jim, and Roger (fictitious names, if you haven't already guessed). I say to myself, "This is not going to be as easy as I thought it was." I did not believe this was the first time Joe, Jim, and Roger had worked over a salesman. I decided all I could do was pretend everything was normal, although everything certainly was not beginning normally. Why? Because we—Michele and I—had already given up 200 hours of consulting/training time! And we had *nothing* in return. How easily Joe gained those 200 hours.

This was *déjà vu*. I knew as soon as I met these three successful businessmen that we were in deep trouble. These buyers loved the ritual of the "wringing of the washcloth." I focused on the VP of finance, pretending everything was normal.]

Mike: Joe, Michele told me of your concern about the customization. She told me the two of you agreed that we'd put an extra 200 hours of support in, same price, and that you said you were ready to do business.

[I pulled out our contract from my briefcase, leaving the case open on the tabletop, and I pointed to the contract, gesturing at the changed lines.]

Mike: You can see that we've modified the contract. It's the same $500,000 price, and . . . here are your extra 200 hours.

[I slid the contract across the table over to Joe.]

Mike: So, let's do business.

[Joe recoiled as though the contract would burn him. He would not touch it. I pushed the contract closer to him. Joe backed away further.]

Joe: Mike, I'm not signing that.

Mike: I don't understand. What's going on?

Joe: No, you don't understand. I needed those 200 hours *just to have this meeting*.

[Michele and I both paled. Now what? What were we to do? He never told Michele on the telephone that the 200 hours were just to get the meeting. I decided to use the *silver bullet word*. My silver bullet word is *fair*. That word is so precious that I only use it two times in a whole sell cycle: once to get access to power, "Is that fair?" and the second time to get a contract signed.]

Mike: Joe, I'm sorry, but from my point of view, this is not *fair*. When I gave you those 200 hours, I did not understand the rules the way you *just now* explained to me. You did not tell us on the phone that those 200 hours were just to have this meeting. You did not say that. From my point of view, the only way that this can be *fair* is for me to *take back* those 200 hours.

[I reached across the table and—making sure Joe, Jim, and Roger watched my motions—pulled back the contract and put it in my briefcase, which remained on top of the table, closed the lid, and snapped the fasteners shut.]

Mike: Now, Joe, let's start over.

[I had watched Joe's eyes follow that contract coming back to me. Joe looked at Jim and Roger, Jim looked at Roger and Joe, and Roger looked at Jim and Joe. Joe, Jim, and Roger eventually all looked across the table at Michele and me.]

Postscript

Literally, within a few minutes, I gave Joe back the 200 hours and the deal was signed. *First*, Joe had to be convinced that he was getting the best deal. Once he saw that I was willing to pull back the contract and leave without doing business today, Joe became convinced he had the best deal.

Lesson 1: Protect Your Price

Protect your price. If you have to concede a thing, concede something other than price, something other than cash. Because, when you discount price, at least two bad things happen: First, you will be squeezed even more (I've said enough about this) and second, competing sellers find out eventually, and they will tell your other buyers. "Call the ABC Company. Ask them what they paid for that system. Bosworth gave them a 20 percent discount off the same price he gave you." If your competitors are smart, they'll beat you over the head with it. They have nothing to lose—they did not get the deal in the first place. Protect your price.

Lesson 2: Don't Give without Getting

Do not give without getting. If you have to concede something, first make the buyer concede something, because, if you give something up and the buyer does not, the buyer will scoop those chips off the table and say, "Yes, we're getting closer, but we're not there yet." The only reliable way to end the squeezing is to take something away from the buyer, too. Memorize the following phrase: "The only way I could do something for you is if you could do something for me in return." The buyer will invariably answer, "Like what?" Now you are in the driver's seat to quickly and profitably end the negotiation.

Lesson 3: The Seller Has to Draw the Line First

If you learn one thing only, learn *the seller has to draw the line first.* The seller should give reluctantly and slowly, because the buyer must appreciate the seller's dripping.

Why did I take three stands in the first role play? Yes, they were prepared ahead of time. So why do it? Because, when I take Stands #1 and #2, something dynamic happens: a line is drawn in the sand. The buyer needs to wring the washcloth and see nothing come out. It is part of the process.

So Stands #1 and #2 are necessary to stop the wringing of the washcloth. Although such stands contain practical, logical business reasons, their real importance is that they tell the buyer the seller is taking a stand. Each stand, each nuance, each gesture is a signal to the buyer saying, "Stop. I, the seller, am drawing a line, taking a stand, stopping the wringing of the washcloth."

At the beginning of the meeting, Frank said, "Your price is unacceptable." If, at the first moment he squeezed me, I replied, "Okay, Frank, what if I throw in an extra 200 hours of Ralph's time? Would that help?" Frank would have jumped on that saying, "Yes, that helps, Mike, but we're still far apart. Far apart." In my prenegotiation planning, I prepared to give those 200 hours, but not until the buyer came up dry a couple of times. Why? Because he would not have appreciated them. He had to work for them. Its part of the *process.* By the time he got them, he appreciated them.

Practice price negotiation role plays, because it is something you must do at least 17 times before it will become a habit. Learn to say, *"The only way I can do something for you is if you can do something for me first."* Most buyers will say, *"Like what?"* Then you get to demand what you want—first, before you have to concede anything. There is an important sequence to it.

NEGOTIATING INVOLVES PLANNING

In both stories we had a written plan agreed upon by the buyer. We had helped the buyer justify the cost. We had created vision. We had done it right: from need development to vision to closing to commitment.

If a seller has sold correctly, despite fierce negotiation, that seller can usually expect to get the business. The buyer and the seller are in alignment. The seller will still have to withstand some squeezing, but that is part of selling.

It takes courage and resolve to withstand the squeezing. The seller's emotional hurdle is to withstand the squeezing—at least to take three good squeezes before price is negotiated.

This point bears repeating, so I repeat it. Who has to stop the dripping? You, the seller, do. The seller has to overcome his emotional hurdle, because the buyer will not stop wringing the washcloth until the seller resolves and asserts—first—"Enough, no more squeezing."

It's that simple.

Implement the *Solution Selling* Process

O, what a tangled web we weave
when first we practice to deceive.

William Shakespeare

SALES FORECASTS—THE "SUNSHINE PUMP"

Do salespeople like to do forecasts? No. Therefore, when they see their manager walking down the hall at forecast time, they rev up the "sunshine pump." The sunshine pump gives the manager bright sales forecasts: ones in which prospects have a "92 percent chance" of closing.

The sales manager explains that he needs the sales forecast. The seller hasn't sold anything for four months but promises that "this is the big month." Here comes the sunshine. "Company X *loves* us," the seller explains. "They love our technology—92 percent chance of closing." "Company Y has at least an 88 percent chance of closing."

What is the seller's mission? To get his sales manager off his back for the next 30 days. (Some companies are so out of control they do a *weekly* forecast.) Once a seller has worked for a manager for about three months, he learns which combination of words and phrases can get the sales manager excited. He learns how to get the sales manager off his back with his sunshine pump.

Does that sales manager have to do his own forecast? Sure he does. So he massages the seller's sales forecast, takes the 92 percent sunshine and downgrades to 88 percent. Then he pumps it up to the next level, using his own sunshine pump.

How useful is that forecast by the time it finally reaches top management? How accurate was it at the first level? And they are not done yet. Now they have to answer specific questions: When a prospect does not close when predicted, why didn't it happen? When will it happen? What's going on? Think about the fax machine, voice mail, administrative effort, and selling and management time devoted to this monthly (or weekly) fiasco! I see companies wasting 15 to 20 percent of their potential selling time each month priming the sunshine pump and asking Why didn't it happen? questions—month after month after month—without ever receiving any hard answers.

I believe the driving force behind the monthly (or weekly) hysteria is the gut level belief by senior executives that the front line sellers really have very little *control* over when a piece of business will really close. This feeling is reinforced each month when they see forecasted business get moved out another time period. I ask sellers, "If you could tell your senior management that Prospect A will close in June, Prospect B in August, and Prospect C in September, and be *right*, wouldn't they leave you alone?"

Solution Selling is about control. The buyer feels in control because he is not being pressured to do something he is not ready to do. Sellers feel in control because they can anticipate buyer behavioral changes as they facilitate the buy cycle—so they can keep better control over both their positive and negative emotions. Managers also gain control through *Solution Selling* as they implement it in their organization. How? By successfully predicting future business.

Top management and first line management support are required to successfully implement *Solution Selling*. Most first line sales managers readily admit to me that they achieved their position because of their ability to sell—their intuitive ability to sell. Most of them are eagles who now find themselves having to manage a group of sellers composed mostly of journeymen. Journeymen sellers need a map to follow. They need a defined process. They need to be managed on a regular basis.

What do I mean by managed? Most sales managers operate within the same model as their former sales manager did: "What are you going to close this month?" "I want to see your top five opportunities and I want a daily status on each of them until the end of the quarter." I believe this style of management is counterproductive.

When you were in college, did you "cram" for exams? Most of us did, and we seem to have carried this bad habit into our working lives. Many managers "cram" the quarterly bookings, shipments, or revenues into the last 10 days of the quarter. When we plot the sales order booking patterns for the year, it looks like four "hockey sticks." One negative outcome of this behavior is that by procrastinating, our buyers now know when to get the best possible price out of us. Another negative outcome is that we do not build an effective organizational selling model. We fail to manage our "pipeline," we predict future business inaccurately, and our revenues are unnecessarily uneven from one period to the next.

A major knock on American business executives, when they are compared to Japanese business executives, is that they are too "short-term" oriented. The Japanese are more willing to sacrifice short-term results for long-term gain. In this strategy, I am going to give you some techniques for balancing the long term with the short term.

THE FARMER IS YOUR MODEL

If you're a farmer and you want a good crop in August, what must you do? You have to plan ahead: soil improvement, tilling, seeding—they are all done in the spring. The farmer does the bulk of the work on the front end. He manages, nurtures, tends on the front end and then waits for everything to grow.

For salespeople, the sell cycle is the growing season. If a salesperson can plant enough seeds, nurture and tend those seeds, plan for damage, he can harvest his crop at the end of the growing season without cramming. As with the farmer, sellers have to plan out one growing season, but, in many cases, salespeople need to plant new crops each month.

Focus on two items: (1) the number of qualified prospects in your sales pipeline and (2) their status in the sales process. How many have you got, how would you grade them, and what are the chances that you can close each prospect?

Shakespeare understood the sunshine pump. Many salespeople, sales managers, and sales executives deceive themselves as well as others—usually not intentionally—and wherever I go, I see salespeople spinning tangled webs of deception and inaccuracy regarding their prospects, pipelines, and forecasts. This wastes resources, wastes time, and causes stress. Honest prospect appraisal and sales management—by both sellers and their com-

FIGURE 15
Letter Edit Stamp

1. Critical Issue:
2. Reasons:
3. Vision:
4. Agree to Explore: ☐ Yes   ☐ No
5. Bargain/Hooks: ☐ Yes   ☐ No
6. Proof/Plan Proposal: ☐ Yes   ☐ No

pany—can result in proactive selling, greater sales, increased profits, and a lot less anxiety.

EDIT LETTERS

The first step in managing the sales process is to bring management as close to the action as possible. Since managers cannot go on every call with their salespeople, they should edit the follow-up letters. I recommend that any "call" for which a salesperson is credited should have a letter to the buyer summarizing that call. Many of our clients are now using an "edit stamp" to reinforce the *Solution Selling* process. When we edit a letter we look for

- The buyer's critical issue (his pain).
- The reasons for the pain.
- The buyer's action vision.
- Confirmation that the buyer has agreed to explore further.
- Documentation of the bargain for access to power.
- Organizational interdependence or "hooks."
- The proof or plan proposal.

Follow-up letters are the manager's "audit" for the qualification of the buying process.

A salesperson can get creative on internal call reports and forecast forms, but the letter he writes to his buyer should be a realistic summary of what transpired. Figure 15 is a representation of the stamp many of our clients are using. We typically ask sales managers to fax us some letters after they edit them during the first 30 days of implementation after the training. We find that they too need some management assistance early in the process.

FIGURE 16
Milestones

T	Territory	☐ In assigned territory
S	Qualified suspect	☐ Interested in your company ☐ Meets marketing criteria ☐ Potential sponsor identified
D	Qualified sponsor	☐ Pain admitted to by sponsor ☐ Vision created for sponsor ☐ Sponsor agreed to explore ☐ Access to power negotiated ☐ Agreed to above in writing
C	Qualified power sponsor	☐ Access to power person ☐ Pain admitted to by power person ☐ Vision created for power person ☐ Power person agreed to explore ☐ Sequence of events proposed ☐ Sequence of events agreed on
B	Decision due	☐ Evaluation plan completed ☐ Preproposal review conducted ☐ Asked for the business ☐ Proposal issued, decision due
A	Pending sale	☐ Verbal approval received ☐ Contract negotiation in process
W	Win	☐ Signed documents
L	Loss	☐ Update prospect database

GRADE YOUR PIPELINE

I use Milestones™ to grade the status of a pipeline. The purpose of Milestones (see Figure 16) is to enable sales executives to view all prospects via a consistent grading system.

Feel free to customize this. About 80 percent of my clients use Milestones grades as explained and illustrated below; the other 20 percent modify them to better fit their business. There are eight grades: T, S, D, C, B, A, W, and L.

T   Territory.   This means the prospect is in your assigned sales territory.

Using Solution
Selling phone
scripts, our clients
report "conversion
rates"—of moving a
T prospect to an S
milestone status—
of from 22 to 98
percent. One
telemarketing sales
rep in an integrated
voice response
business actually has
a 98 percent interest
rate. The average
our clients report is
slightly under 50
percent, which is
far better than
most sellers.

S   Qualified suspect.   It's a suspect if a potential buyer (that meets your marketing criteria) has shown curiosity or interest.

Perhaps a returned "bingo card."

If you made a cold-call phone call using your phone script and the prospect showed interest, then you have a qualified suspect. Or perhaps you met a prospect at a trade show. Somebody called and told you somebody is looking and you contacted them and confirmed their interest in buying.

Frequently, a buyer who formerly bought from you changed jobs and called you up again. If they are interested in your product or service, they meet your marketing criteria, and a potential sponsor is identified, then they are a qualified suspect.

D   Qualified sponsor.   You have a qualified sponsor when the buyer accepts the sponsor letter, which contains six key components: admitted pain, reasons, vision, agreement to explore, bargain for access to power, and proof proposal. I tell my clients that D prospects will close about 20 percent of the time.

C   Qualified power sponsor.   You have a qualified power sponsor when you have access to a power person and your power person has admitted pain, has a vision, has agreed to explore your product or service, and has accepted ownership of the proposed sequence of events with specific go/no-go points and time frames. Your chances of closing a beginning C is 50 percent and gets better with each completed "go" decision. They stay a C until we attempt to close them for the first time. Typically, we close for the first time at the preproposal review—a week before the buyer expects to be closed. Once you attempt to close, the grade changes. Four things can happen: decision due, pending sale, win, or loss.

Note: Four things
can happen when
you attempt to close.
    Agreement to
buy. If they agree to
buy and sign your
purchase order or
your agreement,
then you grade your
buyer a W.
    Turndown. This
is the worst thing
that can happen.
They say no. There-
fore, you put it on
your loss report.
You grade your
buyer an L and
move on to your
next prospect.

B   Decision due.   You have a decision due if, for some reason, your guard was down on the preproposal review day, you completed the plan, you did the preproposal review, you asked for the business, but they said, "Bring us back the proposal next week." You bring the proposal back a week later and they take it and say, "We're going to give this serious consideration. We'll let you know." What's happened? Your prospect has your proposal—the final one, not the preproposal—and you have nothing except the promise of a decision. How much control do you have at that point? Zero. This grade carries a poor probability of success: 10 percent. It might be less. Why? Because you have no control once the buyer has the "final" proposal. All you can do is drop by once a week and ask, "How's it going?"

A Pending sale. You have a pending sale when you have verbal approval (no ink). The buyer looked you in the eye, confirmed he was going to buy, but said he had a few things to work out before he signs the agreement. At this point you have about a 90 percent probability of winning.

W Win. The agreement is signed.

L Loss. It's time to update your database and move on. You lost. Close the file and move on to better prospects and learn by your mistakes. Get back to prospecting.

A major hurdle for my new clients is having the "stomach" to grade their existing prospects using these Milestones. Many discover they have lots of Ss and Bs and very few honest Ds and Cs. A recent new client shared with me that his "pipeline" went from $88 million to $9 million when he applied this grading system. It can be a harsh reality check.

The Milestones can be adapted. Banks and service businesses have made adaptations so that their pipeline/activity summaries and grades match what's going on in their business.

SALES MANAGEMENT TOOLS

We suggest four tools: a first call debriefing log, a prospect qualification form (PQW), a call log, and a pipeline/activity summary. These four tools are easy to learn and practical, and each supports the *Solution Selling* process.

A number of "sales force automation" software companies are in various stages of adding a *Solution Selling* module to their packages. They have realized that it is much easier to sell sales productivity software to organizations when that software supports an organizational selling model. Many of my clients are excited about the software. They realize that the software itself helps to provide an "infrastructure" that makes successful implementation of *Solution Selling* much easier. With the infrastructure in place, top management can easily audit the process with a minimum of time and effort. And when first line managers know that top management has

Conditional agreement to buy. You get a verbal approval, "This looks good, Mike, but there are still a couple of things we have to work out." It might be the discount structure or the terms or the provisions for training. Something like that. There's still a negotiation in process. You grade your buyer an A.

Decision due. Your buyer asks you to type it up and return it. When you do, he takes it from you and tells you that he will give it "serious consideration." You grade your buyer a B. You have little control at this point.

a "window" into their pipeline, they tend to focus more on building a quality pipeline and less on their sunshine pumps.

Let's look at each of these four tools.

First Call Debriefing Log

A key benefit of *Solution Selling* is that it provides a model for first line managers to reinforce the process. We tell our workshop audiences that the key to making *Solution Selling* a habit is to get their calls debriefed and their letters reviewed by their managers. An effective call debriefing requires the seller to describe the six elements that should be in his sponsor or plan letter.

Figure 17 shows a section of the first call debriefing log. We ask sales managers to edit the letters, ask the questions, and record the answers: it's their diary of their seller's ability to qualify needs and the buying process. The editing and review process must support the selling process through the critical first 30–60 days after the training.

The Prospect Qualification Worksheet

The Prospect Qualification Worksheet™ (the "PQW") is the "audit" for the qualification of the needs of the entire buying committee. When does the seller fill out the PQW? It should be filled out by the seller the first time he needs another person from his company to get involved with his buyer. It is a one-page summary of the key decision makers, their pains, reasons, vision, and interdependence. For many of my clients, it is the "ticket" for technical support. It enables each additional person involved to build on the past events. It enables the seller to continue to build and enhance his buyer's vision over time. It prevents the seller from being in the embarrassing position of repeatedly asking the buyer to once again explain to the seller's management why they are looking at this product or service. It enables senior managers who are involved at the end of the sell cycle to appear to be closely involved with the buyer's situation with a minimal investment of time.

Examine our sample PQW in Figure 18. It contains key prospect information: on January 10th, 1993, it was graded **D**: the sponsor and power sponsor have admitted pain and have a vision of a solution. We can also begin to see the organizational interdependence and that the seller still needs to interview three more key people.

FIGURE 17
First Call Debriefing Log

FIRST CALL DEBRIEFING LOG

Manager:_____   Sales Representative:_____

Date	Company/Division		Name & Title		Power Person
Pain:		Reasons:		Capabilities Needed:	
Date	Company/Division		Name & Title		Power Person
Pain:		Reasons:		Capabilities Needed:	
Date	Company/Division		Name & Title		Power Person
Pain:		Reasons:		Capabilities Needed:	
Date	Company/Division		Name & Title		Power Person
Pain:		Reasons:		Capabilities Needed:	
Date	Company/Division		Name & Title		Power Person
Pain:		Reasons:		Capabilities Needed:	
Date	Company/Division		Name & Title		Power Person
Pain:		Reasons:		Capabilities Needed:	

Call Log

I am a proponent of a call log in which the seller logs each significant sales call: it could be a phone call, a face-to-face call—whatever
your company defines as a *real* sales call. A *real* sales call on the
phone, in my opinion, is when the seller was able to take the buyer
through the 9 Boxes. A *real* face-to-face call is when there was an appointment, a written call objective prior to the call, and a follow-up
letter. In either case, a letter should be sent to the buyer (and edited
by the manager).

Let's go through some of columns in the call log (see Figure 19):

FIGURE 18
PQW Example

Date	Sales Representative Bill Hart		Account Name ABC Manufacturing Co.		Business Unit	
Prospect # 0438	Rep # 078	Applic # MRP II	Status (Check one) [X] D [ ] C [ ] B [ ] A			
			Date	1/10/93		

Name/Title Sponsor:	Critical Issues (Pain) Note critical business issues with	Value ($K/Yr)	Reasons for Pain (Problems)	Others Affected (Integration)	Qualified Needs (Visualized solutions)
Steve Jones Materials Manager Other Key Players:	Excessive shortages	$1,000K	Inaccurate inventory Uncontroleed ECNs Last-minute changes in priority by sales executives	VP Sales - Missed customer deliveries VP Mfg - Missing shipment schedule VP Finance - profit & revenue are off	Audit inventory weekly for accuracy Be control point on all ECNs Show VP Sales impact of propsed changes
Jim Smith - VP Manufacturing Jack Berman - VP Sales Don Jones - VP Finance Bill Watkins - D of MIS	Missing shipment schedule Late deliveries to customers Missed revenue targets, eroding profits Unhappy line VPs	$5,000K	Shortages, priority changes by sales, can't plan production	Same as above	Steve Jones must be able to control shortages Need ability to stimulate capacity utilization

Approval	Decision Criteria/Pain	Requirement
Technical Approver Bill Watkins	Pressure to downsize operation	Client/Server environment
Legal Approver Outside		
Administrative Approver NA		
Financial Approver Don Jones	Formal value justification will be required	ROI must be within 15 months

Name & Title, Call #, Status, Call Objective, and Outcome/ Comments. Each column records key selling information that the seller and the manager can use. After we have examined each column, I will take you through an actual, partially completed call log.

Name & Title. This column lets you record at what levels in your prospect's organization you have called: sponsor, power sponsor, beneficiary, administrative—legal, operations.

Call #. How many calls have been made on this potential opportunity? Is this the first time, the second time, the thirtieth time, or the eighty-seventh time? You may have one large client—for example, AT&T—where five different salespeople from your company are selling products or services to three or five different

FIGURE 19
Sample Call Log

Sales Representative: _____John Doe_____ Week _____2/14/92_____

Date	Company/Division	Name & Title	Call #	Status	Call Objective	Outcome/Comments
2/10/94	ABC Manufacturing	Steve Jones - Material Mgr	1	S	Qualify as sponsor	Letter to confirm!
2/11/94	XYZ Manufacturing	Ron Bush - Controller	13	B	Follow up on 12/27 proposal	No decision yet.
2/11/94	DEF Co.	Steve James - VP Finance	6	C	Calculate payback -ROI.	9-month payback— looks good!
2/12/94	DEF Co.	S.J.-Fin; B.B.-Mfg; R.L.-Mktg; B.W.-MIS	7	C	Site visit -Crown Mfg.	Went well, PPR planned for next week.
2/13/94	GHI Co.	Kathy van Pelt - Project Leader	1	S	Qualify lead, gain access to power.	No go, PL insists it's her sole decision & on full control.
2/14/94	JKL Co.	John O'Donohue - VP Finance	11	A	Finalize leasing arrangements.	Pick up contract 2/18!
2/14/94	MNO Co.	Keith Eades - Materials Mgr.	2	D	Proof demonstration.	Go! Appointment with VP Manufacturing next week.

departments. Count these as separate opportunities, and each salesperson keeps his own call log.

Status. Record each prospect's Milestones grade or status at the *beginning* of the call: D, C, B, or A. We typically have to help managers assign the proper status early in an implementation.

Call Objective. Depending on the purpose of the call and whom the seller is meeting, the call objective should have something to do with moving the sell cycle process forward. For example, if the seller has a prospect at a C status (accepted schedule of events), then the call objective is likely to reflect the next step in getting to an agreement to buy. A "red flag" for which we look is too many calls that are showing activity versus progress.

Call Outcome/Comments.   What happened? What was the outcome? Truthful comments will let the seller—and the manager—decide whether he is on course, off course, or wasting time, or needs to make some special effort to save the opportunity.

When we discuss balancing pipeline with activity, a key element in that discussion will be the number of total calls and first calls per month per seller. The call log is an excellent source of this information. If our client has automated *Solution Selling*, these numbers get automatically summarized and sent to the pipeline/activity management system.

Sample Call Log, Some Analysis

The call log is a strong, simple sales management tool. Examine Figure 19, Sample Call Log. Analyze a week in the life of fictitious John Doe.

On February 7, 1994, John Doe made a call on Steve Jones, the materials manager, at ABC Manufacturing. It was a first call—an S status, a suspect: Steve had shown some interest in John Doe's company, he met the marketing criteria, and a potential sponsor was identified. John's call objective was to qualify Steve Jones as sponsor. The outcome was that John sent Steve a confirming letter (sponsor letter). The next time you see the ABC Company on John Doe's call log, the status will be D. That's because on that call he took Steve through need development and created a vision of a solution. He got agreement to explore further, bargained for access to power, and confirmed all of this in his sponsor letter.

On February 8, 1994, John Doe called on Ron Bush, the controller at XYZ Manufacturing. This is the thirteenth call on a B!—a follow-up call on a proposal dated 12/27/93—and the outcome is no decision yet. If you are John's manager, what are you going to advise? Declare it a loss, stop wasting time, and move on. (Probably not all 13 calls were made on the controller, but it was the thirteenth call on the opportunity.)

The second call on February 8, 1994, promises better results. John called on Steve James, the VP of finance at DEF Company. It was the sixth call on a C. What does that mean? The simplest way to analyze a C is to conclude that John has a truly qualified prospect: he's dealing with the *power* to buy, admitted *pain*, a *vision* created for a power person, and an agreed-upon *plan* with an accepted schedule of events. Those are the four key elements of a truly qualified prospect.

The purpose of the meeting was to calculate the payback, which resulted in a nine-month payback. In John's words, it looks good.

The second call on the DEF Company on February 9, 1994—the next day—indicates John is simply progressing through his schedule of events. In this instance, four people representing finance, manufacturing, marketing, and MIS made a visit to one of John's clients to prove his product. It went well and a preproposal review was planned for the coming week. This C is progressing and, by the end of next week, it should be either an A or a W.

On February 10, 1994, John conducted a first call with Kathy van Pelt, a project leader at the GHI Company, which was a bust. Why did John make a first call on a project leader? The answer is that on the day Kathy called John's company, the regular receptionist was sick and a temporary services person operated the switchboard. Kathy van Pelt called and said she wanted to speak with a salesperson. She was put directly through to John. (The regular receptionist would have known never to do that.) Therefore, John had to take the call. This prospect was graded S—a no-go deal, despite Kathy van Pelt's insistence that it was her decision and that she had full control: everyone knows a project leader can't buy. But John should not end there; after a cool-down period of a week, he should cold call "above the line" and try to come back to her via a power person.

February 8, 1994, John Doe called on an A. What's an A? A verbal approval, but no ink. It cannot be a win until you have ink: a check or a signed purchase order. John Doe and John O'Donohue, the VP of finance of JKL Company, finalized leasing arrangements. After 11 calls, he was told to pick up the signed contract on February 18th.

And last, on February 11, 1994, John met with Keith Eades, the materials manager at MNO Company. It was his second call on a D status prospect. What's John's objective? A proof demo. How did he do? He got a "go" decision. Because Keith agreed that John proved it, he now has the appointment with the VP, manufacturing. Keith kept his bargain. After next week's call, what will the grade be? If you answered D, you are right. It will stay a D until the VP of manufacturing—John's power sponsor—admits pain, has a vision, receives a plan letter with a proposed schedule of events, and agrees to the plan and schedule. It must stay a D until John has a qualified power sponsor. That's why C's have such a good chance of closing: you have a truly qualified prospect—power, pain, vision, and an agreed-upon plan.

Balancing Activity with Quality Pipeline: A "Farming" Algorithm

I promised you, earlier in this strategy, some ideas on balancing the long term with the short term. I work with my clients to manage pipeline ("long term") and prospecting activity ("short term") on a monthly basis, regardless of the length of their sell cycle. What we try to do is *balance* quality pipeline with prospecting activity by creating a "farming algorithm."

The *C pipeline* is the long term component of our farming algorithm. If you remember, a C has *power*, *pain*, *vision*, and an agreed-upon *plan*. If a seller has a strong C pipeline, he can ease up on the prospecting. If he has a weak C pipeline, he should be actively prospecting: direct mail, cold calls, seminars, and so on.

First calls are the short term component of our farming algorithm. If you remember, most of my clients record a first call if either

- The seller took the buyer through the 9 Boxes *on the phone* and followed the call with a letter, documenting the pain, reasons, impact, and vision.

or

- The seller had an appointment, a documented call objective, and a letter summarizing whatever happened on the call.

In either case, the "audit" on the first call is the follow-up letter.

We help our clients create a custom tailored farming algorithm designed to help them balance the long term with the short term on a monthly basis. We initially create one for an organization, but with automation and some performance history, we can eventually create custom farming algorithms for each *individual* salesperson. This algorithm, for instance, could enable you to calculate your prospecting requirements—given an assigned monthly sales quota, the length of your sale cycle, the probability of closing a C prospect, and the minimum first call prospecting requirements needed to maintain each salesperson's C pipeline.

Let's build a farming algorithm for a fictitious software company.

> Annual quota per salesperson: $1.2 million ($100,000/month)
> Average sale: $300K
> Sell cycle: 6 months (one "growing season")
> Probability of closing a C: 50 percent

So, if I am a salesperson for this company, my quota for one sell cycle of six months is $600,000 (or $100,000/month). If I know I will close 50 percent of my C pipeline, how much will I always need in my C pipeline to cover quota for one growing season? $1.2 million. Therefore, the goal for C pipeline dollars is $1.2 million. We want every salesperson to always have $1.2 million in Cs. That means, if you have a 50 percent close rate on Cs and you close an order for $300K, you have to add another $600K that month. If you don't have $600K to add to your C pipeline that month, you have to make up the difference in first calls.

The vice president of sales of our fictitious company feels very strongly about continuous prospecting. He does not want any seller to completely forget how to pick up the phone and call a stranger no matter how strong his C pipeline is. He therefore insists on a *minimum* of three first calls each month per salesperson.

In this particular case we will use these two key variables to make our farming algorithm: minimum first calls per month and targeted C pipeline dollars.

This is about apples and oranges. If we add apples (first calls) and oranges (C pipeline dollars)

Goal #1: Minimum # of first calls   3
Goal #2: C pipeline dollars target ($M)   <u>1.2</u>
    The "farming algorithm" target becomes   15
    because ignoring the decimal in 1.2 makes it 12. 3 plus 12 equals 15.

Bear with me and watch what happens. Let's look at two sales-people, John Doe and Mary Smith. Assume that seller John Doe has been "dogging it." When his manager reviewed his monthly pipeline versus his monthly activity (see below), he only has $500,000 ($.5M) in his C pipeline against a target of $1.2M. In order for his first calls and C pipeline to "add" up to 15, John would need 10 first calls this month.

If Mary Smith decided to convert from customer support to sales and in her first month selling had a zero ($0M) C pipeline, she would have to make 15 first calls this month.

	Target	John Doe	Mary Smith
C pipeline dollars	1.2	.5	0
First calls this month	3	10	15
Farming algorithm	15	15	15

Some clients customize their farming algorithms for each salesperson because they have compiled a history of the individual "conversion rates" of Ss into Ds and Ds into Cs—for each seller.

Not all of our clients use first calls and C pipeline dollars. The variables must be meaningful to your business.

Monthly Pipeline/Activity Report

Once a month, each manager can sit down with each salesperson and in a 30- to 60-minute meeting take a "snapshot" of the seller's pipeline and activity. Here's a sample monthly pipeline/activity summary report. Let's examine the numbers in Figure 20 for each of Ned Daily's five salespeople and see what we can learn.

Let's start with Dave B. Since he has no C prospects, according to his farming algorithm, Dave should have made 15 first calls, but he made 3. Do we have a prospecting problem? He has a satisfactory number of total calls, but too few first calls. He has many suspects, but only 2 D prospects and no C prospects, indicating poor need development and qualification skills. YTD sales are $200,000 versus a YTD quota of $500,000. His career prospects are poor. I recommend he dramatically increase his first call prospecting and his manager accompany him on these calls to assess his ability to develop needs and qualify buyers. A decision on whether or not to keep Dave B. can be made in 30 days.

Brad N. is new with the company. He missed his farming algorithm target, but he spent eight days in training. He has only one D prospect and, although he has a reasonable number of first calls and suspects, he is having difficulty in qualifying needs and buyers. His B prospect represents an outstanding proposal delivered by his predecessor that is over three months old. Brad's manager should observe some first calls, give him a tag-team guru for need processing, consistently debrief his first calls, and edit his prospect control letters.

Susan H. has an ideal pipeline. (Her first calls and C pipeline add up to 16.) Her C pipeline exceeds her annual quota, and she has four more D prospects right behind her Cs. Susan is able to develop and qualify needs, which is the *Solution Selling* key skill. She has no B prospects, which shows she is an eagle. Eagles don't leave proposals with prospects who now owe them decisions.

Mike T. appears to have a qualifying problem. He has many suspects, one D, *no* Cs, and *four* outstanding proposals (Bs), which indicate that Mike is proposing prematurely. His B prospects probably lack access to power, pain, and vision. Mike should take back all outstanding proposals and see if he can develop needs and personal

FIGURE 20
Sample Monthly Pipeline/Activity Summary

Manager: _____ Ned Daily _____   Month Ending: _____ 5/31/94 _____

		Sales Rep: Dave B.	Sales Rep: Brad N.	Sales Rep: Susan H.	Sales Rep: Mike T.	Sales Rep: Gordon J.
Total Calls	#	23	11	24	25	13
First Calls	#	3	9	3	4	0
Territory	#	120	110	115	112	123
Suspects	#	14	11	5	9	2
D Prospects	#	2	1	4	1	3
D Prospects	$	400K	150K	700K	200K	500K
C Prospects	#	0	0	5	0	1
C Prospects	$	0	0	1300K	0	1500K
B Prospects	#	0	1	0	4	0
B Prospects	$	0	200K	0	900K	0
A Prospects	#	0	0	1	0	0
A Prospects	$	0	0	200K	0	0
MTD Business Booked	$	0	0	150K	0	0
YTD Business Booked	$	200K	on board 3 months	800K	150K	600K
Short-Term Activity Recommended:		Performance plan; 15 first calls in June with guru or sales manager	Send guru out on next 10 need-development calls to "tag team" with Brad.	Leave her alone!	Manager to take over outstanding proposals over 30 days old; 15 first calls in June.	No more than 50% of time on "elephant," move Ds to C; 5 first calls in June.

credibility. His manager will probably have to help him. He should have made 15 first calls this month; however, he made only four, so prospecting will have to be a bigger priority next month.

Gordon J.'s C pipeline exceeds his annual quota, which allows him to achieve his farming algorithm. In spite of his first calls and C pipeline adding up to 15, I see two red flags: his entire C pipeline is made up of *one* prospect and there are *no* first calls—Gordon has completely quit prospecting. All his eggs are in one basket. He is hunting the big one—one that will make him rich and famous. Gordon is an "elephant hunter." He should spend no more than 50 percent of his time on his large C prospect, convert the three D prospects to C, and make 10 first calls in the next 30 days. Gordon must rebuild his pipeline. If he doesn't, even if he closes his "elephant," he will be looking for another job next year.

The previous example is designed to demonstrate that even in a long sell cycle environment, "farming" can be done on a monthly basis. We are shifting the primary focus of the first line manager from "cramming" ("What are you going to close this month") to helping salespeople build a quality pipeline. That quality pipeline has something that is very useful to senior management—scheduled and completed go/no-go steps in a written plan approved by the buyer. This will be the foundation of an accurate sales forecast.

FORECASTING

We talked earlier about the "sunshine pump" and the monthly hysteria. Is there a better way to forecast? I believe there is. I don't think salespeople should do forecasts at all! My idea is that once each month, after the sales manager has had his 30–60 minute meeting with each salesperson, the sales *manager*—not the salesperson—updates a forecasting database.

The first line manager should go through each seller's pipeline and adjust the database to reflect current status: additions, deletions, changes such as changing a prospect's status from a D to a C, and so on. The manager (not the seller) should assign the pipeline grades based on personally reviewing the Milestones.

Look at Figure 21. The information is pretty basic. Most of it is self-explanatory, but there are a few subtleties. Estimate $ versus Actual $ allows us to see which of our managers is the best negotiator. Total go/no-go steps in plan and Completed go/no-go steps allow us to compute a percent complete on our C prospects. By asking for an earliest and latest estimated close date, we get a much better feel for the amount of control the seller feels he has. The Manager gut feel asks the manager to put his best guess as to whether the prospect will close. He has three choices: 25 percent, 50 percent, 75 percent—no other percentages, no in-betweens—just three choices.

If all first line managers updated this database for all of their salespeople once a month and the vice president of sales had access to that database with a report writer, could he do his own forecast? In other words, the only person in the company doing forecasts would be the VP of sales.

If I were a VP, sales, and I wanted to do a *pessimistic* forecast off such a database, I would ask the computer for only As and Cs that are at least 75 percent complete with the latest close date of this quarter and with a manager gut feel of 75 percent.

If I wanted to do a more *optimistic* forecast, I would ask the computer for the Bs, as well as the As and Cs, that are 60 percent complete with the earliest close date of this quarter and with a manager

FIGURE 21
Forecasting Database

Prospect name, address, contact, phone number
Prospect number
Status (S, D, C, B, A, Win, Loss)
Salesperson (branch, region, etc.)
Manager
Assigned quota
Product(s)
Estimated $
Actual $
Date of first call
Total calls-to-date
Length of sell cycle*
Total go/no-go steps in plan
Completed go/no-go steps
Percent complete*
Estimated earliest close date
Estimated latest close date
Actual close date
Competition
Manager gut feel (25%, 50%, 75%)

---

* Calculated

gut feel of 50 percent and above. Would I not get a very different list of prospects? Eventually, over a few months of trial and error, I would learn which view of my database is most predictive.

I am not the originator of this idea. One of my creative clients came up with the idea of the database. Here's the story using the *Solution Selling* reference story format.

Situation.   He was the SVP of a software company that at the time did about $150 million in sales.

Critical issue.   He was in deep trouble at the time. He was getting tremendous pressure from senior management. Their share price was getting hammered because analysts were criticizing the company for not being able to predict how much business they were going to close on a quarterly basis. He got demoted, figuratively speaking. They let him keep his office and his title but took away all of his direct reports. The region VPs now reported directly to the CEO. He was motivated to try something new.

Reasons.   He had region, district, and branch managers with a variety of backgrounds, selling models, and forecasting methods. Field salespeople hated doing forecasts and subsequently figured out how to "get their manager off their back" every 30 days.

Vision.   He told me he needed a way to view all prospects companywide via a consistent grading system that would reflect both quantity and *quality* of his pipeline.

Solution Selling **provided him with this capability.**   I trained his entire sales force in *Solution Selling*. His administrative assistant set up a forecasting database on a PC. They had a paper system in the field, and each month all of his first line managers would update the paper system and send the pipeline forms in to his assistant, who would key in the changes. He would run multiple "views" of that database and prepare his own forecast.

Result.   That year he never missed a quarterly forecast by more than $300,000. One quarter he was only $100,000 off. His quota was $175 million. He came in at $191 million. No salespeople did forecasts. No first line managers did forecasts. One person did the forecast. He did and he got his direct reports back.

Sounds great, right? Well it is, but there is a price to pay, and that price is *change*. In order for this forecasting methodology to work, some changes are necessary in the organization.

- First line managers must shift from pressuring sellers to close business this month to helping sellers build quality pipeline.

- Senior management must shift from pressuring field management to close business this month to encouraging them to build and accurately report quality pipeline.

- Compensation plans must motivate all managers to manage the process.

- The pipeline must be graded consistently and accurately across the entire organization—a C prospect in New Jersey must fit the exact same criteria as a C prospect in London or Los Angeles.

- Senior management must ask to see the pipeline on a regular basis—they must be willing to conduct periodic quality and consistency audits.

We've got one client where the CFO now does the forecast. Nobody in that sales organization even has to mess with it anymore. Field sales managers update the database; then the CFO goes in once a month and does the forecast.

AUTOMATING *SOLUTION SELLING*

A number of sales force automation software firms are now adding a *Solution Selling* module to their packages. By automating the forecast database, the PQW, Pain Sheets, Milestones, the call log, and the sponsor and plan letters, it is possible to add a new dimension to the decision-making ability of sellers, sales management, marketing, and senior management. "What ifs" can be answered with clarity, certainty, and accuracy. Here are some examples.

About the past, you can

- Benchmark and compare the patterns of successful and unsuccessful representatives, products, and organizations.
- Find differences in the life cycles of winning and losing prospects.
- Find points in the sell cycle where performance is being lost.

Common questions asked about the past are

- How much time and effort do we spend getting prospects through the Milestones? To win? To lose? Does it differ by branch? By competitor?
- What is the percentage chance of success at each Milestone—that is, at C or B or A by individual seller? By product? By branch?
- Can you recognize early signs of a winning or losing prospect?
- Where is our competition the weakest? The strongest?

About the present, you can

- Balance and maintain the pipeline by seller and organization.
- Rank managers by actual to estimate percentage.

Common questions asked about the present are

- What is the total probable value of the current pipeline? (Is it enough to meet quota?)
- How much is in the current pipeline at its various Milestone stages?

- Where are "stale" prospects "clogging up" the pipeline?
- On which prospects should I concentrate my efforts? Which ones should I drop?

About the future, you can

- Forecast the value and timing of orders with improved accuracy.

Common questions asked about the future are

- How much can we expect to win?
- When will it be won?
- How much do the sales reps/sales managers think will be won?

Such questions can be answered for a variety of pipelines: individual salespeople, a sales group or region, or the entire company. Information is available to all stakeholders in the sales process: CEOs, CFOs, executives, managers, and salespeople.

As I get new ideas, I communicate them to the sales force automation software companies. For instance, an area with which I now would like to see some help is computing actual cost of sales per seller. Some sellers use heavy resources to make the sale, some don't. If we could track this information, we might be able to create compensation plans that would pay sellers on true gross profit. I believe this would encourage sellers to operate more like stakeholders than employees.

Whether we manually implement *Solution Selling* or use automated tools, *Solution Selling* is a change not only in the selling process but in the sales management process. If systems didn't improve performance, most of my clients wouldn't have a business.

III

SOLUTION SELLING IN ACTION

Solution Selling has enabled both businesses and individuals to become more effective. In this section you see both. You will learn how my personal clients as well as clients of my associates have reengineered their organizational sales processes. You will meet executives dealing with serious organizational selling problems, and you will see examples of how individual sellers used *Solution Selling* to improve their own effectiveness. You will also see that the customer wins as well. By utilizing the *Solution Selling* concepts of vision, proper expectation levels, and ownership, you will see that the probability of customers succeeding with the products and services they buy from Solution Sellers increases as well. I will continue to use the *Solution Selling* success story format: situation, critical issue, reasons, vision, capabilities provided, and result. In future editions of this book, I hope to include many more examples of sales success, and I encourage you to write me and share your *Solution Selling* experiences with me.

Solution Selling
Reference Stories

Most people don't want to be first; most people won't even go to a movie or read a book without a recommendation from someone they trust.

DEMAX Software

AT&T Global Business Communications Systems

National Computer Systems

Lawson Software

TRW Business Credit Services

Shared Systems Corporation

Information Mapping, Inc.

Zymark Corporation

Keane, Inc.

Great Western Bank Retail Banking Group

Wheat, First Securities, Inc.

IMRS

Lucas Management Systems

REFERENCE STORIES

People naturally resist change. The laws of inertia apply to people as well. *Solution Selling* requires behavioral change by *both* sellers and managers. We talk about sellers having the courage to "branch to door" when the buyer is not meeting them halfway. Managers have to have courage as well: the courage to persist in the face of resistance to change.

There are two emotional hurdles executives frequently encounter when attempting to implement *Solution Selling*. The first is the willingness to hold salespeople accountable for vision processing and buyer qualification *before* corporate resources are spent trying to land the business. The second is the reality check they face the first time they grade their existing pipelines with the *Solution Selling* Milestones.

The following stories are examples of executives and managers having the courage to reengineer their corporate selling and managing models. There are also some examples of how front line sellers have used *Solution Selling* to close business. These stories were submitted to me by executives, salespeople, and *Solution Selling* licensed affiliates. In this section I want to share with you examples of success some organizations have had implementing *Solution Selling*.

DEMAX Software

Mike "Mac" McLoughlin, licensed *Solution Selling* affiliate, spent over 20 years in the information technology industry. His experience encompasses operations, software development, sales, and marketing. Since 1991, he has focused almost exclusively on helping companies learn and implement the principles of *Solution Selling.* He has developed custom *Solution Selling* course materials for many companies, helping them to learn the *Solution Selling* process while using their own products and services as examples. Mac prepared the value justification exercise in Appendix C. He has a BS degree in economics and an MBA.

DEMAX Software operated eight offices worldwide, including the main headquarters in San Mateo, California. DEMAX sold application software to major corporations that helped them maintain security from a central location over a wide network of computers. Mike McLoughlin and I jointly worked with DEMAX Software and their CEO, Richard Earnest.

Richard Earnest was president and CEO of DEMAX Software until July 1993, when DEMAX was acquired by Open Vision Technologies. Richard now serves as a consultant for that company. Richard has 20 years' experience in the information processing industry, the last 9 of which have been in the capacity of COO or CEO. He attended the US Naval Academy, receiving a BS in engineering, and also holds an MS from the Naval Post Graduate School.

Situation. DEMAX had approximately 55 employees, which included a sales department of approximately 18 people.

Critical issue. The company's pricing structure and resultant sales productivity were slowly draining the company's cash position, threatening its survival.

Reasons. Mac, Richard, and I came up with a number of reasons for the problems:

- There was *no* sales process in place and no way to determine why they were or were not successful. They had no repeatable model.
- There had been high turnover in the sales force and no continuity within accounts. This lengthened an already long

sell cycle with no predictability for closing and subsequent forecasting.
- Low productivity meant low incomes for the sales staff, and this caused difficulty in attracting top performers.
- Selling was being conducted at a low level in the buyer organization and targeted at a very tactical audience. "Feature wars" were the name of the game. This led to deep discounting and adding capabilities to the products that weren't necessary.
- Management reporting was nonexistent, and decisions regarding competition and marketing positioning were guesses.
- Many of the salespeople were inexperienced and had no formal sales training of any kind in their careers.
- The company had a great reputation for its technology and with its customers but could not seem to differentiate itself from other vendors.

Vision. Richard told us DEMAX sellers needed a way to differentiate themselves through the sales process itself. He wanted his people to be taught to get to higher level buyers in prospect companies. He said he needed to get the average sale raised from $15K to $55K in order for the company to reach its financial goals. He needed to be able to do this without adding products and only marginally raising prices.

Solution Selling gave Richard these capabilities. He and his VP sales attended an open *Solution Selling* workshop conducted by Mac McLoughlin and me in Del Mar, California. They decided that it provided the capabilities they needed. Rather than just train the sales staff, however, Richard felt that the very survival of the company was at stake and a new way of communicating critical issues could be achieved through the *Solution Selling* process. Richard put everyone who directly or indirectly touched a customer through the training. This included marketing, customer support, administration, and all the executives. Key executives attended the course first and became the role play coaches for the rest of the DEMAX people at the company training.

Result. The initial discoveries were predictable yet disturbing. Their "pipeline" upon which they were relying was dramatically reduced once graded via the *Solution Selling* Milestones. Richard discovered that they had been spending time on prospects who would *never* buy and had not been getting to those who *needed* to buy.

The sell cycle became shorter and the sales became much larger. Management now had the ability to predict future business with much more certainty. Morale of the sales force improved with their increased success. DEMAX created a new playing field in their market by changing the way they were selling. The company was acquired shortly after the training, but a number of significant events occurred in a short time:

- A relatively new salesperson closed the biggest sale in company history, which proved to be material in the acquisition negotiations.
- Success was demonstrated in a remote office where it was believed the process would not work.
- After the acquisition, the *Solution Selling*–trained salespeople continued their success and became critical to the performance of the acquiring organization.
- The decision to undergo the implementation literally saved DEMAX.

A quote from Richard Earnest when asked what lessons were learned:

The most effective lesson to take advantage of in the *Solution Selling* process was getting commitment from the top. And I mean from the CEO. Everyone in the company is involved in the sales process and it is the most important activity of any company. If the CEO doesn't understand the need to take a hands-on leadership role in this, the results will be diluted. Don't let the CEO tell you he or she doesn't have time to take the course. They don't have time NOT to!!

AT&T Global Business Communications Systems

Bob Populorum, licensed *Solution Selling* affiliate, received a Bachelor of Science degree in psychology from Northwestern University. He began his career in the information technology field in 1966. Bob held positions as sales representative, sales manager, branch manager, region manager, general manager, and manager of market planning at IBM, Xerox Computer Services (where I first met Bob in 1974), and System Software Associates. One of Bob's *Solution Selling* clients is AT&T Global Business Communications Systems.

AT&T Global Business Communications Systems (GBCS) develops, manufactures, sells, and services telecommunications systems for small and large businesses nationally and in fifty countries worldwide. A market leader in business communications, GBCS would rank approximately 130 in the Fortune 500 listing—were it a stand-alone company.

GBCS is staffed by more than 25,000 associates who work in over 800 locations around the world. It is dedicated to providing the highest quality business communications products, services, and solutions. To achieve its goals, this AT&T business unit offers a full line of systems to meet ever-increasing sophisticated and global needs of its customers.

A number of GBCS salespeople have attended the *Solution Selling* workshop conducted by Bob Populorum. Here is an example of how a GBCS seller was able to use the process to land an account.

AUTOMOTIVE PARTS MANUFACTURER

Situation. Carol, a GBCS sales representative, was attempting to increase business with the communications systems manager of a manufacturer and supplier of automotive products to automotive manufacturers.

Critical issue. Eroding profits were causing pressure on this manager to reduce the increasing acquisition costs of communications systems and of operating such systems.

Reasons. Because of automotive industry price pressure on purchases of automotive parts manufacturers, the company had decided not to purchase any more communications equipment. An additional problem for the seller was that the company was unhappy with AT&T.

Vision. The system manager said that if she had a way to *prove* to her senior management that a communications system (that is, voice processing, telemarketing/call centers) would boost productivity, increase revenues, reduce operating expenses, and improve customer service, then she would introduce the AT&T GBCS salesperson to her company president.

Carol, using *Solution Selling* provided her with that proof.

Result. Following her *Solution Selling* sales methodology, Carol processed her buyer's needs, explored the impact, and then— with her buyer—mutually created a vision for a solution. By becoming a true allied resource of the system manager, she won the confidence of the buyer, who then took her to her president. Using *Solution Selling* techniques, she also won the president's support and was able to match AT&T's product capabilities with the buyer's requirements.

The resulting sale exceeded $400,000. AT&T GBCS sold a complete telemarketing system, including software and telephone upgrades. The seller is now discussing a $300,000 video conferencing system with the president.

National Computer Systems

Situation.   National Computer Systems (NCS) is one of my personal clients. NCS operates 14 offices nationally. It develops and sells education hardware and software products and services for education departments, districts, and schools. The NCS Education Systems Division employs over 200 people. Their vice president of sales is Bob Whelan.

Bob Whelan graduated from the University of Alabama. Therefore, it is not surprising that his idol is Paul "Bear" Bryant. He began working in Atlanta in the banking industry as a financial officer. He brought that expertise to the Financial Systems Division of NCS, selling trust systems to large banks. Bob moved to Minneapolis and has held various positions in the Education Systems Division of NCS for the last 12 years: from sales support manager and product manager to 3 years back in Georgia as the region manager of the number one NCS region, the Southern Region.

Critical issue.   Bob was charged with maintaining ESD's momentum and growth during its transition from a hardware-oriented company to a software/solutions company.

Reasons.   Four primary reasons for NCS's sales difficulties were identified: an unstructured selling process, lots of "feature" selling where the hardware demonstration was the primary selling vehicle, an increasing lengthy sell cycle, and, due to several recent mergers, using a variety of selling techniques and sales management reports in different regions.

Vision.   Bob said he needed a way to get the field salespeople to use a *consultative sale approach* as opposed to product "feature" selling. He was also looking for a way by which NCS could establish credibility as a comprehensive solutions provider in the education market. His ultimate goal was to help NCS grow revenues and profits at an established 20 percent annual goal.

Solution Selling provided Bob with these capabilities.

Results.   NCS trained over 200 sales organization staff, marketing personnel, product managers, customer support and training staff, development organization, and divisional executives over a six-month period in a customized *Solution Selling* program.

NCS has implemented a structured sales process allowing sales and support personnel to focus on the specific needs of each client. The company now uses a consultative selling approach that stresses building relationships with potential customers.

Sales cycles have been shortened for the more comprehensive, complex software products, and sales forecasting accuracy has improved by 50 percent.

What follows are NCS Education Systems Division sales success stories submitted by Jane Ehmiller, the director of training.

STORY #1: AN IMPOVERISHED SOUTHERN SCHOOL DISTRICT

Situation. Karen Condon is an experienced NCS Education sales representative who has been in business for more than a decade. Karen made a call on the director of curriculum of an impoverished school district in the South.

Critical issue. On the first call, Karen learned that the district was in desperate need of a way to identify students at risk of dropping out of school so that early intervention preventative measures could be taken. The district's loss of students was affecting their state and federal funding allocations. In turn, such losses limited the district's ability to upgrade programs to deter the continuing drop-out trend.

Reasons. Through a discussion of their reasons, the critical issue became even more complex than just the drop-out problem.

- The state had mandated that each district have an effective procedure in place for managing the instructional and assessment information for all students (not just the at-risk group), but the state had not allocated any funds to support this all-student assessment and instruction procedure.
- The district was already financially strapped.
- If the district did not comply, their state funding allocation would be cut.
- If their funding was cut, such action would impact all programs offered by the district, from community outreach services to extracurricular programs.
- Teachers were already working unpaid overtime trying to track student progress through a manual, paper-based record-keeping system.

- Because of unpaid overtime, teachers were threatening to demand overtime pay, which was not included in their current contract—and which the district did not have the funding to pay anyway.

Vision. The director of curriculum told Karen that if she had the ability to diagnose weak areas in a student's learning, then specific area remedial actions could be pursued, saving the student from having to repeat an entire year; and she said that this approach would meet state guidelines and reduce the drop-out rate.

She also said that she needed a way to use multiple methods of assessment for diagnosing student progress as part of the state mandate.

She agreed that if she had a way to minimize the drop-out rate while complying with the state mandates, it would have a positive effect on the district's monetary allocations.

She said if NCS could prove that she could get the capability to monitor each student's progress through a computerized process—tracking individual learning objectives by subject and grade level and identifying at-risk students—and provide immediate appropriate instruction to bring students up to grade level and track their achievements using multiple types of assessment, then she would sponsor NCS at a school board meeting.

Karen used *Solution Selling* to discover these needs and provide these capabilities.

Results. NCS helped the director of curriculum calculate a value justification and set up success criteria with her school board to track their success and to make adjustments. Early warning measures were put into place and were able to pinpoint deficient areas of instruction, and immediate remedial steps were implemented.

Within two years of implementation, the graduation rate is currently 90 percent and funding has increased accordingly.

A personal note from Karen Condon:

If I had used my former sales approach, the sell cycle would have been much longer, but—more importantly—I would not have known about the underlying issues which contributed to this impoverished school district's problems. Nor would I have been able to position NCS to provide the capabilities needed by all of the district staff to work with the multitude of student learning and district financial issues that surfaced.

STORY #2: A LARGE SCHOOL DISTRICT

Situation. The first sales call on the director of technology of a large school district ended in *no action*. The seller then attended an NCS *Solution Selling* workshop. Determined to try again, she was successful in arranging a second meeting—only this time using her *Solution Selling* sales tools.

Critical issue. The district was under pressure to fully integrate—not just automate—district financial and student information to ensure accuracy of data reported to the state. Because of past discrepancies in reported data, the state threatened audits of the district books with direct implications on funding allocations and their management.

Reasons. Cash disbursements, payroll, fixed asset inventory, bank reconciliation, class scheduling, and report cards were all processed on an outdated computer system no longer supported by the original vendor.

- Software for these applications had been written for another school district and were maintained by a local software company.
- Changes in federal or state laws required the school district to seek program coding changes by the local software company.
- At the school level, non-networked PCs were used to record student attendance data; however, at the district level, such information was rekeyed manually, at which point errors occurred.
- Because the state suspected the district's accuracy, the district was required to maintain two sets of this manual data.
- The associate superintendent of curriculum and many principals were involved, and they reported an increasing need to have access to the district's databases for planning and reporting purposes.
- Their shared attitude can best be summed up by the deputy superintendent's words: "We perceive ourselves to be like Indianapolis 500 drivers trying to compete for limited state funding using soap box cars held together by Band-Aids and bailing wire."

Vision. The director of technology said he needed technology that was "integrated," not "isolated." He said that if he could get a data processing system that would allow all departments to utilize, share, and communicate commonly needed data, then they could solve their problems.

NCS provided these capabilities. Incidentally, because of the consultative relationship the seller had formed with many people on the district's buying committee, NCS was able to provide *proof* through research on written information, presentations, and site visits to other school districts of similar enrollment.

Results. The school district purchased the entire NCS software module line. Following implementation of the NCS system, all school buildings were connected to the central system; district personnel could enter transactions in a real-time mode, inquire into relevant data instantly, and prepare and route the building reports necessary to operate their departments efficiently.

The state has approved the automated system and dropped its requirement for a manual backup system: the deputy superintendent took all the attendance secretaries to a victory lunch.

The ability of the NCS system to customize reports has saved the district money previously paid to the local software company for system updates. The district takes great pride in being able to solve their own problems.

STORY #3: A FAST-GROWING SCHOOL DISTRICT

Situation. The seller, Nancy Fortenberry, was about to make yet another call on the assistant superintendent of a once-remote, small school district who found himself being rapidly overwhelmed by the growth of a nearby large city. Prior to *Solution Selling*, Nancy had only provided information; she had not created *pain*. She had not brought the assistant superintendent and his buying committee from latent pain to admitted pain. This time she diagnosed their real needs and was able to assist them in creating visions of solutions to their problems.

Critical issue. The assistant superintendent knew he needed to upgrade his systems, but viewed himself as having the "inability to purchase an updated, automated system."

Reasons.

- District budgets were currently based on a historic no-growth experience.

- Explosive growth of a nearby city was causing the school district to enter a phase of rapid growth. Almost overnight the district had become a bedroom community serving the larger city.

- The district's "leading edge" but small computerized administrative system suddenly became obsolete. Given its equipment architecture, it could not handle the new mass of data being generated. This had become especially problematic for their general ledger and payroll requirements.

- Old equipment leases, budgetary constraints, and political conservatism worked against their being able to purchase a newer, more capable system.

Vision. The buying committee agreed that if they could find a way to tie into their present equipment with upgraded software applications—they did not want to waste years of computer hardware equipment—and not have their budgets affected until a year hence, the school district would be able to take a look at NCS products and services. (How to afford such a system upgrade was important.)

(Note: Using *Solution Selling* tools, Nancy was able to create anxiety about the cost of *not* acting and the even greater costs that would be incurred if they did not solve the problem quickly. This was all based on facts and information that *they* supplied during her need development sessions.)

NCS provided the school district with those capabilities with flexible financing terms.

Results. The school district upgraded its administrative system to the newest IBM platform. Previously, IBM salespeople had been discouraged about their inability to sell equipment to the district; however, they agreed to accompany Nancy on her calls. They were amazed at her success.

The school district is now able to keep pace with growth. With this growth, state funding has grown so the district is financially healthy.

The assistant superintendent said simply, "Thank you for *helping me buy* my new system. . . . "

Lawson Software

Michele Wrzesinski is one of my *Solution Selling* affiliates. Michele has her M.A. in economics (University of California at Riverside) and has over 20 years of sales and sales management success, including Xerox Computer Services, where she achieved 160 percent or greater of her annual sales quota for five years. One of those years she worked for me. She also has worked for Martin Marietta Data Systems and Apple Computer. Michele's business expertise and *Solution Selling* clients include businesses and organizations that sell software, hardware, and professional services in the information technology industry.

Situation. Lawson Software, with 12 offices worldwide, is a global provider of business application software: accounting applications, human resources systems, distribution management systems, retail management systems, and materials management systems. Michele Wrzesinski was working with Don Slusarski, the vice president of sales. Don had seven regional managers who managed 65 account executives and product consultants. Don's salespeople sell business application software to Fortune 1000 companies.

Critical issue. Don was having difficulty meeting senior management's expectation of increased sales in the face of severe competition from other software providers.

Reasons. Michele and Don soon identified the following reasons:

- Their software products and services lacked differentiation from competing software.
- They were unable to position their strong technological advantages.
- Their salespeople sold "features/functions" in a mature, crowded marketplace.

Vision. Don Slusarski told Michele that if there were a way for his account executives to identify buyers' critical business issues, allowing them to participate in and create mutual visions of solutions, Lawson's strong technology could then be brought to bear on those buyer needs. He also needed a way for them to in-

crease the number of sales opportunities they could simultaneously manage. With these capabilities, then—despite a massively
crowded marketplace—he said Lawson could increase sales.

Solution Selling via Michele Wrzesinski provided these
capabilities.

Result. In one year Lawson Software increased its North
American sales by over 40 percent. Lawson salespeople are now
able to win accounts because they have learned the elements of
Solution Selling: They develop buyer need, create a mutually shared
vision of the solution, match those visions with their capabilities
and technology, and keep control of the buy cycle.

TRW Business Credit Services

In another Michele Wrzesinski client, TRW Business Credit Services (BCS), we found Merrylue Langdon, who eventually became a *Solution Selling* instructor.

Merrylue Langdon, as the national training manager, introduced Michele to BCS. Merrylue combines a background in education with sales experience. As a former secondary school administrator, she made the transition into the business world as a territory manager for a major pharmaceutical company. She holds a BA and MA in education and is currently completing a doctoral degree in institutional management at Pepperdine University. Merrylue is now a licensed *Solution Selling* affiliate.

Situation. TRW Business Credit Services is a division of TRW Information Systems & Services, based in Orange, California, which is a unit of TRW Inc. BCS provides commercial credit information on-line to businesses nationwide for the purposes of commercial risk management and evaluation.

Michele and Merrylue were working with Don Lavoie, vice president and general manager, TRW BCS. Prior to TRW, Don Lavoie spent 18 years in sales and marketing positions with Xerox Corporation. Most recently he was national sales manager for advanced products. Don holds three degrees: a BS in business administration (California State University); an MBA (Pepperdine University); and a PhD in business administration (Pacific Western University).

Critical issue. In 1989, BCS's sales performance was flat, which was hurting TRW's ability to grow profits and therefore the business. There was pressure from senior management to improve penetration in a market held by a well-entrenched competitor.

Reasons. TRW salespeople lacked situational knowledge necessary to reposition multiple complex products and services in a variety of industries, and the start-up time required for new hires was taking too long.

Vision. Don said he needed a standard process or "roadmap" for selling intangible, difficult-to-sell products and services in a variety of industries.

Solution Selling via Michele provided Don with these capabilities.

Results. They were able to improve new salesperson start-up time (time to first sale) from six months to two months, and reduce their average sell cycle from 45 days to 20. Additionally, TRW Business Credit Services has experienced significant increases in customer retention and satisfaction.

What follows are three actual TRW Business Credit Services reference stories where the seller utilized *Solution Selling*. These reference stories reflect TRW BCS's ability to interact with their customers on a business level rather than a product or feature level. BCS salespeople are now able to win accounts because they use the elements of *Solution Selling:* they develop buyer need, create mutually shared visions of solutions, don't lead with their company history and list of services, and keep control of the buy cycle.

STORY #1: A MAJOR AUTOMOTIVE CREDIT COMPANY

Situation. Tom Nance, an account executive, Midwest District, TRW BCS, called on an automotive credit company. Tom's prospect's situation involved the vice president of risk management and the supervisor of operations services.

Critical issue. The company was experiencing lost business opportunities and falling sales.

Reasons. The credit decision process was taking too long, and credit approval was processed through many different branch offices, resulting in highly subjective credit decisions. Their policy was to turn around a credit decision in one hour. In fact, it often took much longer, and credit politics interfered at many levels. These two factors—lost time and subjective decision making—were costing this credit company a great deal of money.

Vision. They said they needed an automated risk scoring system that would reflect their credit policies and produce a credit score with backup detail to speed up the decision-making process. They also wanted to ensure that each prospective credit application was analyzed using the same criteria.

TRW BCS provided these capabilities.

Result.   A customized product was developed for the large American automotive credit company and launched with amazing results: credit applications now have a one-hour or less turnaround and credit decisions are objective and standardized. Overall costs have been reduced and revenues have been increased.

STORY #2: COMPUTER AFFILIATE

Situation.   Jan Field, an account executive, Northwest District, TRW BCS, was calling on the CFO of a computer distributor.

Critical issue.   Credit losses combined with rising costs of processing credit applications and rising costs of collection processing adversely impacted profits.

Reasons.   The company had experienced a major increase in the volume—a doubling—of credit applications bringing smaller dollar value sales and rising credit risk, and their present provider's credit information was incomplete, which resulted in increased losses.

Vision.   He said if he could find a way to evaluate business risk, especially of smaller companies, and if he had the ability to integrate a proprietor's personal and business credit data, then he could reduce credit losses and improve profits.
TRW BCS provided these capabilities.

Result.   Using TRW BCS products and services, he was able to reduce his operational cost by 30 percent, which enabled them to increase their permanent credit processing staff by only one person, while cutting four temporary employees. And, significantly, by using TRW Business Profile, TRW Small Business Advisory Reports, and TRW Intelliscore, the computer affiliate cut its direct checking costs by 50 percent.

STORY #3: CERAMIC/GIFTWARE MANUFACTURER

Situation.   Bernice Campagnoni, and account executive, Southwest District, TRW BCS, called on the CFO of a major ceramics/giftware manufacturer.

Critical issue. The high cost of obtaining credit approvals on sales was impacting gross profits.

Reasons. Their current credit information provider supplied very poor, often no credit data on the manufacturer's buyers. This was because most of the manufacturer's buyers were small gift shops that did not have an established credit history. The company had to rely on its own slow, costly internal manual credit processing, which took two days per transaction—averaging $2,000 per purchase order.

Vision. He said he needed the ability to compare these small accounts against a statistical model of predictive business credit variables that assigns a credit risk score to the account, with backup data to support the score.
TRW BCS gave him that capability.

Result. He was able to achieve a *60 percent* hit rate, more than doubling their previous hit rate, and it reduced their credit decision turnaround time from two days to about one hour. They now process an average of 10 applications a day. They can now update over 14,000 accounts automatically and on a same-day basis. Overall sales have improved dramatically.

Shared Systems Corporation

This story is from one of my personal clients.

Situation. Shared Financial Systems, now known as Shared Systems Corporation, was founded in 1982 to develop and deliver on-line transaction processing software to drive the banking industry's new, at the time, automated teller machines (ATMs). Currently, the company provides OLTP software, consulting services, and systems integration for more than 325 banking, retail, and health care customers in 46 countries. Revenues are $25 million.

Phil Yarbrough is senior vice president of sales and marketing for Shared Systems Corp. Prior to joining Shared in 1990, Phil was president/COO of CompuTrac, and VP/general manager of BankTec corporation.

Critical issue. Sales goals were not being met. The sell cycle was too long. Phil's cost of sales was too high, they had numerous losses to "no decision," and he had high turnover in his sales force.

Reasons. Phil and I came up with the following reasons:

- 80 percent of "lost" sales were to "no decision," not to competitors.
- Salespeople were selling at technical levels rather than to decision makers, requiring expensive "multi-legged" sales calls.
- Too many proposals were being sent to unqualified "prospects" with little or no results.

Vision. Phil told me that he needed a way to lower his cost of sales while shortening the sell cycle and improving his salesperson's closing ratios.

Solution Selling provided Phil with the capabilities he needed. Phil put all of his field managers, application support people, salespeople, and marketing people through the *Solution Selling* workshop.

Result. Close ratios initially improved from 12 to 23 percent. Cost of sales dropped 24 percent. Sell cycles shortened from 18–24 months to 6–12 months within two years. Turnover within the sales force decreased from 50 percent per year to less than 10 percent over a two-year period, and for the 1993 fiscal year, 17 percent of his salespeople had already achieved quota by the end of the FY93 third quarter.

Information Mapping Inc.

Mary Ann Cluggish is a licensed *Solution Selling* affiliate located in Wellesley, Massachusetts. Formerly a vice president of sales and marketing at Information Mapping, Inc. (IMI), in Waltham, Massachusetts, Mary Ann introduced *Solution Selling* to IMI. She was so impressed with her results after implementing the process that she became a *Solution Selling* affiliate. Mary Ann effectively led her division, increasing revenues by more than 40 percent for 7 years.

With over 15 years of sales experience, Mary Ann has sold financial services, medical products, and real estate. She is a frequent speaker at national and regional sales conferences.

Situation. Information Mapping, Inc., sells training and consulting services. The core product is a methodology for simplifying and restructuring complex technical information and presenting it in an easy-to-access visual form. Doug Gorman is their president.

Critical issue. Sell cycles were averaging five to nine plus months or more. New hires were taking over six months to make their first big sale.

Reasons. Mary Ann and Doug discussed the situation and came up with these reasons:

- Products and services were intangible and difficult to sell.
- IMI was a new and unknown company.
- IMI was selling to the Fortune 1000 and high technology companies.
- Salespeople were calling too low.

Vision. Doug Gorman and Mary Ann needed a way to shorten the learning curve for his new salespeople and they needed a selling methodology for selling intangible, sophisticated services. They also wanted to find a way for their salespeople to shorten the sell cycle and be comfortable discussing business issues with senior executives.

Solution Selling provided them with these capabilities.

Result.   After implementation of *Solution Selling* sales and sales management training, new hires began to bring in their first significant sales in about six weeks. Sell cycles now average 2.5 months instead of 6 months. IMI has experienced consistent growth of over 30 percent annually in both revenues and profits. They have also established a significant market presence and are known as the industry leader.

Zymark Corporation

Situation. Another Mary Ann Cluggish client, Michael J. Marshall is the senior vice president of sales at Zymark Corporation, located in Hopkington, Massachusetts. Zymark is a laboratory robotics manufacturer that sells primarily to the pharmaceutical and petrochemical industries.

Critical issue. Only 31 percent of sales reps were making their sales goals.

Reasons. Mary Ann and Michael came up with a list of reasons why so few sellers were achieving their goals:

- Products were technically sophisticated.
- Sellers had technical backgrounds.
- Selling was being addressed to laboratory end users.
- Sellers were selling technical features.
- Sale cycles were usually long—over six months.

Vision. Michael Marshall told Mary Ann that he needed a way to get his sales force calling higher—on top management—and to get his sales reps comfortable discussing business issues, not just technical issues and product features. He also said he wanted them to be able to translate highly technical products into business solutions.

Solution Selling via Mary Ann provided him with these capabilities.

Result. After one year of implementing *Solution Selling* sales methodology and sales management training, over 60 percent of Zymark's sales reps made their sales goals. Bookings have increased at the rate of 27 percent annually in a flat market. The company's domestic growth has gone from $17 million per year to $28 million in three years.

Keane, Inc.

Situation. Mary Ann Cluggish worked with Ray Becker, who is vice president of Keane, Inc., located in Boston, Massachusetts. Keane sells software development services to a wide range of industries.

Critical issue. Keane was having difficulty selling new sophisticated consulting services.

Reasons. Ray and Mary Ann came up with the following reasons:

- Only five or six consultants understood the new services well enough to sell them. The bulk of the sales force was not familiar with the new services.
- At the time, Keane had over 15 branch offices located across the United States; therefore, travel and training were costly.
- The consultants were traveling extensively selling the new services and also explaining them to Keane's sales force: each consultant was working up to 80 hours per week.

Vision. Ray Becker said that he needed a way to leverage the expertise of the few who understood the new services, to get branch offices trained to sell the new services, and to enhance the sales of their traditional service lines while the new services were being launched.
Solution Selling via Mary Ann Cluggish provided him with these capabilities.

Result. Within six months of training, all of the branches were able to handle selling the new services with the support of only one consultant. Within one year, the new services became a routine part of Keane's consulting services, and in two years became responsible for 30 to 40 percent of revenue.

Great Western Bank Retail Banking Group

Howard Eaton is a licensed *Solution Selling* affiliate who specializes in the financial services arena. He has over 28 years' experience in business covering a number of industries: financial services (banking—international, retail, wholesale, and mortgage), investment banking, commercial real estate, information technology, and publishing. His first 18 years were spent in banking, including positions as COO and CEO. He helped start two banks that achieved top quartile performance. His years of business experience plus the knowledge he obtained from *Solution Selling* seminars inspired Howard to become a licensed affiliate.

Situation.   Great Western Bank (GWB) is a multi-regional, consumer-oriented financial services company focused on mortgage lending. Total assets exceed $38 billion. Insured by the FDIC, Great Western Bank operates more than 1,100 retail banking, mortgage lending, and consumer finance offices nationwide.

Phil Altman, senior vice president, branch administration, discovered *Solution Selling* at a breakfast briefing at Stanford University and introduced it to his bank. Phil is responsible for GWB's retail branch administration in California. Other key GWB people include

- Michele Maddock, first vice president, Management Services Department.
- Randy Wellen, senior vice president, Florida.
- Mike Struzik, vice president, Training and Development, California.

Critical issue.   Retail buyers object to bank products early in the sales call and resist switching banks. Existing customers resist additional products and services cross-selling.

Reasons.   Several GWB participants and Howard Eaton mutually identified that banking generally—and retail banking specifically—suffers common reasons for buyer objections and resistance to bank selling. Four prominent reasons account for GWB's critical issue:

- Buyers see bank products as *undifferentiated*—that is, all banks' retail products and services are believed to contain generally the same features.

- Buyers believe, generally, that banks offer products and services *without personal service.*
- Feature selling results in buyer objections, as opposed to creating curiosity.
- Almost all prospects are already banking at another bank, and, despite their unhappiness, prospective buyers are reluctant to switch to a better-service, better-relationship bank. This reluctance occurs even when lower prices and/or higher interest rates are offered.

Vision.   Phil and his three-member buying committee said to Howard that if there was a way for the bank to *prove* that it could differentiate itself from other banks *by the way it sells,* then the bank would be able to attract more new customers and increase its cross-sales of related retail banking products and services, such as checking accounts, CDs, money-market accounts, savings accounts, business checking services, direct deposit, and payroll services.

Solution Selling via Howard Eaton provided this capability in the form of a pilot program.

Result.   Great Western Bank's participating salespeople now make *the way they sell* as much of an advantage as their products' and services' benefits. Salespeople in the pilot program no longer lead with their products and services. They hold them back as *proof.* More customers and prospects alike are buying the bank's retail products and services.

Salespeople—from FSRs/FSAs up to top management—are finding that their buyers object less, volunteer more personal financial information, and are buying more bank products and services. Comments from GWB *Solution Selling*–trained sellers form part of our measurement. Here are typical comments about the bank's pilot sales training and post-training activity:

In 26 years of commercial banking, I have attended numerous sales seminars . . . None has had the immediate impact on me as *Solution Selling.* [A vice president, region manager.]

Now I know how to avoid no, and how to get to Is there any reason we can't do business today? [An FSA.]

After the course, [a VP, branch manager] made 84 phone calls and got a 50 percent interest rate in the bank's products. He's doing great. He's setting the example for all of us. [A vice president, training.]

Now I understand that selling is a process from beginning to close. [An FSR.]

Although the benchmark periods of the bank's pilot program are not yet fully completed and analyzed, the early results are encouraging. Regional reports show certain branch phone prospecting up by over 200 percent. Face-to-face meetings are up over 100 percent. Cross-selling is more commonplace, and the bank's branch participants enthusiastically report encouraging progress with their buyers.

Wheat, First Securities, Inc.

Phil McCrory is a licensed *Solution Selling* affiliate located in Charlotte, North Carolina. Phil has experience in the financial services industry as a salesperson, sales manager, and manager of corporate marketing. Phil has used this background to help expand *Solution Selling* from information technology to financial services and professional practices.

Situation.   Wheat, First Securities, Inc., and its sister company, Butcher & Singer, were founded in 1934. They are headquartered in Richmond, Virginia, and are the largest stock brokerage firm in the Mid-Atlantic region with over 800 financial consultants in 92 offices. Christopher Davis, CFP and senior vice president, has 12 years' experience with Wheat and is one of those financial consultants.

Critical issue.   Chris felt he was not growing his business enough for someone with his years of experience.

Reasons.   Phil and Chris discussed several selling problems they believed contributed to the slow growth:

- Chris was telling people about stocks in which they were not interested.
- He knew he wasn't listening carefully enough to the needs of his clients and prospects.
- He was spending too much time on small accounts.
- He found himself reacting more to what his prospects said they needed.

Vision.   Chris said he needed to be able to position himself more as a problem solver than a product seller. He also said he needed to be able to listen better to his clients—to have the patience to truly understand their needs *before* he made recommendations.

Solution Selling via Phil McCrory gave him these capabilities. Chris attended one of Phil's "open" workshops.

Result.   Out of 800+ financial consultants, Chris moved into the top 10 percent in revenue generated. All financial consultants that have been in the field for 9–12 months and who have opened a minimum number of accounts are now being trained in *Solution Selling.*

IMRS

Keith Eades was my first licensed affiliate, starting his *Solution Selling* business in 1988. Keith knows first hand the enormous effect *Solution Selling* has on increasing sales effectiveness. While employed as director of training, Keith was responsible for implementing *Solution Selling* at Management Science America (MSA). Prior to MSA, Keith was the number one salesperson in the nation for Milliken and Company. Keith's *Solution Selling* client list includes D&B Software, Software 2000, Computer Task Group, EDS, and the following company, IMRS.

Situation.   Headquartered in Stamford, Connecticut, IMRS® develops, markets, and supports financial management applications for enterprise client/server environments. They offer a wide variety of financial software products, as well as a complete range of support and training services. Keith was working with David Sample, senior vice president of IMRS. David is responsible for the sales function in North America plus all international business. He joined IMRS in 1986 as vice president of sales. He was promoted to senior vice president in 1993. Prior to IMRS, David worked for Control Data Corporation. He has a BA in history from Trinity College.

Critical issue.   IMRS was losing market share; it had slipped to 60 percent.

Reasons.   David and Keith came up with the following reasons:

- Increased competition was pulling them into "feature wars."
- IMRS lacked a corporate framework for consultative-type selling.
- Sellers were having difficulty selling high-priced value-added capabilities in a price-sensitive market.

Vision.   David told Keith he needed his salespeople to sell more than just features. He said he needed a consultative-type methodology that would differentiate IMRS not just with technology, but by their approach and by the solution actually delivered.

Solution Selling via Keith Eades gave David Sample these capabilities. IMRS has trained all their salespeople, sales support, sales management, and marketing personnel either by in-house programs or at open *Solution Selling* workshops for the past four years. Additionally, they continue to reinforce the process on a regular basis at their sales meetings.

Result. Over the past four years, despite increasing competition, IMRS has been able to capture close to 80 percent of their market share. They have also been able to maintain price stability and reduce the average length of their sell cycle.

Lucas Management Systems

Bob Junke is one of my *Solution Selling* affiliates. Bob brings over 15 years of experience in the management consulting, information technology, communication technology, and systems integration industries (including 10 years of sales and sales management experience) to his *Solution Selling* clients. His prior experience includes Andersen Consulting and Computer Task Group. While at CTG, he became exposed to *Solution Selling* and implemented it in the division he headed.

Situation.   Lucas Management Systems (LMS), a division of UK–based Lucas Industries Plc, is in the business of providing project management software and related services to a variety of industries. LMS was founded in 1977. Since that time, LMS has had strong, steady growth: revenues in 1992 exceeded $100 million. LMS was rated as one of the world's top 50 software companies by *SOFTWARE*™ magazine. The company employs over 600 people in over 40 offices worldwide.

Jon Swain is a programme manager with LMS. He has worked with LMS for the past six years. He began his career as a salesperson, and three years ago was promoted from PC business unit manager to programme manager. He has responsibility for approximately one-third of all UK income.

Critical issue.   Jon was facing an increasing challenge to make profit goals in a highly competitive marketplace.

Reasons.   Bob and Jon came up with the following reasons:

- Inconsistent approaches to selling and qualification in particular.
- Inconsistent methods of communicating prospect and pipeline status to senior executives.
- Difficulty in differentiating themselves from their competition.
- Inability to repeat successes.

Vision.   Jon told Bob he needed a sales model for the organization that would provide him with a consistent, repeatable set of sales processes. He also said he needed a way to uniformly conduct prospect reviews, allocate support resources, and accurately and predictably manage their pipeline and forecast.

Solution Selling via Bob Junke gave Jon these capabilities.

Result. By applying *Solution Selling* techniques, the day after a four-day workshop, Rob Legge, a member of Jon's team, closed a £23K consulting engagement six weeks earlier than forecasted. As a group, during their first year of using *Solution Selling*, they achieved 132 percent of quota. During their second year, even though their quota increased significantly, they achieved 120 percent of quota. Jon Swain also received his most recent promotion.

Getting Started with *Solution Selling*

What can you do to get started with *Solution Selling?* Decide to start right away. Don't put it off. Here some suggestions.

During the next week, convert your top three prospects to a full C status: pain, power, vision, and plan. Also, take the time to sit down, create a good telephone script using a *Solution Selling* sample telephone script, and make 20 cold calls. And *take back* all inactive proposals over 30 days old.

Within the first month, establish your own "farming algorithm"—and start farming. Using the Milestones, honestly grade all of your prospect opportunities. Build a C pipeline to *Solution Selling* standards. Begin to include written value justification as a standard element in your C status pipeline accounts. And get someone to debrief at least 17 of your vision processing calls.

Here is further explanation on the above points.

FIRST WEEK

Convert top three opportunities to C status. How many of your prospects are not going as well as they should? Take your top three opportunities, ones in which you have invested blood, sweat, and tears. Make a copy of the letter edit stamp (Figure 15). Now apply to these top three opportunities the elements of the edit stamp—pain, reasons, vision, access to power, others impacted, evaluation plan. What will you discover when you do this? Missing information? Information critical to the sale? Information critical for your buyer to be able to buy?

Telephone your prospect, review your file with him, and say, "I've been reviewing my file on you and I see that we've been at this four months. I'm losing my focus. Would you spend a few minutes with me and help me to get refocused?" Your prospect will agree. You have a relationship. What is your purpose for doing this? To take him through the 9 Boxes. And what happens after you take your prospect through the boxes on the telephone? If he has the power to buy, you can send him a control letter confirming his primary critical issue, the reasons, the key capabilities he needs to deal with his problem, and a proposed sequence of events schedule— yes, even if your proposed sequence only has two steps.

In most cases, you can do this over the phone. It will not require a face-to-face visit. And in a lot of cases, it's *better* to do this over the telephone, because if you have to take somebody through the boxes, you can have your pain sheet and strategic prompter in front of you on your desk. You will probably be more successful on the telephone.

The primary two reasons we see buyers languishing in the "Land of No Decision" are lack of vision and lack of value justification. By taking your prospect through the 9 Boxes, you can help your buyer accomplish both.

Make three vision processing calls and debrief. Separate from the first step, make three vision creation calls on new prospects. And do it soon, because you will lose your new ability to take people through the boxes if you do not do it soon.

If you have a serious intent to use these 9 Boxes, I suggest you get a commitment from someone, preferably your first line manager or someone with whom you work closely, and practice role plays of going through the boxes. Further, ask him to debrief your first 17 calls—no less than 17—after you have resolved to take your buyers through the 9 Boxes. Have him use the call debriefing log.

If you don't have someone to debrief you, what will happen? You will forget. You are going to slide back into your old habits, your old ways, and selling difficulties will remain.

Create a phone script and make 20 cold calls. I recommend that you make 20 telephone calls—most eagles do this weekly. If you don't try the phone script next week, what will happen? The probability of you ever trying it again will drop dramatically for each subsequent week you delay. Procrastination is the unsuccessful salesperson's greatest bad habit.

Take back any proposals over 30 days old. How do you take back a proposal? The best way is to send the buyer a letter saying, "I was going through my file and I reread the proposal I sent you six weeks ago. I am embarrassed to say that in reviewing it I realize that I did not do a good job for you. That proposal is now *null and void*. I'd like an opportunity to make it up to you and to do a better job for you. I'll call you in a couple of days." Send those letters out.

After they receive such "take backs," if your prospects do not call, guess what? That opportunity is gone. Take it off your prospect list. Still, in a number of instances, they'll call and ask what's wrong with the proposal, or something to that effect. Then you can say, "I realize that though I sent you a proposal, I did not have a good understanding of your primary critical issue from your perspective. I'm embarrassed to tell you that." Then take him through the 9 Boxes. In most cases, those proposals are hanging around with no action because your buyer has no vision and no value justification. No wonder your buyer couldn't take action!

FIRST MONTH

Establish farming algorithm.   Depending on your sales objectives, establish the minimum number of first calls you will have to make so your C pipeline will be sufficient. Go back and read Strategy 10 so you can balance the short term with the long term.

Honestly grade all opportunities.   This is a major hurdle for most salespeople and managers starting to use *Solution Selling*. Honestly grade all existing opportunities against those Milestones at which we just looked.

Build a C pipeline to a standard.   I don't need to say more about this, except: Just do it.

Attempt written value justification for all Cs.   Go back to Strategy 7, "Advance the Buyer's Vision with Value Justification." Study how to do one incorporating *Solution Selling* principles. Make sure all measurements are owned by your prospect—this is no time for your ego—and make value justification a habit. When incorporated into your sales strategy and tactics, value justification will increase your success rate.

Debrief at least 17 vision processing calls. Steven Covey, in his book *The 7 Habits of Highly Effective People*, says to develop a habit, you need to integrate knowledge (what to, why to) with skills (how to) with desire (want to). He also says, "Creating a habit requires hard work in all three areas . . . It's sometimes a painful process. It's a change that has to be motivated by a higher purpose, by the willingness to subordinate what you think you want now for what you want later."

The number 17 is not magic. Some say more; others say less. I say for you to develop new habits, you've got to have the desire to stay out of your comfort zone 17 times. Avoid "winging" those 17 calls. What's going to motivate you to not "wing it"? Ideally, it's the belief that, if you sell the *Solution Selling* way, you will have more control, less stress, more wins, and more money.

Sample Value Justification Presentation

The following sample value justification was created by Mike "Mac" McLoughlin, one of my distributors. (Mac's bio is in Part III of this book.) Mike prepared it for a company selling software that supports *Solution Selling*. As you go through it, remember the concept of ownership and discover the answers to the following questions:

- What will be measured?
- Who is responsible?
- How much is possible?
- What capabilities will be needed?
- When will this investment pay for itself?

The scenario we have is an anonymous sales force automation software company attempting to sell its software to a fictitious project management software company with 106 direct salespeople.

SAMPLE VALUE JUSTIFICATION EXERCISE

Current Environment

X-Y-Z Software, Inc., is a 10-year-old company that specializes in project management software applications. The sales staff consists of 106 direct salespeople who are located in nine district offices. Not one of the direct sales offices was within 20 percent of their quarterly forecasts for the last year, and the international distributors did not prepare forecasts. In June 1992, at the semiannual sales meeting, the CEO announced that the direct sales staff and all distributors would be required to produce *accurate monthly* sales forecasts. During this last six months of the year, sales revenue decreased by 11 percent from the same period of the prior year. According to the district sales managers, sales were declining because the sales staff were spending too much time doing their monthly sales forecasts and were not selling enough project management software.

Four X-Y-Z clerks work full time on compiling the sales data and producing the monthly forecast reports. Because the management team wants the reports issued no later than three working days after the end of the month, the clerks will have to work 75 hours of overtime each month. Additionally, the cost to bring the international distributors into the process will require three additional clerks. The clerks make $10 per hour base pay with overtime pay at $15 per hour. The clerk's benefits costs are calculated by the company at 40 percent of the base pay rate, with no benefits costs assigned to overtime pay. The clerks work an average of 20 days per month.

The 1992 sales revenue for X-Y-Z Software was $78 million, distributed evenly over the year. The average sale is $31,000, with an average profit margin of 10 percent. The average sales cycle is three months, and sales projections are based on four weeks per month. The sales force converts an average of 10 percent of first calls into sales.

Buyer Vision

The management of X-Y-Z Software had a vision that during the fourth quarter of 1992, the entire sales force would attend *Solution Selling* sales training and that the company would install pipeline management software that supports the *Solution Selling* process. Management believed that by relieving the salespeople of the burden of developing monthly forecasts, each salesperson could make two more first calls per week. Additionally, management believes that the pipeline management software will enable managers to do the forecasts without any clerical assistance. Based on the increased sales revenue and the decreased clerical costs, management believes the pipeline management software is justified.

Value Justification Elements

1. What will be measured?

Increased profit	Increased number of sales.
Displaced costs	Clerks preparing the monthly forecast.
Avoided costs	Clerks needed to prepare monthly forecasts

for Europe, South America, and Pacific Rim
distributors. Overtime to prepare the reports
in three working days.

2. Who is responsible?

Increased number of sales	VP sales
Decreased clerks	VP operations
Avoided clerks	VP operations
Avoided overtime	VP operations

3. How much is possible?

Increased profit	21 sales/week at $31,000 (10 percent margin)
Displaced costs	4 clerks at $14/hr
Avoided costs	3 clerks at $14/hr
	75 hours of overtime at $15/hr

4. What capabilities are needed?

Allow each salesperson additional time to make two extra calls each week.
Eliminate the resources needed to compile the monthly sales forecasts.
Produce standard sales forecasts for the worldwide distributors.

5. When will this investment pay for itself?

Increased sales are expected to start three months after the implementation
in a sales territory because of the three-month sales cycle. The displaced
clerks, the avoided overtime, and the avoided clerks will take effect upon
implementation. The cost break-even point is expected to be nine months
after project start, and four months after full cutover.

Pricing Agreement

One-time costs:

Pipeline management software (Compliant with *Solution Selling*) and installation (due 50% in Feb., 50% in April)	$149,000
Hardware equipment: $4,500 × 106 sales reps. (due $50,000 in Feb., $79,400 in April, $158,800 in May, and $158,800 in June)	$447,000
Total one-time costs	$596,000

Maintenance costs:

Base Products ($3,500/mo) − 20% of original sales price = $2,483 per month (due to start in April)	$ 29,800
Total maintenance costs	$ 29,800

Summary of Benefits

Increased profits:

106 Salespeople[a] × 2 additional sales calls/week[a]
    = 212 additional calls/week
10% of first calls converted to sales[a] × 212 calls
    = 21 additional sales/week (84 sales/mo)
$31,000 average per sale[b] × 84 additional sales
    = $2.604 million/mo
10% profit margin[b] × $2.604 million additional revenue
    = $260,400[b] expected additional profit/mo
    (Three months after complete cut-over. The actual conversion will be staged in four groups. The pilot in June, and 1/3 of the remainder in August, September, and October.)

Displaced costs:

4 employees[e] × $10/hr[b] + overhead $4/hr[b] × 8 hrs/day × 20 days/mo
    = $8,960/mo[b]

Avoided costs:

3 employees[e] × $10/hr[b] + overhead $4/hr[b] × 8 hrs/day × 20 days/mo
    = $6,720/mo[b]
75 hours overtime[e] × $15/hr[b]
    = $1,125/mo[b]

Intangible benefits:

Improved morale of the sales staff.[a]
No overtime during peak workload periods.[a]
Improved morale in the entire company.[b,c]
Improved professional image with college recruits.[a,d]
Avoidance of budget "cuts" and spending "freezes" by departments.[b,d]

[a] VP, sales.

[b] CFO.

[c] VP, sales marketing.

[d] President.

[e] VP, operations.

Implementation Plan (Preliminary)

Implementation kick-off meeting	2/2/93
Install hardware for pilot territories	2/5/93–2/9/93
Education for the pilot salespeople	2/12/93–2/13/93
Education for HQ MIS technical personnel	2/15/93
Pilot test period	2/26/93–2/28/93
Review the results with management	4/7/93
Finalize the production cut-over plan	
Production cut-over	4/15/93–6/27/93
Educate and install one field office per week; three weeks/mo	
Review the production cut-over	7/9/93
Perform sales rep and management	9/15/93
Satisfaction review	
Report usage and satisfaction	9/25/93

Net Customer Benefits

Costs:

One-time:

Software applications	$ 149,000	
Hardware equipment	$ 447,000	
Total one-time costs		$ 596,000

Ongoing costs:

Hardware and software maintenance	$ 2,483/mo	$ 29,800
Total first year operating costs		$ 625,800/yr

Benefits:

Increased revenue/mo	$ 2,604,000/mo	
Profit margin	10%	
Increased profit	$ 260,400/mo	
Total annual increase in profit		$3,124,800
Displaced clerks	$8,960/mo	
Avoided clerks	$6,720/mo	
Avoided overtime	$1,125/mo	
Total annual decreased costs		$ 201,660
First operational year net benefits		$2,700,660
Monthly net benefit	$ 225,055	
Payback period	9 months	
Break-even month	October 1993	
(see cash flow, Figure B2)		

Mac does a few subtle things in the example I'd like to touch on. You will notice that he computes a *monthly benefit* amount. This is the cost of delay. If a buyer gets cold feet at the end, or decides to look at one more alternative, knowing the cost of delay can help put things in perspective.

Mac also likes to schedule a *satisfaction review* as part of the implementation plan. Typically, when a buyer signs a contract, who is the last person he expects to see again? The seller, of course. Helping the buyer do a value justification gives the seller power. It tells the buyer, "We are so confident in the value of our capabilities, we *want* you to measure that value." This is why he includes proposed success criteria with each value justification exercise. The success criteria enables the buyer to prove to himself and others that it was a good decision to buy. The seller's power can be enhanced again by the satisfaction review. By returning after implementation, it again demonstrates to the buyer the seller's belief and confidence in his capabilities.

FIGURE B1
Proposed Success Criteria

	3/Q/93	4/Q/93	1/Q/94	2/Q/94
Average calls/sell cycle				
Average first calls per salesperson				
Percent deviation of actual to forecast				
Percent increase in profit from additional sales				
Number of salespeople making quota				
Overtime worked by the sales staff during the last week of the quarter				

FIGURE B2
Cash Flow Spread Sheet

X-Y-Z Software
Solution Selling® Software
1993–1994

	Jan	Feb	Mar	Apr	May	June	July	Aug	Sept	Oct	Nov	Dec
Benefits:												
Increased profit												
Pilot cut-over						26,000	26,000	26,000	26,000	26,000	26,000	26,000
April cut-over								46,800	46,800	46,800	46,800	46,800
May cut-over									93,600	93,600	93,600	93,600
June cut-over										93,600	93,600	93,600
Displaced clerks			9,000	9,000	9,000	9,000	9,000	9,000	9,000	9,000	9,000	9,000
Avoided clerks			7,000	7,000	7,000	7,000	7,000	7,000	7,000	7,000	7,000	7,000
Avoided overtime			1,000	1,000	1,000	1,000	1,000	1,000	1,000	1,000	1,000	1,000
Total monthly benefits			17,000	17,000	17,000	43,000	43,000	89,800	183,400	277,000	277,000	277,000
Cumulative total benefits			17,000	34,000	51,000	94,000	137,000	226,800	410,200	687,200	964,200	1,241,200
Cost:												
One-time costs												
Software		74,500		74,500								
Hardware		79,400		79,400	158,800	158,800						
Ongoing												
SW maint		2,483		2,483	2,483	2,483	2,483	2,483	2,483	2,483	2,483	2,483
Total monthly costs	0	156,383	0	156,383	161,283	161,283	2,483	2,483	2,483	2,483	2,483	2,483
Cumulative total costs	0	280,883	124,500	280,883	442,166	603,449	605,932	608,415	610,898	613,381	615,864	618,347
Net benefits:												
Monthly	0	−124,500	17,000	−139,383	−144,283	−118,283	40,517	87,317	180,917	274,517	274,517	274,517
Cumulative net benefits	0	−124,500	−107,500	−246,883	−391,166	−509,449	−468,932	−381,615	−200,698	73,819	348,336	622,853

X-Y-Z Software

Break-even point

■ Cumulative total benefits
● Cumulative total costs
▲ Cumulative net benefit

Dollars (000): 1,000 / 840 / 680 / 520 / 360 / 200 / 40 / −120 / −280 / −440 / −600

Months: 1 2 3 4 5 6 7 8 9 10 11 12

FIGURE B3
Implementation Plan

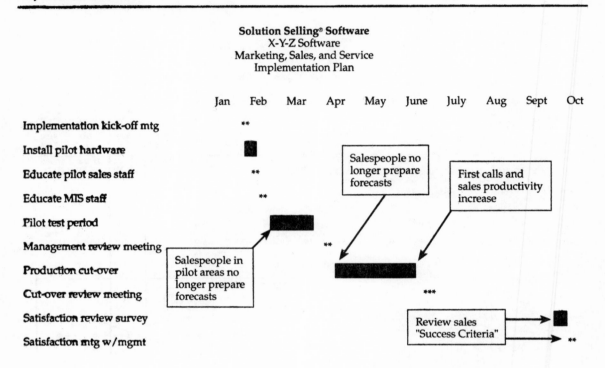

Solution Selling® Software
X-Y-Z Software
Marketing, Sales, and Service
Implementation Plan

	Jan	Feb	Mar	Apr	May	June	July	Aug	Sept	Oct
Implementation kick-off mtg		**								
Install pilot hardware		■								
Educate pilot sales staff		**								
Educate MIS staff		**								
Pilot test period			■							
Management review meeting				**						
Production cut-over					■					
Cut-over review meeting						***				
Satisfaction review survey										■
Satisfaction mtg w/mgmt										**

Salespeople no longer prepare forecasts

First calls and sales productivity increase

Salespeople in pilot areas no longer prepare forecasts

Review sales "Success Criteria"

Resources

Selected Bibliography on Sales, Sales Management, Change Management, and Personal Empowerment Books

Alessandra, T. and R. Barrera. *Collaborative Selling, How to Gain the Competitive Edge in Sales.* New York: John Wiley & Sons, 1993. Accents solving customers' problems and developing long-term relationships with buyers.

Barker, J. A. *Future Edge.* New York: Morrow, 1992. Getting your mind and your organization ready to accept, embrace, and relish change. Recommended prerequisite for participation in *Solution Selling* workshops.

Covey, S. R. *Principle-Centered Leadership.* Provo, UT: The Institute for Principle Centered Leadership, 1990. This book can empower you to empower others.

Covey, S. R. *The 7 Habits of Highly Effective People: Restoring the Character Ethic.* New York: Simon & Schuster, 1989. Self-management, understanding ourselves and our impact on other people, and maximizing both your professional effectiveness and quality of life.

Davis, S. and B. Davidson *2020 Vision.* New York: Fireside, 1991. Must reading for all information technology professionals.

Ford, E. E. *Freedom from Stress.* Scottsdale, AZ: Brandt Publishing, 1989. Based on cybernetic control theory, deals with the causes of stress.

Gordon, T. *P.E.T. in Action.* New York: Bantam Books, 1978. The best book I have read on listening and win-win conflict resolution. Skills are directly transferable to the workplace.

Hanan, M. *Key Account Selling.* New York: AMACOM, 1989. If you are interested in key account selection and how to get them, then this book will interest you.

Hanan, M.; J. Cribben; and H. Heiser. *Consultative Selling.* New York: AMACOM, 1973. Focus on the long-term business partnership.

Merrill, R. A. *Connections: Quadrant II Time Management.* Salt Lake City, UT: Publishers Press, 1990. "Give a man a fish, and you feed him for a day; teach him how to fish, and you feed him for a lifetime." Roger Merrill will teach you how to fish.

Miller, R. B. and S. E. Heiman. *Conceptual Selling.* New York: Warner Books, 1989. Authors of the book *Strategic Selling* and of *Conceptual Selling* seminars teach selling from the buyers' point of view.

Moore, G. A. *Crossing the Chasm.* HarperBusiness, 1991. An aid to understanding how the majority of buyers of innovative technology will not buy like the early ones.

Rackham, N. *SPIN Selling.* New York: McGraw-Hill, 1988. If you are still not convinced that traditional selling techniques will get you in trouble, read this book.

Robbins, A. *Unlimited Power.* New York: Fawcett Columbine, 1987. Focuses on peak personal power.

Tannen, D. *You Just Don't Understand.* New York: Ballentine Books, 1990. Will allow you to take your alignment skills to a new level with both men and women.

Waitley, D. E. and R. B. Tucker. *Winning the Innovation Game.* Old Tappen, NJ: Revell, 1986. A meaty approach to innovation and innovators.

Webster, B. *The Power of Consultative Selling.* Englewood Cliffs, NJ: Prentice Hall, 1987. Another book on consultative selling.

Selected Bibliography on Business Management, Strategic Planning, Innovation, and Business Turnarounds

Albrecht, K. and R. Zemke. *Service America.* New York: Warner Books, 1990. The national bestseller on how to make your company customer-driven and service-oriented.

Drucker, P. F. *The Practice of Management.* New York: Harper & Row, 1954. A great book for understanding the objectives of a business and then managing the business. Drucker remains the "guru" of modern business management.

Heibroner, R. L. *The Worldly Philosophers: The Lives, Times and Ideas of the Great Economic Thinkers,* New York: Simon & Schuster, 1972.

Kami, M. J. *Trigger Points: How to Make Decisions Three Times Faster, Innovate Smarter, and Beat Your Competition by Ten Percent (It Ain't Easy!).* New York: McGraw-Hill, 1988. This management book provides solutions and actions to cope with the ever-changing marketplace and need for innovation.

Naisbitt, J. and P. Aburdene. *Megatrends 2000.* London: Pan Books, 1990. Leading social forecasters discuss the 1990s in terms of likely trends and markets.

Peters, T. *Thriving on Chaos.* New York: Alfred A. Knopf, 1985. Maintains that perpetual change is now a permanent condition and tells us why we must accept it, adapt to it, and live with it.

Walton, M. *The Deming Management Method.* New York: Dodd, Mead, 1986. Whether your business is large or small, this practical book can lead you to higher productivity and profits. Discusses applications by some of America's leading businesses.

Waterman, R. H. *The Renewal Factor: How the Best Get and Keep the Competitive Edge.* New York: Bantam Books, 1987. This is a book about businesses that have achieved successful turnarounds.

Index

Other books of interest to you

THE SALES MANAGER'S GUIDE TO TRAINING AND DEVELOPING YOUR TEAM
National Society of Sales Training Executives

This essential resource includes checklists to assist in managing a staff; forms for training, planning, and evaluating performance; and a listing of additional sources of information for sales managers.

1-55623-652-2   188 pages

NETWORKING WITH THE AFFLUENT AND THEIR ADVISORS
Dr. Thomas J. Stanley

Shows the most productive way to penetrate the affluent market and network with members, advisors, and key members of their important affinity groups.

1-55623-891-6   250 pages

SELLING TO THE AFFLUENT
The Professional's Guide to Closing the Sales That Count
Dr. Thomas J. Stanley

After finding potential groups of affluent clients, use this book to land those prospects. Shows the key indicators that reveal when a prospect is about to make significant dollar transactions.

1-55623-418-X   280 pages

MARKETING TO THE AFFLUENT
Dr. Thomas J. Stanley

The first book in the Affluent Library, this premier guide gives the true demographics, psychographics, buying, and patronage habits of the wealthy. Includes in-depth interviews with some of the nation's top sales and marketing professionals who have successfully identified affluent prospects.

1-55623-105-9   324 pages

. . . AND IT TASTES JUST LIKE CHICKEN
Endless Retail Sales and Management Success
Gregory L. Will

This unique book approaches sales and management from the retail perspective, covering the cornerstone principles and showing how to achieve success.

0-7863-0194-5   240 pages